中国政府白皮书汇编
（2022 年）

人民出版社　外文出版社
FOREIGN LANGUAGES PRESS

目　录

第一部分　中文版

2021 中国的航天

（2022 年 1 月）

前　言 ……………………………………………………………（5）

一、开启全面建设航天强国新征程 …………………………（6）

二、发展空间技术与系统 ……………………………………（8）

三、培育壮大空间应用产业 …………………………………（15）

四、开展空间科学探索与研究 ………………………………（18）

五、推进航天治理现代化 ……………………………………（20）

六、构建航天国际合作新格局 ………………………………（24）

结束语 …………………………………………………………（33）

中国残疾人体育事业发展和权利保障

（2022 年 3 月）

前　言 ………………………………………………………（37）

一、国家发展促进残疾人体育进步 …………………………（38）

二、残疾人群众性体育活动广泛开展 ………………………（42）

三、残疾人竞技体育水平不断提高 …………………………（45）

四、为世界残疾人体育运动作出贡献 ………………………（48）

五、残疾人体育展现中国人权事业发展进步 ………………（53）

结束语 ………………………………………………………（57）

新时代的中国青年

（2022 年 4 月）

前　言 ………………………………………………………（61）

一、新时代中国青年生逢盛世、共享机遇 …………………（64）

二、新时代中国青年素质过硬、全面发展 …………………（73）

三、新时代中国青年勇挑重担、堪当大任 …………………（80）

四、新时代中国青年胸怀世界、展现担当 …………………（88）

结束语 ………………………………………………………（94）

台湾问题与新时代中国统一事业

（2022 年 8 月）

前　言 ……………………………………………………………（97）

一、台湾是中国的一部分不容置疑也不容改变 …………（99）

二、中国共产党坚定不移推进祖国完全统一 ……………（104）

三、祖国完全统一进程不可阻挡 …………………………（109）

四、在新时代新征程上推进祖国统一 ……………………（115）

五、实现祖国和平统一的光明前景 ………………………（121）

结束语 ……………………………………………………………（124）

新时代的中国北斗

（2022 年 11 月）

前　言 ……………………………………………………………（127）

一、北斗发展进入新时代 …………………………………（129）

二、跻身世界一流的中国北斗 ……………………………（133）

三、提高系统运行管理水平 ………………………………（137）

四、推动应用产业可持续发展 ……………………………（140）

五、提升现代化治理水平 …………………………………（145）

六、助力构建人类命运共同体 ……………………………（149）

结束语 ……………………………………………………………（153）

携手构建网络空间命运共同体

（2022 年 11 月）

前　言 ·· （157）

一、构建网络空间命运共同体是信息时代的必然选择 ······ （159）

二、中国的互联网发展治理实践 ·························· （165）

三、构建网络空间命运共同体的中国贡献 ·············· （178）

四、构建更加紧密的网络空间命运共同体的中国主张 ······ （196）

结束语 ·· （202）

第二部分　英文版

China's Space Program：
A 2021 Perspective

（January 2022）

Preamble ·· （207）

I. A New Journey Towards a Strong Space Presence ··········· （208）

II. Development of Space Technology and Systems ··········· （210）

III. Developing and Expanding Space Application Industry ·········· （218）

IV. Research on Space Science ·························· （221）

V. Modernizing Space Governance ·························· （224）

VI. International Cooperation ·························· （228）

Conclusion ·· （239）

China's Parasports

Progress and the Protection of Rights

（March 2022）

Preamble ·· （243）

I. Parasports Have Progressed Through National Development ··········· （244）

II. Physical Activities for Persons with Disabilities Have Flourished ··· （249）

III. Performances in Parasports Are Improving Steadily ················· （253）

IV. Contributing to International Parasports ···························· （257）

V. Achievements in Parasports Reflect Improvements in China's

    Human Rights ··· （263）

Conclusion ··· （268）

Youth of China in the New Era

（April 2022）

Preamble ·· （271）

I. The New Era: Great Times with Ample Opportunities ················ （274）

II. All-Round Development in the New Era ···························· （285）

III. Shouldering Heavy Tasks and Responsibilities ····················· （293）

IV. Having a Global Vision and a Strong Sense of Responsibility ······ （303）

Conclusion ··· （310）

The Taiwan Question and China's

Reunification in the New Era

（August 2022）

Preamble ·· （313）

I. Taiwan Is Part of China-This Is an Indisputable Fact ················ (315)

II. Resolute Efforts of the CPC to Realize China's Complete

  Reunification ··· (321)

III. China's Complete Reunification Is a Process That Cannot

  Be Halted ·· (327)

IV. National Reunification in the New Era ························· (334)

V. Bright Prospects for Peaceful Reunification ·················· (341)

Conclusion ·· (344)

China's BeiDou Navigation Satellite System in the New Era

(November 2022)

Preamble ·· (347)

I. BeiDou in the New Era ·· (349)

II. A World-Class Navigation Satellite System ·················· (354)

III. Improving BDS Operation Management ······················· (358)

IV. Promoting Sustainable Development of the BDS Applications

  Industry ·· (362)

V. Upgrading BDS Governance ····································· (368)

VI. Contributing to Building a Global Community of Shared Future ····· (373)

Conclusion ·· (378)

Jointly Build a Community with a Shared Future in Cyberspace

(November 2022)

Preface ··· (381)

I. Building a Community with a Shared Future in Cyberspace Is
   Essential in the Information Age ······································· (383)
II. Development and Management of the Internet in China ·············· (389)
III. China's Contribution to Building a Community with a Shared
   Future in Cyberspace ·· (402)
IV. China's Proposals on Creating a Community with a Shared
   Future in Cyberspace ·· (423)
Conclusion ··· (429)

第一部分　中文版

2021 中国的航天

（2022 年 1 月）

中华人民共和国
国务院新闻办公室

前　言

习近平总书记指出，"探索浩瀚宇宙，发展航天事业，建设航天强国，是我们不懈追求的航天梦。"中国始终把发展航天事业作为国家整体发展战略的重要组成部分，始终坚持为和平目的探索和利用外层空间。

2016年以来，中国航天进入创新发展"快车道"，空间基础设施建设稳步推进，北斗全球卫星导航系统建成开通，高分辨率对地观测系统基本建成，卫星通信广播服务能力稳步增强，探月工程"三步走"圆满收官，中国空间站建设全面开启，"天问一号"实现从地月系到行星际探测的跨越，取得了举世瞩目的辉煌成就。

未来五年，中国航天将立足新发展阶段，贯彻新发展理念，构建新发展格局，按照高质量发展要求，推动空间科学、空间技术、空间应用全面发展，开启全面建设航天强国新征程，为服务国家发展大局、在外空领域推动构建人类命运共同体、促进人类文明进步作出更大贡献。

为介绍2016年以来中国航天活动主要进展、未来五年主要任务，进一步增进国际社会对中国航天事业的了解，特发布本白皮书。

一、开启全面建设航天强国新征程

（一）发展宗旨

探索外层空间,扩展对地球和宇宙的认识;和平利用外层空间,维护外层空间安全,在外空领域推动构建人类命运共同体,造福全人类;满足经济建设、科技发展、国家安全和社会进步等方面的需求,提高全民科学文化素质,维护国家权益,增强综合国力。

（二）发展愿景

全面建成航天强国,持续提升科学认知太空能力、自由进出太空能力、高效利用太空能力、有效治理太空能力,成为国家安全的维护者、科技自立自强的引领者、经济社会高质量发展的推动者、外空科学治理的倡导者和人类文明发展的开拓者,为建设社会主义现代化强国、推动人类和平与发展的崇高事业作出积极贡献。

（三）发展原则

中国发展航天事业服从和服务于国家整体发展战略,坚持创新引领、协同高效、和平发展、合作共享的原则,推动航天高质量发展。

　　——创新引领。坚持创新在航天事业发展中的核心地位,建强航天领域国家战略科技力量,实施航天重大科技工程,强化原创引领的科技创新,持续优化创新生态,加快产品化进程,不断提升航天自主发展能力和安全发展能力。

　　——协同高效。坚持系统观念,更好发挥新型举国体制优势,引导各方力量有序参与航天发展,科学统筹部署航天活动,强化空间技术对空间科学、空间应用的推动牵引作用,培育壮大新模式新业态,提升航天发展的质量效益和整体效能。

　　——和平发展。始终坚持和平利用外层空间,反对外空武器化、战场化和外空军备竞赛,合理开发和利用空间资源,切实保护空间环境,维护一个和平、清洁的外层空间,使航天活动造福全人类。

　　——合作共享。坚持独立自主与开放合作相结合,深化高水平国际交流与合作,拓展航天技术和产品全球公共服务,积极参与解决人类面临的重大挑战,助力联合国 2030 年可持续发展议程目标实现,在外空领域推动构建人类命运共同体。

二、发展空间技术与系统

中国航天面向世界科技前沿和国家重大战略需求,以航天重大工程为牵引,加快关键核心技术攻关和应用,大力发展空间技术与系统,全面提升进出、探索、利用和治理空间能力,推动航天可持续发展。

(一)航天运输系统

2016年以来,截至2021年12月,共完成207次发射任务,其中长征系列运载火箭发射共完成183次,总发射次数突破400次。长征系列运载火箭加速向无毒、无污染、模块化、智慧化方向升级换代,"长征五号""长征五号乙"运载火箭实现应用发射,"长征八号""长征七号甲"实现首飞,运载能力持续增强。运载火箭多样化发射服务能力迈上新台阶,"长征十一号"实现海上商业化应用发射,"捷龙一号""快舟一号甲""双曲线一号""谷神星一号"等商业运载火箭成功发射。可重复使用运载器飞行演示验证试验取得成功。

未来五年,中国将持续提升航天运输系统综合性能,加速实现运载火箭升级换代。推动运载火箭型谱发展,研制发射新一代载人运载火箭和大推力固体运载火箭,加快推动重型运载火箭工程研制。

持续开展重复使用航天运输系统关键技术攻关和演示验证。面向航班化发射需求,发展新型火箭发动机、组合动力、上面级等技术,拓展多样化便利进出空间能力。

(二)空间基础设施

卫星遥感系统。高分辨率对地观测系统天基部分基本建成,对地观测迈进高空间分辨率、高时间分辨率、高光谱分辨率时代。陆地观测业务服务综合能力大幅提升,成功发射"资源三号"03星、"环境减灾二号"A/B星、高分多模综合成像卫星、高光谱观测卫星以及多颗商业遥感卫星等。海洋观测实现全球海域多要素、多尺度、高分辨率连续覆盖,成功发射"海洋一号"C/D星、"海洋二号"B/C/D星。大气全球化、精细化综合观测能力实现跃升,成功发射新一代静止轨道气象卫星"风云四号"A/B星,实现全天候、精细化、连续大气立体综合探测和快速响应灾害监测,成功发射"风云三号"D/E星,形成上午、下午、晨昏星业务组网观测能力,成功发射"风云二号"H星,为"一带一路"沿线国家和地区提供卫星监测服务。遥感卫星地面系统进一步完善,基本具备卫星遥感数据全球接收、快速处理与业务化服务能力。

卫星通信广播系统。固定通信广播卫星系统建设稳步推进,覆盖区域、通信容量等性能进一步提升,成功发射"中星"6C、"中星"9B等卫星,支持广播电视业务连续稳定运行;成功发射"中星"16、

"亚太"6D卫星,单星通信容量达到50Gbps,中国卫星通信进入"高通量"时代。移动通信广播卫星系统逐步完善,成功发射"天通一号"02/03星,与"天通一号"01星组网运行,具备为中国及周边、亚太部分地区手持终端用户提供语音、短消息和数据等移动通信服务能力。中继卫星系统建设迈入升级换代新阶段,成功发射"天链一号"05星和"天链二号"01星,综合性能大幅提升。卫星通信广播地面系统持续完善,形成全球覆盖天地融合的卫星通信广播、互联网、物联网及信息服务能力。

卫星导航系统。北斗三号全球卫星导航系统全面建成开通,完成30颗卫星发射组网,北斗系统"三步走"战略圆满完成,正式进入服务全球新时代。北斗系统具备定位导航授时、全球短报文通信、区域短报文通信、国际搜救、星基增强、地基增强、精密单点定位共七类服务能力,服务性能达到世界先进水平。

未来五年,中国将持续完善国家空间基础设施,推动遥感、通信、导航卫星融合技术发展,加快提升泛在通联、精准时空、全维感知的空间信息服务能力。研制静止轨道微波探测、新一代海洋水色、陆地生态系统碳监测、大气环境监测等卫星,发展双天线X波段干涉合成孔径雷达、陆地水资源等卫星技术,形成综合高效的全球对地观测和数据获取能力。推动构建高低轨协同的卫星通信系统,开展新型通信卫星技术验证与商业应用,建设第二代数据中继卫星系统。开展下一代北斗卫星导航系统导航通信融合、低轨增强等深化研究和技术攻关,推动构建更加泛在、更加融合、更加智能的国家综合定位导航授时(PNT)体系。持续完善卫星遥感、通信、导航地面系统。

（三）载人航天

"天舟一号"货运飞船成功发射并与"天宫二号"空间实验室成功交会对接,突破并掌握货物运输、推进剂在轨补加等关键技术,载人航天工程第二步圆满收官。"天和"核心舱成功发射,标志着中国空间站建造进入全面实施阶段。"天舟二号""天舟三号"货运飞船和"神舟十二号""神舟十三号"载人飞船成功发射,先后与"天和"核心舱快速对接,形成空间站组合体并稳定运行,6名航天员先后进驻中国空间站,实施出舱活动、舱外操作、在轨维护、科学实验等任务。

未来五年,中国将继续实施载人航天工程,发射"问天"实验舱、"梦天"实验舱、"巡天"空间望远镜以及"神舟"载人飞船和"天舟"货运飞船,全面建成并运营中国空间站,打造国家太空实验室,开展航天员长期驻留、大规模空间科学实验、空间站平台维护等工作。深化载人登月方案论证,组织开展关键技术攻关,研制新一代载人飞船,夯实载人探索开发地月空间基础。

（四）深空探测

月球探测工程。"嫦娥四号"探测器通过"鹊桥"卫星中继通信,首次实现航天器在月球背面软着陆和巡视勘察。"嫦娥五号"探测器实现中国首次地外天体采样返回,将1731克月球样品成功带回地球,标志着探月工程"绕、落、回"三步走圆满收官。

行星探测工程。"天问一号"火星探测器成功发射,实现火星环绕、着陆,"祝融号"火星车开展巡视探测,在火星上首次留下中国人的印迹,中国航天实现从地月系到行星际探测的跨越。

未来五年,中国将继续实施月球探测工程,发射"嫦娥六号"探测器、完成月球极区采样返回,发射"嫦娥七号"探测器、完成月球极区高精度着陆和阴影坑飞跃探测,完成"嫦娥八号"任务关键技术攻关,与相关国家、国际组织和国际合作伙伴共同开展国际月球科研站建设。继续实施行星探测工程,发射小行星探测器、完成近地小行星采样和主带彗星探测,完成火星采样返回、木星系探测等关键技术攻关。论证太阳系边际探测等实施方案。

（五） 发射场与测控

航天发射场。酒泉、太原、西昌发射场适应性改造全面完成,酒泉发射场新增液体火箭商业发射工位,文昌航天发射场进入业务化应用阶段,基本建成沿海内陆相结合、高低纬度相结合、各种射向范围相结合的航天发射格局,能够满足载人飞船、空间站舱段、深空探测器及各类卫星的多样化发射需求。海上发射平台投入使用,填补了中国海上发射火箭的空白。

航天测控。测控通信能力实现由地月空间向行星际空间跨越,天基测控能力持续增强,国家航天测控网布局进一步优化,形成安全可靠、响应迅速、接入灵活、运行高效、服务广泛的天地一体化航天测控体系,圆满完成"神舟""天舟"系列飞船、"天和"核心舱、"嫦娥"系列月球探测器、"天问一号"火星探测器等为代表的航天测控任务。商业卫星测控站网加快发展。

未来五年,中国将在强化航天产品统一技术体制的基础上,进一步完善现有航天发射场系统,统筹开展发射场通用化、集约化、智能化建设,增强发射场系统任务适应性和可靠性,提升高密度、多样化发射任务支撑能力。建设商业发射工位和商业航天发射场,满足各类商业发射需求。持续完善现有航天测控系统,优化组织模式,创新测控技术和手段,强化天地基测控资源融合运用能力,推动构建全域覆盖、泛在互联的航天测控体系,统筹实施国家太空系统运行管理,提高管理和使用效益。建强深空测控通信网,保障月球、火星等深空探测任务实施。

(六) 新技术试验

成功发射多颗新技术试验卫星,开展新一代通信卫星公用平台、甚高通量通信载荷、Ka 频段宽带通信、星地高速激光通信、新型电推进等技术试验验证。

未来五年,中国将面向新技术工程化应用,开展航天器智能自主管理、空间扩展飞行器、新型空间动力、航天器在轨服务与维护、空间碎片清除等新技术验证,以及航天领域新材料、新器件、新工艺在轨试验验证,提升技术成熟度和工程应用能力。

（七）空间环境治理

空间碎片监测网络初具规模,基础数据库不断完善,碰撞预警和空间事件感知应对能力逐步提升,有力保障在轨航天器运行安全。落实国际空间碎片减缓准则、外空活动长期可持续准则,全面实施运载火箭末级钝化,成功实施"天宫二号"等航天器任务末期主动离轨,为空间碎片减缓作出积极贡献。近地小天体搜索跟踪和数据分析研究取得积极进展。初步建成空间天气保障业务体系,具备监测、预警和预报能力,应用服务效益不断拓展。

未来五年,中国将统筹推进空间环境治理体系建设。加强太空交通管理,建设完善空间碎片监测设施体系、编目数据库和预警服务系统,统筹做好航天器在轨维护、碰撞规避控制、空间碎片减缓等工作,确保太空系统安全稳定有序运行。全面加强防护力量建设,提高容灾备份、抗毁生存、信息防护能力,维护国家太空活动、资产和其他利益的安全。论证建设近地小天体防御系统,提升监测、编目、预警和应对处置能力。建设天地结合的空间天气监测系统,持续完善业务保障体系,有效应对灾害性空间天气事件。

三、培育壮大空间应用产业

中国航天面向经济社会发展重大需求,加强卫星公益服务和商业应用,加速航天技术成果转移转化,推动空间应用产业发展,提升航天发展效益效能。

（一）卫星公益服务

卫星应用业务服务能力显著增强,在资源环境与生态保护、防灾减灾与应急管理、气象预报与气候变化应对、社会管理与公共服务、城镇化建设与区域协调发展、脱贫攻坚等方面发挥重要作用,航天创造更加美好生活。卫星遥感基本实现了国家和省级政府部门业务化应用,对100余次国内重特大自然灾害开展应急监测,为国内数万家各类用户和全球100多个国家提供服务,累计分发数据超亿景。卫星通信广播累计为国内农村及边远地区的1.4亿多户家庭提供直播卫星电视服务、500多个手机通信基站提供数据回传,在四川凉山特大森林火灾、河南郑州特大暴雨等灾害救援中提供高效应急通信服务。北斗导航为超过700万辆道路运营车辆提供安全保障服务,为超过4万艘海洋渔船提供定位和短报文通信服务,为新冠肺炎疫情防控物资运输、人员流动管理、医院建设等提供精准位置服务。

未来五年，围绕平安中国、健康中国、美丽中国、数字中国建设，强化卫星应用与行业区域发展深度融合，强化空间信息与大数据、物联网等新一代信息技术深度融合，深化陆地、海洋、气象遥感卫星数据综合应用，推进北斗导航+卫星通信+地面通信网络融合应用基础设施建设，加快提升精细化精准化业务化服务能力，更好服务支撑碳达峰与碳中和、乡村振兴、新型城镇化、区域协调发展和生态文明建设。

（二）空间应用产业

卫星应用商业化发展方兴未艾，面向政府、企业和个人的应用市场持续扩大，涌现出一批具有较强竞争力的商业航天企业，产业化规模化发展格局初步形成。卫星遥感高精地图、全维影像、数据加工、应用软件等产品和服务更好满足了不同用户特色需求，广泛应用于大众出行、电子商务、农产品交易、灾害损失评估与保险理赔、不动产登记等领域。卫星通信广播商业服务能力进一步提升，实现国内 4 个 4K 超高清频道上星和 100 多套节目高清化，为远洋船舶、民航客机提供互联网接入服务，"天通一号"卫星移动通信系统实现商业化运营。卫星导航产业快速发展，北斗兼容型芯片模块销量超过亿级规模，北斗应用广泛进入大众消费、共享经济和民生领域。航天技术成果加速赋能传统产业转型升级，助推新能源、新材料、绿色环保等新兴产业和智慧城市、智慧农业、无人驾驶等新业态发展，为建设科技强国、制造强国、网络强国、交通强国作出重要贡献。

　　未来五年，中国航天将紧紧抓住数字产业化、产业数字化发展机遇，面向经济社会发展和大众多样化需求，加大航天成果转化和技术转移，丰富应用场景，创新商业模式，推动空间应用与数字经济发展深度融合。拓展卫星遥感、卫星通信应用广度深度，实施北斗产业化工程，为国民经济各行业领域和大众消费提供更先进更经济的优质产品和便利服务。培育发展太空旅游、太空生物制药、空间碎片清除、空间试验服务等太空经济新业态，提升航天产业规模效益。

四、开展空间科学探索与研究

中国航天围绕宇宙起源和演化、太阳系与人类的关系等科学主题,论证实施空间科学计划,开展空间科学探索和空间环境下的科学实验,深化基础理论研究,孵化重大空间科学研究成果。

(一)空间科学探索

空间天文。"悟空"号暗物质粒子探测卫星获取了宇宙射线电子、质子和氦核能谱精细结构。成功发射"慧眼"硬 X 射线调制望远镜卫星,实现宇宙磁场测量和黑洞双星爆发过程全景观测。成功发射"羲和号"太阳探测科学技术试验卫星,获得多幅 Hα 波段不同波长点的太阳光谱图像。

月球与行星科学。依托月球探测工程,开展月球地质和月表浅层结构综合探测,在月球岩浆活动定年、矿物学特征和化学元素分析等方面取得重大成果。依托行星探测工程,开展火星地表结构、土壤和岩石物质成分分析,深化火星地质演化认知。

空间地球科学。"张衡一号"电磁监测试验卫星获取了全球地磁场和电离层原位数据,构建了全球地磁场参考模型。全球二氧化碳监测科学实验卫星获取了全球高精度二氧化碳分布图,卫星数据向全球免费共享。

空间基础物理。利用"墨子"号量子科学实验卫星,开展千公里级星地量子纠缠分发和隐形传态实验、引力诱导量子纠缠退相干实验,完成基于纠缠的无中继千公里量子密钥分发。成功发射"太极一号"和"天琴一号"空间引力波探测试验卫星。

未来五年,中国将围绕极端宇宙、时空涟漪、日地全景、宜居行星等科学主题,研制空间引力波探测卫星、爱因斯坦探针、先进天基太阳天文台、太阳风—磁层相互作用全景成像卫星、高精度地磁场测量卫星等,持续开展空间天文、日球物理、月球与行星科学、空间地球科学、空间基础物理等领域的前瞻探索和基础研究,催生更多原创性科学成果。

(二) 空间环境下的科学实验

利用"神舟"系列飞船、"天宫二号"空间实验室、"实践十号"卫星等,在太空实现了哺乳动物细胞胚胎发育,完成世界首台空间冷原子钟在轨验证,深化了微重力颗粒分聚和煤粉燃烧、材料制备等机理认识,取得了一批有国际影响力的空间科学研究成果。

未来五年,中国将利用天宫空间站、"嫦娥"系列探测器、"天问一号"探测器等空间实验平台,开展空间环境下的生物、生命、医学、材料等方面的实验和研究,持续深化人类对基础科学的认知。

五、推进航天治理现代化

中国政府积极制定发展航天事业的政策与措施,科学部署各项航天活动,充分发挥有效市场和有为政府作用,营造良好发展环境,推动航天事业高质量发展。

（一）持续提升航天创新能力

建设航天战略科技力量,打造以科研院所为主体的原始创新策源地,建立健全产学研用深度融合的航天技术创新体系,构建关键领域航天科技创新联盟,形成上中下游协同、大中小企业融通的创新发展格局。

推进实施一批航天重大工程和重大科技项目,推动航天科技跨越发展,带动国家科技整体跃升。

勇攀航天科技高峰,超前部署战略性、基础性、前瞻性科学研究和技术攻关,推进新一代信息技术在航天领域融合应用,加速先进技术特别是颠覆性技术的工程应用。

加强航天技术二次开发,推动航天科技成果转化应用,辐射带动国民经济发展。

（二）强化航天工业基础能力

持续完善基于系统集成商、专业承包商、市场供应商和公共服务机构，根植于国民经济，融合开放的航天科研生产组织体系。

优化产业结构布局，做强研发制造，做优发射运营，做大应用服务，强健产业链供应链。

加快工业化与信息化深度融合，建设智能化脉动生产线、智能车间、智慧院所，持续推动航天工业能力转型升级。

（三）加快发展空间应用产业

完善卫星应用产业发展政策，统筹公益和市场需求，统合设施资源建设，统一数据与产品标准，畅通共享共用渠道，构建产品标准化、服务个性化的卫星应用服务体系。

加快培育卫星应用市场，支持各类市场主体开展卫星应用增值产品开发，创新卫星应用模式，培育"航天+"产业生态，加快发展航天战略性新兴产业。

（四）鼓励引导商业航天发展

研究制定商业航天发展指导意见，促进商业航天快速发展。扩大政府采购商业航天产品和服务范围,推动重大科研设施设备向商业航天企业开放共享,支持商业航天企业参与航天重大工程项目研制,建立航天活动市场准入负面清单制度,确保商业航天企业有序进入退出、公平参与竞争。

优化商业航天在产业链中布局,鼓励引导商业航天企业从事卫星应用和航天技术转移转化。

（五）积极推进法治航天建设

加快推进航天法立法,构建完善以航天法为核心的航天法制体系,促进法治航天建设。研究制定卫星导航条例,规范和加强卫星导航活动管理。修订空间物体登记管理办法,持续规范空间数据共享和使用管理、民用航天发射许可管理。研究制定卫星频率轨道资源管理条例,加强卫星频率轨道资源申报、协调和登记,维护我国卫星频率轨道资源合法权益,助力航天事业发展。

加强国际空间法研究,积极参与外空国际规则、国际电联规则制定,维护以国际法为基础的外空国际秩序,推动构建公正、合理的外空全球治理体系。

（六）建设高水平航天人才队伍

加快建设航天领域世界重要人才中心和创新高地,厚植人才发展沃土,壮大人才队伍规模。完善人才培养机制,加强战略科学家、科技领军人才、青年科技人才和创新团队建设,培养一大批卓越工程师、高素质技术技能人才和大国工匠,造就一批具有国际视野和社会责任感的优秀企业家。完善人才交流机制,规范和引导航天人才合理流动。完善人才激励机制,加大奖励支持力度。加强航天特色学科专业建设,培养航天后备人才队伍。

（七）大力开展航天科普教育和文化建设

继续组织开展"中国航天日"系列活动,充分利用"世界空间周""全国科技活动周"以及"天宫课堂"等平台,加强航天科普教育,普及航天知识,传播航天文化,传承弘扬"两弹一星"精神和载人航天精神、探月精神、新时代北斗精神,激发全民尤其是青少年崇尚科学、探索未知、敢于创新的热情,提高全民科学文化素养。

做好重大航天遗产保护,持续推动航天博物馆、航天体验园等科普教育基地建设。鼓励支持航天题材文艺作品创作,繁荣航天文化。

六、构建航天国际合作新格局

和平探索、开发和利用外层空间是世界各国都享有的平等权利。中国倡导世界各国一起推动构建人类命运共同体，坚持在平等互利、和平利用、包容发展的基础上，深入开展航天国际交流合作。

（一）基本政策

中国政府在开展航天国际交流合作中，采取以下基本政策：

——维护联合国在外空事务中的核心作用，遵循联合国《关于各国探索和利用包括月球和其他天体在内外层空间活动的原则条约》，重视联合国相关原则、宣言、决议的指导意义，积极参与外空国际规则制定，促进外空活动长期可持续发展。

——加强空间科学、技术及应用等领域的国际交流与合作，与国际社会一道提供全球公共产品与服务，为人类应对共同挑战作出贡献。

——加强基于共同目标、服务"一带一路"建设的空间合作，使航天发展成果惠及沿线国家，特别是发展中国家。

——支持亚太空间合作组织发挥重要作用，重视在金砖国家合作机制、上海合作组织框架、二十国集团合作机制下的空间合作。

——鼓励和支持国内科研机构、企业、高等院校、社会团体,依据有关政策和法规,开展多层次、多形式的国际空间交流与合作。

(二) 主要进展

2016 年以来,中国与 19 个国家和地区、4 个国际组织,签署 46 项空间合作协定或谅解备忘录;积极推动外空全球治理;利用双边、多边合作机制,开展空间科学、空间技术、空间应用等领域国际合作,取得丰硕成果。

1. 外空全球治理。

——参加联合国框架下外空活动长期可持续性、空间资源开发利用、防止外空军备竞赛等议题磋商,共同创建空间探索与创新等新议题,持续推进联合国空间 2030 议程。

——支持联合国灾害管理与应急反应天基信息平台北京办公室工作,深度参与联合国全球卫星导航系统国际委员会各项活动,加入空间任务规划咨询组和国际小行星预警网等国际机制。

——发挥亚太空间合作组织东道国作用,支持《亚太空间合作组织 2030 年发展愿景》。

——利用中俄航天合作分委会空间碎片工作组、中美空间碎片与空间飞行安全专家研讨会等机制加强在空间碎片、外空活动长期可持续等领域的交流。

——支持国际电信联盟、地球观测组织、机构间空间碎片协调委员会、国际空间数据系统咨询委员会、国际空间探索协调组、机构间互操作顾问委员会等国际组织活动。

2. 载人航天。

——利用"天宫二号"空间实验室与欧洲空间局合作开展伽马暴偏振探测研究,在"神舟十一号"载人飞行任务期间与法国合作开展微重力环境下人体医学研究,与欧洲航天员中心联合进行洞穴训练、海上救生训练。

——完成中国空间站首批空间科学国际合作实验项目遴选,围绕空间科学实验、空间站舱段研制与德国、意大利、俄罗斯开展技术合作与交流。

3. 北斗导航。

——推动中国北斗卫星导航系统与美国全球定位系统、俄罗斯格罗纳斯系统、欧洲伽利略系统协调发展,在兼容与互操作、监测评估、联合应用等领域深入合作。

——推动北斗国际标准化工作,相继进入民航、海事、国际搜救、移动通信、电工委员会等多个国际组织标准体系。

——推动北斗系统全球服务,与阿盟、非盟分别建立北斗合作论坛机制,在突尼斯建成首个海外北斗中心,与巴基斯坦、沙特阿拉伯、阿根廷、南非、阿尔及利亚、泰国等国家开展卫星导航合作。

4. 深空探测。

——与俄罗斯联合发起国际月球科研站计划,启动中俄月球与深空探测联合数据中心建设,推动中国"嫦娥七号"月球极区探测任务与俄罗斯月球—资源—1轨道器任务联合实施。

——利用月球探测工程"嫦娥四号"任务，与俄罗斯、欧洲空间局开展了工程技术合作，与瑞典、德国、荷兰、沙特开展了科学载荷合作。启动月球探测工程"嫦娥六号"任务国际载荷搭载合作。

——利用首次火星探测"天问一号"任务，与欧洲空间局开展了工程技术合作，与奥地利、法国开展了科学载荷合作。与美国建立火星探测器轨道数据交换机制。启动小行星探测任务国际载荷搭载合作。

——与欧洲空间局、阿根廷、纳米比亚、巴基斯坦开展月球与深空探测领域的测控合作。

5.空间技术。

——联合研制并成功发射中法海洋卫星、中巴（西）地球资源04A星、埃塞俄比亚遥感微小卫星，为亚太空间合作组织成功搭载发射大学生小卫星。持续推进埃及二号遥感卫星等联合研制。

——完成巴基斯坦遥感卫星一号、委内瑞拉遥感卫星二号、苏丹一号遥感卫星、阿尔及利亚一号通信卫星等在轨交付。

——为沙特阿拉伯、巴基斯坦、阿根廷、巴西、加拿大、卢森堡等国家提供卫星搭载发射服务。

——与俄罗斯、乌克兰、白俄罗斯、阿根廷、巴基斯坦、尼日利亚等国家开展宇航产品技术合作。

——助力发展中国家航天能力建设。与埃及、巴基斯坦、尼日利亚等国家合作建设卫星研制基础设施。推动"一带一路"空间信息走廊建设,向发展中国家开放中国空间设施资源。

6. 空间应用。

——建立风云气象卫星国际用户防灾减灾应急保障机制,中国气象卫星数据广泛应用于 121 个国家和地区。

——签署金砖国家遥感卫星星座合作协定。与欧洲空间局开展对地观测卫星数据交换合作。建设中国—东盟卫星信息(海上)服务平台和遥感卫星数据共享服务平台。与老挝、泰国、柬埔寨、缅甸等国家共同建设澜沧江—湄公河空间信息交流中心。

——与玻利维亚、印度尼西亚、纳米比亚、泰国、南非等国家合作建设卫星数据接收站。

——积极参与空间与重大灾害国际宪章机制,为近 40 个国家的减灾提供卫星遥感数据近 800 景,新增 8 颗(座)卫星和星座作为值班卫星和星座,提升国际社会防灾减灾能力。

——积极开展卫星应急监测和服务,针对 15 个国家的 17 次重特大灾害事故启动应急监测,就 2018 年阿富汗大旱、2018 年老挝溃坝事故、2019 年莫桑比克台风向受灾国相关部门提供监测产品服务。

——发布《中国面向全球的综合地球观测系统十年执行计划(2016—2025 年)》,担任地球观测组织 2020 年轮值主席国,推动全球综合地球观测系统建设。

——参与国际空间气候观测(SCO)平台机制,推动中国利用空间技术应对气候变化的最佳实践,助力国际空间气候观测合作。

7. 空间科学。

——与瑞士、意大利、奥地利、英国、日本等国家联合开展"悟空"号、"墨子"号、"实践十号"和"慧眼"等科学卫星的联合科学研究和实验。

——联合研制并成功发射中意电磁监测试验卫星,持续推进中欧太阳风—磁层相互作用全景成像卫星、中法天文卫星、中意电磁监测卫星 02 星联合研制,与意大利、德国等国家开展先进天基太阳天文台、爱因斯坦探针、增强型 X 射线时变与偏振空间天文台等科学卫星有效载荷的联合研制和定标。

——利用中国—巴西空间天气联合实验室,共同建设南美地区空间环境综合监测研究平台。

8. 人才与学术交流。

——参与国际宇航联合会、国际空间研究委员会、国际宇航科学院、国际空间法学会等活动,举办全球空间探索大会、全球卫星导航系统国际委员会第十三届大会、中国/联合国航天助力可持续发展大会、文昌国际航空航天论坛、珠海论坛、北斗规模应用国际峰会、风云气象卫星国际用户大会等。

——助力发展中国家人才培养。依托联合国空间科技教育亚太区域中心(中国)为 60 余个国家培养了近千名航天人才,并建立"一带一路"航天创新联盟和中俄工科大学联盟;通过发展中国家技术培训班等渠道,促进遥感与导航方向的人才交流。

——通过中欧空间科学研讨会、中欧空间科技合作对话、中欧

"龙计划"等渠道,促进空间科学、遥感与导航方向的科技交流。

（三）未来合作重点

未来五年,中国将以更加积极开放的姿态,拓展双边、多边合作机制,在以下重点领域广泛开展国际空间交流与合作:

1. 外空全球治理。

——在联合国框架下,积极参与外空国际规则制定,共同应对外空活动长期可持续发展面临的挑战。

——积极参与空间环境治理、近地小天体监测与应对、行星保护、太空交通管理、空间资源开发利用等领域国际议题讨论和机制构建。

——开展空间环境治理合作,提高太空危机管控和综合治理效能,支持与俄、美等国及有关国际组织开展外空治理对话,推动亚太空间合作组织空间科学观测台建设。

2. 载人航天。

——依托中国空间站,开展空间天文观测、地球科学研究,以及微重力环境下的空间科学实验。

——推动开展航天员联合选拔培训、联合飞行等更广泛的国际合作。

3. 北斗导航。

——持续参加联合国全球卫星导航系统国际委员会有关活动,

推动建立公正合理的卫星导航秩序。

——积极推进北斗卫星导航系统和其他卫星导航系统、星基增强系统的兼容与互操作合作,促进全球卫星导航系统兼容共用。

——重点推进北斗卫星导航系统应用合作与交流,共享北斗系统成熟应用解决方案,助力各国经济社会发展。

4. 深空探测。

——重点推进国际月球科研站合作,欢迎国际伙伴在项目的各个阶段、在任务的各个层级参与国际月球科研站的论证和建设。

——拓展在小行星、行星际探测领域合作。

5. 空间技术。

——支持卫星工程和技术合作,完成埃及二号卫星联合研制,发射中法天文卫星、中意电磁监测卫星 02 星,推动中巴(西)资源系列后续卫星合作。

——开展航天测控支持合作,继续开展与欧洲空间局在测控支持领域合作,进一步推进地面站网建设。

——支持商业航天国际合作,包括发射服务,以及卫星整星、卫星及运载火箭分系统、零部件、电子元器件、地面设施设备等产品技术合作。重点推动巴基斯坦通信卫星研制,以及巴基斯坦航天中心、埃及航天城建设合作进程。

6. 空间应用。

——推动中国气象卫星数据全球应用,支持中法海洋卫星数据向世界气象卫星组织开放,推动"张衡一号"电磁监测卫星数据全球共享和科学应用。

——推动"一带一路"空间信息走廊建设,加强遥感、导航、通信卫星的应用合作。

——推动亚太空间合作组织数据共享服务平台建设。

——推动金砖国家遥感卫星星座建设与应用。

——参与空间气候观测平台建设与实践。

7. 空间科学。

——依托深空探测工程,利用地外样品和探测数据,开展空间环境、行星起源演化等领域的联合研究;通过联合国向国际社会开放"嫦娥四号"卫星科学数据。

——推动空间科学卫星联合研制,开展以暗物质粒子、太阳爆发活动及其影响、空间引力波等为重点的空间科学探索研究。

8. 人才与学术交流。

——开展航天领域人员交流与培训。

——举办高水平国际学术交流会议和论坛。

结　束　语

当今世界,越来越多的国家高度重视并大力发展航天事业,世界航天进入大发展大变革的新阶段,将对人类社会发展产生重大而深远的影响。

站在全面建设社会主义现代化国家新征程的历史起点上,中国将加快推进航天强国建设,秉持人类命运共同体理念,继续同各国一道,积极参与外空全球治理与交流合作,维护外空安全,促进外空活动长期可持续发展,为保护地球家园、增进民生福祉、服务人类文明进步作出新的更大贡献。

中国残疾人体育事业发展和权利保障

（2022 年 3 月）

中华人民共和国
国务院新闻办公室

前　言

　　体育对包括残疾人在内的每个人的生活都具有重要价值。残疾人体育是残疾人增强体质、康复身心、参与社会、实现全面发展的有效途径；是人们认识残疾人潜能与价值、促进社会和谐共进的独特渠道。发展残疾人体育，对于保障残疾人平等权利、促进残疾人融合发展、推动残疾人共享经济社会发展成果，具有重要意义。残疾人体育重在参与，这是残疾人的一项重要权利，是人权保障的重要内容。

　　以习近平同志为核心的党中央十分关心残疾人，高度重视残疾人事业发展。中共十八大以来，在习近平新时代中国特色社会主义思想指引下，中国将残疾人事业纳入"五位一体"总体布局和"四个全面"战略布局，采取切实有效措施促进残疾人体育蓬勃发展。残疾人体育运动水平不断提高，残疾人运动员自强不息、顽强拼搏、为国争光、激励社会，残疾人体育事业取得历史性成就。

　　北京 2022 年冬残奥会开幕在即，全世界的目光再次聚焦残疾人体育健儿，中国残疾人体育迎来新的发展机遇，必将推动国际残疾人体育运动"一起向未来"。

一、国家发展促进残疾人体育进步

新中国成立以来,在社会主义革命和建设、改革开放和社会主义现代化建设、新时代中国特色社会主义伟大进程中,伴随着残疾人事业的发展,残疾人体育不断发展壮大,走出一条具有中国特色、符合时代潮流的残疾人体育发展之路。

1. 新中国成立后残疾人体育活动逐步开展。1949 年中华人民共和国成立,实现了人民当家作主,残疾人在政治上获得了和其他人平等的地位,享受应有的公民权利和义务。1954 年制定的《中华人民共和国宪法》规定,残疾人"有获得物质帮助的权利"。福利工厂、福利机构、特殊教育学校、残疾人社会组织和友善的社会环境保障了残疾人的基本权益,改善了残疾人的生活。新中国成立初期,中国共产党和中国政府就非常重视全民体育运动,基于学校、工厂、疗养院的残疾人体育逐步发展起来。广大残疾人积极参与体育活动,开展了广播操、生产操、乒乓球、篮球、拔河等体育活动,为残疾人体育的发展奠定了基础。1957 年,第一届全国青年盲人运动会在上海举办。全国各地建立了聋人体育组织,积极举办区域性聋人体育运动会。1959 年,举办了全国首届聋人男子篮球赛。全国性残疾人体育比赛的开展,推动更多残疾人参加体育活动,增强了残疾人体质,激发了残疾人社会参与的热情。

2. 残疾人体育在改革开放中快速发展。改革开放后,中国实现了人民生活从温饱不足到总体小康、奔向全面小康的历史性跨越,推进了中华民族从站起来到富起来的伟大飞跃。中国共产党和中国政府实施了一系列发展残疾人事业、改善残疾人状况的重大举措。中国制定了《中华人民共和国残疾人保障法》,批准了联合国《残疾人权利公约》。残疾人事业由改革开放初期以救济为主的社会福利工作,逐步发展成为综合性社会事业。残疾人参与社会生活的环境大为改善,残疾人各方面的权利得到尊重和保障,为发展残疾人体育奠定了基础。《中华人民共和国体育法》规定,全社会应当关心、支持残疾人参加体育活动,各级政府应当采取措施为残疾人参加体育活动提供方便,公共体育设施要对残疾人实行优惠办法,学校应当创造条件为病残学生组织适合其特点的体育活动。残疾人体育纳入国家发展战略和残疾人事业发展规划,残疾人体育工作机制逐步健全,公共服务全面开展,残疾人体育迎来了快速发展阶段。1983 年,在天津举办全国伤残人体育邀请赛。1984 年,在安徽合肥举办首届全国残疾人运动会。同年,中国残奥代表团首次赴美国纽约参加第七届残奥会,并实现中国残奥史上金牌"零的突破"。1994 年,北京承办第六届远东及南太平洋地区残疾人运动会(以下简称"远南运动会"),这是中国首次承办综合性国际残疾人体育赛事。2001 年,北京获得 2008 年奥运会和残奥会举办权。2004 年,中国残奥代表团在雅典残奥会上首次获得金牌数和奖牌数双第一。2007 年,举办上海世界夏季特殊奥林匹克运动会(以下简称"上海特奥会")。2008

年,举办北京残奥会。2010年,举办广州亚洲残疾人运动会(以下简称"广州亚残运会")。这一时期,先后成立了中国伤残人体育协会(后更名为中国残疾人体育协会、中国残奥委员会)、中国聋人体育协会、中国智残人体育协会(后更名为中国特奥委员会)等残疾人体育组织,并相继加入国际残奥委员会等多个国际残疾人体育组织。各地也先后成立了各类残疾人体育组织。

3. 新时代残疾人体育取得历史性成就。中共十八大以来,中国特色社会主义进入新时代,中国如期全面建成小康社会,中华民族迎来了从站起来、富起来到强起来的伟大飞跃。中共中央总书记、中国国家主席习近平对残疾人格外关心、格外关注,强调"残疾人是社会大家庭的平等成员,是人类文明发展的一支重要力量,是坚持和发展中国特色社会主义的一支重要力量""健全人可以活出精彩的人生,残疾人也可以活出精彩的人生""2020年全面建成小康社会,残疾人一个也不能少""中国将进一步发展残疾人事业,促进残疾人全面发展和共同富裕""努力实现残疾人'人人享有康复服务'的目标";强调"把北京冬奥会、冬残奥会办成一届精彩、非凡、卓越的奥运盛会""要想运动员之所想、办运动员之所需,为运动员提供方便、快捷、精准、细致的服务,特别是针对残疾人运动员的特殊需求,增设相关无障碍设施"。这些重要论述为中国残疾人事业发展指明了前进方向。在以习近平同志为核心的党中央坚强领导下,中国把残疾人事业持续纳入国家经济社会发展总体规划和国家人权行动计划,残疾人权益保障更加有力,残疾人"平等、参与、共享"的目标得到更好实现,残疾人获得感、幸福感、安全感持续提升,残疾人体育迎来前所未有的历史性发展机遇。

残疾人体育纳入全民健身、健康中国、体育强国等国家战略。《中华人民共和国公共文化服务保障法》和《无障碍环境建设条例》规定优先推进体育等公共服务场所的无障碍设施改造,配置无障碍的设施设备。投资建设国家残疾人冰上运动比赛训练馆。残疾人康复健身体育广泛开展,残疾人体育活动进入社区和残疾人家庭,越来越多残疾人走出家门参与体育活动。实施全民健身助残工程,培养残疾人社会体育指导员,为重度残疾人提供居家康复健身服务。全力备战北京2022年冬季残奥会,实现冬残奥参赛大项全覆盖。残疾人运动员在平昌冬季残奥会上勇夺轮椅冰壶金牌,实现冬季残奥会金牌和奖牌"零的突破";在东京残奥会上表现"神勇",实现金牌数和奖牌数五连冠;参加听障奥运会、世界特奥会等重大国际赛事取得历史最好成绩。

中国残疾人体育发展水平快速提升,彰显了中国推动残疾人事业发展的制度优势,展现了中国尊重和保障残疾人权益的显著成就,理解、尊重、关心、帮助残疾人的社会氛围更加浓厚,越来越多残疾人通过参与体育运动成就出彩人生,实现人生梦想。残疾人挑战极限、锐意进取、顽强拼搏的精神激励了全国人民,促进了社会文明进步。

二、残疾人群众性体育活动广泛开展

中国将残疾人康复健身体育作为实施全民健身、健康中国、体育强国等国家战略的重要组成部分,开展全国性残疾人体育活动,改善体育服务,丰富活动内容,加强科研教育,残疾人群众性康复健身体育活动日益活跃。

1. 残疾人体育活动丰富多彩。城乡基层残疾人康复健身体育活动因地制宜,活跃开展。通过推广社区残疾人康复健身体育项目、政府购买体育健身服务等方式,推动残疾人在基层社区开展体育健身和竞赛活动。全国残疾人社区文体活动参与率由 2015 年的 6.8% 持续提升至 2021 年的 23.9%。各级各类学校组织残疾学生开展适合其特点的日常体育活动,创编推广排舞、啦啦操、旱地冰壶等适合残疾学生集体参与的运动项目。鼓励大中小学生参与特奥大学计划和融合活动等项目,动员医务工作者参与体育康复、运动员分级、特奥运动员健康计划等活动,组织体育工作者参与残疾人体育健身、竞赛训练等专业工作,为残疾人体育提供志愿服务。全国残疾人运动会设有康复健身类体育比赛项目。举办残疾人民间足球赛,设盲人、聋人、智力残疾人等多个组别。全国残疾人排舞公开赛参与队伍扩展至近 20 个省(区、市),越来越多的特殊教育学校将排舞项目列为大课间体育活动。

2.全国性残疾人体育活动风生水起。各类残疾人每年定期参加"全国特奥日""残疾人健身周"和"残疾人冰雪运动季"等全国性残疾人体育活动。自2007年起,每年7月20日开展"全国特奥日"活动,智力残疾人通过参加特奥运动,挖掘潜力、增强信心、融入社会。自2011年起,每年"全民健身日"所在周全国集中开展"残疾人健身周"活动,举办轮椅太极拳、柔力球、盲人足球等健身运动项目。残疾人通过参加康复健身体育赛事和活动,学习残疾人体育文化知识,开展体验运动项目,了解各种康复健身器材,展示和交流康复健身技能,增强了身体素质,陶冶了性情,激发了生活热情,培养了融入社会的自信。肢残人轮椅马拉松、盲人象棋交流挑战赛、全国聋人柔力球交流赛等赛事已成为全国性品牌活动。

3.残疾人大众冰雪运动蓬勃发展。自2016年起,连续6年举办"残疾人冰雪运动季",为残疾人参与冰雪运动搭建平台,带动残疾人融入"3亿人参与冰雪运动"。从首届开展的14个省级单位发展到现在的31个省(区、市)。各地因地制宜举办冬季残疾人体育活动,开展冬残奥项目体验、大众冰雪体育赛事、冬季康复健身训练营、冰雪嘉年华等形式多样、内容丰富的活动。创编和推广了迷你滑雪、旱地滑雪、旱地冰壶、冰蹴球、滑冰、冰橇、雪橇、冰上自行车、雪地足球、冰上龙舟、雪地拔河、冰河钓鱼等新颖有趣、深受残疾人喜爱的大众冰雪运动项目。通过编制发放《残疾人冬季体育健身项目和活动方法指导手册》等,为基层残疾人冬季体育健身提供服务和支持。

4.残疾人康复健身体育服务不断改善。实施"自强健身工程"

和"康复体育关爱工程",促进残疾人康复健身。加强残疾人康复健身体育服务队伍建设,创编推广残疾人康复体育、健身体育项目和方法,研发推广康复体育、健身体育器材,丰富残疾人体育服务产品,推进社区残疾人健身体育和居家重度残疾人康复体育服务。《全民健身基本公共服务标准(2021年版)》等国家政策法规明确要求改善残疾人健身环境,要求公共体育设施免费或低收费向残疾人开放。截至2020年,全国残疾人健身示范点累计建设10675个,共培养、发展残疾人社会体育指导员12.5万名,为43.4万户重度残疾人提供了康复体育进家庭等服务。同时,面向经济欠发达地区和乡镇、农村地区给予重点支持,积极引导建设残疾人冬季健身活动服务站点。

5.残疾人体育教学科研取得进步。中国把残疾人体育纳入特殊教育和师范、体育教学计划,残疾人体育科研机构建设步伐加快,中国残疾人体育运动管理中心、中国残疾人事业发展研究会体育发展专业委员会以及多所高校成立的残疾人体育科研机构成为残疾人体育科研的重要力量。残疾人体育人才培养初步形成体系,部分高校开设残疾人体育相关选修课程,培养了一批残疾人体育专业人才。残疾人体育科研成果不断丰富。截至2021年,关于残疾人体育研究的国家社科基金项目累计超过20项。

三、残疾人竞技体育水平不断提高

残疾人参与体育赛事日益增多，越来越多的残疾人运动员参加国内国际残疾人体育赛事，勇于挑战，超越自我，展现自强不息、顽强拼搏的精神，成就出彩人生。

1. 在重大国际残疾人体育赛事中表现优异。自 1987 年起，中国智力残疾人参加了 9 届世界夏季特奥会和 7 届世界冬季特奥会，展示了"勇敢尝试、争取胜利"的特奥精神。1989 年，中国聋人体育首次走出国门，参加了新西兰克赖斯特彻奇第 16 届世界聋人运动会。2007 年，在美国盐湖城第 16 届冬季聋奥会上，中国代表团获得 1 枚铜牌，首次在冬季聋奥会上夺得奖牌。此后在多届夏季和冬季聋奥会上取得佳绩。积极参加亚洲残疾人体育赛事，屡获殊荣。1984 年，中国残奥体育代表团 24 名残疾人运动员在纽约第 7 届残奥会上参加了田径、游泳、乒乓球三个大项的比赛，获得 2 枚金牌、24 枚奖牌，在残疾人群体中掀起了参与体育运动的热潮。此后中国残奥体育代表团相继参加了历届残奥会，成绩稳步提升。2004 年，在雅典第 12 届残奥会上，中国体育代表团获得 63 枚金牌、141 枚奖牌，金牌数和奖牌数跃居第一。2021 年，在东京第 16 届残奥会上，中国体育代表团获得 96 枚金牌、207 枚奖牌，连续五届实现金牌、奖牌榜双第一。"十三五"时期，中国残疾人体育代表团共参加 160 项国际赛事,取得 1114 枚金牌。

2. 全国性残疾人体育赛事影响不断扩大。自 1984 年举办首届全国残运会以来,中国已先后举办 11 届全国残运会,比赛项目从田径、游泳、乒乓球发展到 34 个项目。自 1992 年第三届全国残疾人运动会起,全国残疾人运动会正式列入国务院审批的大型运动会系列,形成每四年举办一次的机制,残疾人体育逐步进入制度化、规范化的发展轨道。2019 年,在天津举办的第十届全国残运会暨第七届全国特奥会首次实现全国残运会和全国运动会同城举办。2021 年,在陕西举办的第十一届残运会暨第八届特奥会首次实现全国残特奥会和全国运动会同城同年举办,促进了两个运动会的同步规划、同步实施、同样精彩。除了举办全国残运会,还在各地举办全国性肢残人、盲人、聋人等各类单项赛事,吸引各类残疾人广泛参与体育运动。通过举办经常性全国残疾人体育赛事,培养了残疾人运动员队伍,提升了残疾人运动水平。

3. 冬残奥运动水平快速提升。北京冬残奥会的成功申办,为中国冬残奥运动发展带来重大机遇。中国高度重视冬残奥会备战工作,制定实施了系列行动方案,积极推动项目布局,统筹训练设施、器材保障、科研服务,组织训练营选拔优秀运动员,加强技术力量培养和国际合作,聘请国内外高水平教练员,组建国家集训队,高山滑雪、冬季两项、越野滑雪、单板滑雪、冰球、轮椅冰壶等 6 个冬残奥大项全部纳入全国残运会赛事,推动 29 个省(区、市)开展冬季项目。自 2015 年至 2021 年,全国开展的冬残奥会大项由 2 个拓展到 6 个,实现了比赛大项全覆盖;运动员由不足 50 人发展至近千人,技术官员从无到有发展到 100 多人。自 2018 年起,每年举办全国性冬残奥项目比赛,并纳入 2019 年和 2021 年全国残运会赛事。2016 年以来,中国残疾人运动员参加冬残奥系列国际赛事,共获得 47 枚金牌、54 枚银牌、52 枚铜牌。中国将有 96 名运动员参加北京冬残奥会全部 6 个大项 73 个小项的比赛,与 2014 年索契冬残奥会相比,参赛运动员增加了 80 余名,参赛大项增加了 4 个、小项增加了 67 个。

4. 残疾人运动员培养保障机制逐步完善。根据残疾人运动员的类别及适宜开展的体育项目,对残疾人运动员进行医学和功能分级,为残疾人运动员公平参与各类体育项目提供了前提和保障。建立完善县级发现选送、市级培养提高、省级集训参赛和国家重点培养四级联动的残疾人运动员业余训练体系,举办青少年选拔赛、训练营,加强后备人才培养。加强残疾人体育教练员、裁判员、分级员等专业人才队伍建设。加强残疾人体育训练基地建设,命名 45 个国家残疾人体育训练基地,为残疾人运动员竞赛、训练、培训、科研等提供保障和服务。各级政府采取措施,切实解决残疾人运动员就学、就业和社会保障问题,开展优秀运动员免试进入高校试点工作。制定《残疾人体育赛事活动管理办法》,促进残疾人体育赛事规范、有序发展。加强残疾人体育道德作风建设,严禁使用违禁药物和各种违规行为,维护残疾人体育比赛的公平、公正。

四、为世界残疾人体育运动作出贡献

开放的中国积极承担国际义务,成功举办北京残奥会、上海特奥会、北京远南运动会、广州亚残运会,全力筹办北京冬残奥会、杭州亚残运会,有力促进了中国残疾人事业发展,为国际残疾人体育运动发展作出了突出贡献。中国全面参与国际残疾人体育事务,不断加强与其他国家和国际残疾人组织交流合作,增进各国人民包括残疾人之间的友谊。

1. 成功举办亚洲综合性残疾人体育赛事。1994 年,北京举办第六届远南运动会,42 个国家和地区的残疾人代表团共 1927 人参加,规模超过历届。这是中国首次举办国际综合性残疾人运动会,展示了改革开放和现代化建设的丰硕成果,加深了社会对残疾人的了解,助推了中国残疾人事业发展,对推进"亚太残疾人十年"行动产生了积极影响。2010 年,在广州举办首届亚残运会,41 个国家和地区的运动员参赛。这是亚洲残疾人体育组织重组后举办的首届运动会,也是亚运会与亚残运会历史上首次在同城同年举行,进一步推动了广州的无障碍环境建设。通过举办亚残运会,在全社会广泛传播了残疾人体育精神,营造了扶残助残、残健融合的良好氛围,使更多残疾人共享社会发展成果,提高了亚洲残疾人体育运动水平。2022 年,第四届亚残运会将在杭州举办。届时,40 多个国家和地区的约

3800 名残疾人运动员将参加 22 个大项、604 个小项的竞赛,必将有力促进亚洲人民的友谊与合作。

2. 圆满举办上海特奥会。2007 年,上海举办第 12 届上海特奥会,164 个国家和地区的 1 万多名特奥运动员、教练员参与了 25 个项目比赛。这是第一次在发展中国家、在亚洲举办的特奥会,鼓励了智力残疾人参与社会的勇气,推动了中国特奥运动的发展。为迎接并纪念上海特奥会,中国将每年 7 月 20 日定为“全国特奥日”,上海成立了“阳光之家”,帮助智力残疾人进行康复训练、教育培训、日间照料、职业康复。在此基础上,全国推广“阳光家园”计划,支持各地智力、精神和重度残疾人托养服务机构和家庭开展托养服务工作。

3. 高水平举办北京残奥会。2008 年,北京举办第 13 届残奥会,147 个国家和地区的 4032 名运动员参加了比赛。赛会设 20 个大项、472 个小项,运动员人数、参赛国家和地区数、比赛项目数都创残奥会历史新高。北京残奥会开启了残奥会与奥运会“同时申办、同城举办”的新模式,兑现了“两个奥运,同样精彩”的承诺,为世界奉献了一届高水平、有特色的残奥会,“超越、融合、共享”理念是中国对国际残奥运动的精神贡献。残奥会在体育设施、城市交通、无障碍环境建设、志愿服务等方面留下了丰富遗产,有力促进了中国残疾人事业发展。北京市建设了一批规范化、标准化的“温馨家园”,残疾人及其家庭可以就近就便享受职业康复、教育培训、日间照料、文体活动等服务,为平等融入社会生活创造了条件。社会各界进一步增进了对残疾人事业和残疾人体育的认识,“平等、参与、共享”的理念更加深入人心,全社会尊重、理解、关心、帮助残疾人的氛围更加浓厚。中国履行了对国际社会的郑重承诺,广泛弘扬了"团结、友谊、和平"的奥林匹克精神,促进了世界各国人民的相互了解和友谊,让"同一个世界、同一个梦想"的口号响彻寰球,赢得了国际社会高度评价。

4. 全力筹办北京 2022 年冬残奥会。2015 年,北京携手张家口赢得了 2022 年冬奥会和冬残奥会的举办权,北京成为第一个既举办过夏季残奥会又举办冬季残奥会的城市,冬残奥运动迎来重大发展机遇。中国全面落实"绿色、共享、开放、廉洁"的办奥理念,突出"简约、安全、精彩"的办赛要求,积极与国际残奥委员会等国际体育组织沟通合作,落实新冠肺炎疫情防控各项措施,精心做好赛会组织、赛会服务、科技应用、文化活动等各项筹办工作。北京自 2019 年起实施无障碍环境建设专项行动,确定城市道路整改、公共交通、公共服务场所、信息交流等重点领域 17 项重点任务,累计完成 33.6 万个点位改造,基本实现首都功能核心区无障碍化,城市无障碍环境规范性、适用性、系统化水平显著提升。张家口积极推进公共设施无障碍建设,城市无障碍环境显著改善。建立完善以残疾人冰雪运动为支撑的残疾人冬季活动体系,加快推动残疾人冰雪运动普及。北京冬残奥会将于 2022 年 3 月 4 日至 13 日举办。截至 2022 年 2 月 20 日,来自 48 个国家(地区)的 647 名运动员注册参赛。中国已做好准备,迎接世界冬残奥运动员参赛。

5. 积极参与国际残疾人体育事务。随着中国残疾人体育走向世界,中国在国际残疾人体育事务中发挥着越来越重要的作用,话语权和影响力逐步扩大。自 1984 年起,中国相继加入国际残奥委员会、国际伤残人体育组织、国际盲人体育联合会、国际脑瘫人体育协会、世界聋人体育联合会、国际轮椅运动联合会、国际特殊奥林匹克委员会、远东及南太平洋地区残疾人运动联合会等世界残疾人体育组织,与一些国家和地区的残疾人体育组织建立了友好关系。中国残疾人体育协会、中国聋人体育协会、中国特奥委员会已经成为世界残疾人体育组织的重要成员。积极参加国际残奥委员会代表大会等国际残疾人体育有关重要会议,共商国际残疾人体育发展大计。中国残疾人体育官员、裁判员、专家等获任远南运动会联合会执委会、世界聋人体育联合会、国际盲人体育联合会执委和专项委员会负责人。为培养残疾人体育技术力量,先后推荐和委派专业人员担任有关国际残疾人体育组织的技术官员和国际裁判。

6. 深入开展残疾人体育国际交流。1982 年,中国首次组派体育代表团参加第三届远南运动会,中国残疾人体育逐步融入世界残疾人体育。中国积极开展国际残疾人体育友好交流与合作。在共建"一带一路"、中非合作论坛等多边合作机制和双边交往中,把残疾人体育作为人文交流的重要内容。2017 年,举办共建"一带一路"框架下残疾人事务主题活动,发布《关于促进"一带一路"残疾人事务合作交流的倡议》和相关文件,搭建体育设施资源共享机制,向共建"一带一路"国家残疾人运动员、教练员开放 45 个国家级残疾人夏季和冬季体育训练中心。2019 年,举办共建"一带一路"框架下残疾人事务主题活动体育分论坛,促成各残疾人体育组织间互学互鉴,共同打造残疾人体育事业交流合作典范。同年,中国残奥委员会与芬兰、俄罗斯、希腊等国残奥委员会签订了残疾人体育发展战略合作协议。与此同时,中外地方和城市间的残疾人体育交流日趋活跃。

五、残疾人体育展现中国人权事业发展进步

中国残疾人体育事业蓬勃发展,不仅体现出残疾人的体育精神与实力,更体现出中国式的人权与国家发展的成绩。中国坚持以人民为中心,将人民幸福生活作为最大的人权,促进人权事业全面发展,切实保障包括残疾人在内的特定群体的各项权益。参与体育活动的权利是残疾人全面实现生存权和发展权的重要内容。中国残疾人体育事业发展,符合中国国情,有效回应残疾人群体的需要,促进残疾人身心健康。残疾人体育是中国人权事业发展进步的生动写照,弘扬了全人类共同价值,促进了各国人民的交往、了解和友谊,为构建公平公正合理包容的全球人权治理秩序、维护世界和平发展贡献了中国智慧。

1. 坚持以人民为中心,促进残疾人身心健康。中国坚持以人民为中心的人权理念,以发展促进残疾人权益保障。国家在发展战略中纳入残疾人事业,实现了"全面建成小康社会,残疾人一个也不能少"的目标。体育是提高人民健康水平的重要途径,是满足人民群众对美好生活向往的重要手段。残疾人通过参与体育活动,有助于改善身体机能,减轻和消除功能障碍,增强独立生活能力,满足兴趣爱好,增加社会交往,提高生活品质,实现人生价值。中国高度重视

残疾人健康权利保障,强调残疾人"人人享有康复服务"。中国把残疾人康复健身体育纳入残疾人康复服务。各级政府面向基层,创新服务方式,开展广泛的残疾人康复健身体育工作。在学校教育中保障残疾学生平等参与体育、增进身心健康和发育。残疾人的健康权利通过体育活动得到更好保障。

2. 坚持立足中国国情,促进残疾人平等融合。中国坚持把人权的普遍性原则同本国实际相结合,坚持生存权和发展权是首要的基本人权,把增进人民福祉、保障人民当家作主、促进人的全面发展作为发展的出发点和落脚点,努力维护社会公平正义。中国的法律制度规定残疾人享有与所有人平等的参与文化体育生活的权利,在实施中加强对残疾人权利的平等保护和特殊扶助。国家建立和完善公共体育设施及服务,确保残疾人获得公共体育服务的均等化。国家采取有力措施,全面推进体育领域的无障碍环境建设,加强全民健身场地设施无障碍改造,完善各类体育场馆设施并向所有残疾人开放,落实合理便利支持,消除残疾人充分参与体育活动的外部障碍。北京冬残奥会等体育赛事为残疾人全面参与社会生活创造了体育、经济、社会、文化、环境、城市发展和区域发展方面的丰厚遗产。各地举办残疾人重大体育赛事的场馆,在赛后继续服务残疾人,并为城市无障碍环境建设提供了样板。各级政府完善社区残疾人体育设施,培育扶持残疾人体育组织和文艺团体,购买多样的社会服务,举办残健融合的体育活动,促进残疾人社区文体活动参与率不断提高。相关组织和机构研发推广适合国情和各类别残疾人锻炼的小型康复体育和健身体育器材,创编普及项目和方法。残疾人充分参与体育活动,追求卓越,突破自我,团结拼搏,共享平等融合,实现人生出彩。残疾人体育弘扬中华优秀传统文化,关爱生命、弱有所扶、和合包容,鼓舞和激励更多残疾人热爱体育、参与运动。广大残疾人自尊、自信、自立、自强,发扬中华体育精神,在体育中展现生命力量和卓越品格。残疾人通过体育活动,平等参与社会生活的权利得到更好保障。

3. 坚持同等重视各类人权,实现残疾人全面发展。残疾人体育是一面镜子,折射出残疾人的生活水平和人权状况。中国确保残疾人享有各项经济、政治、社会、文化权利,为残疾人参与体育活动和社会生活、实现全面发展奠定了坚实基础。在发展全过程人民民主中充分吸收残疾人及其社会组织、群众代表的意见,使国家体育制度更加公平和包容。不断加强残疾人社会保障和福利服务,稳步提高残疾人受教育水平,更好保障残疾人就业权利。完善残疾人公共法律服务体系,加大对残疾人人身财产的保护力度,消除基于残疾的歧视。定期开展残疾人体育先进评选,表彰在残疾人体育发展中作出积极贡献的单位和个人。加强对残疾人体育活动的宣传报道,通过各种渠道和形式,传播残疾人体育新观念新风尚,营造良好社会环境。社会大众深入了解"勇气、决心、激励、平等"的残奥会价值,认同无障碍理念,增强平等融合意识,对残疾人事业各项工作更加关注和支持。社会各界通过"残疾人健身周""残疾人文化周""全国特奥日""残疾人冰雪运动季"等契机,以活动赞助、志愿服务、拉拉队等形式支持促进残疾人参与体育活动,共享社会文明成果。残疾人体育活动推动全社会增强尊重和保障残疾人固有尊严和平等权利的社会氛围,有力地促进了社会文明进步。

4. 坚持推进国际合作,加强残疾人体育交流。中国主张加强不同文明交流互鉴,将残疾人体育作为残疾人领域国际友好交流的重要部分。作为体育大国,中国在国际残疾人体育事务中发挥着越来越重要的作用,有力促进了区域和全球残疾人体育发展。中国残疾人体育蓬勃发展,是中国积极履行联合国《残疾人权利公约》、落实联合国 2030 年可持续发展议程取得的丰硕成果。中国尊重各国文化、体育和社会制度的多样性,强调国际体育活动和规则中的公平正义。中国不附加任何条件,积极向国际残奥委员会发展基金捐款,搭建体育设施资源共享机制,向国外残疾人运动员、教练员开放国家级残疾人体育训练中心。中国促进残疾人广泛参与国际体育活动,增进民间交流了解和民心相通,推动构建更加公平公正合理包容的全球人权治理秩序,升华了世界各国人民之间的友谊,促进了世界和平与发展。中国强调残疾人是人类大家庭的平等成员,始终高扬人道主义和国际主义精神,推动残疾人体育国际交流合作,以残疾人体育交流合作描绘不同文明交流互鉴的宏伟画卷,积极构建人类命运共同体。

结　束　语

　　关心残疾人,是社会文明的重要标志。发展残疾人体育,对于激励广大残疾人自尊、自信、自立、自强,弘扬自强不息时代精神,营造全社会理解、尊重、关心、支持残疾人和残疾人事业,共同促进残疾人全面发展和共同富裕有着十分重要的作用。新中国成立以来,特别是中共十八大以来,中国残疾人体育事业取得举世瞩目的成绩。同时也要看到,中国残疾人体育发展仍然不平衡、不充分,存在较大的地区和城乡差距,服务能力仍然不足,康复健身体育的参与率还需进一步提高,残疾人冰雪运动还需进一步普及,发展残疾人体育依然任重道远。

　　在以习近平同志为核心的党中央坚强领导下,在全面建设社会主义现代化国家新征程中,中国共产党和中国政府坚持以人民为中心的发展思想,坚持弱有所扶,保障残疾人平等权利,增进残疾人民生福祉,提高残疾人自我发展能力,切实尊重和保障包括残疾人参与体育运动的权利在内的各项权益,推动残疾人事业向现代化迈进,不断满足广大残疾人对美好生活的向往。

新时代的中国青年

（2022 年 4 月）

中华人民共和国
国务院新闻办公室

前　言

青年是整个社会力量中最积极、最有生气的力量,国家的希望在青年,民族的未来在青年。中国青年始终是实现中华民族伟大复兴的先锋力量。

近代以后,中国逐步沦为半殖民地半封建社会,国家蒙辱、人民蒙难、文明蒙尘,中华民族遭受了前所未有的劫难,中国青年深切感受到日益深重的民族危机。

中国青年的觉醒,点燃了中华民族伟大复兴的希望之光。五四运动前后,一大批率先接受新思想、新文化、新知识的有志青年在反复比较中选择了马克思列宁主义,促进中国人民和中华民族实现了自鸦片战争以来的第一次全面觉醒。1921 年 7 月,平均年龄仅 28 岁的 13 位代表参加中国共产党第一次全国代表大会,宣告了中国共产党诞生这一开天辟地的大事变,吹响了全民族觉醒和奋起的号角,开启了民族复兴的新纪元。在中国共产党的领导下,中国共产主义青年团于 1922 年成立,中国青年运动翻开了新的历史篇章。

回首百年,无论风云变幻、沧海桑田,中国青年爱党、爱国、爱人民的赤诚追求始终未改,坚定不移听党话、跟党走的忠贞初心始终未变。在新民主主义革命时期,中国青年不怕牺牲、敢于斗争,经受了生与死的考验,为争取民族独立、人民解放冲锋陷阵、抛洒热血。在社会主义革命和建设时期,中国青年勇于拼搏、甘于奉献,经受了苦与乐的考验,在新中国的广阔天地忘我劳动、发愤图强。在改革开放和社会主义现代化建设新时期,中国青年开拓创新、勇立潮头,经受了得与失的考验,为推动中国大踏步赶上时代锐意改革、拼搏奋进。

党的十八大以来,中国特色社会主义进入新时代。以习近平同志为核心的党中央高度重视青年、热情关怀青年、充分信任青年,鲜明提出党管青年原则,大力倡导青年优先发展理念,着力发挥共青团作为党的助手和后备军作用,推动青年发展事业实现全方位进步、取得历史性成就。在这个伟大的新时代,中国青年展现了亮丽的青春风采、迸发出豪迈的青春激情。

新时代中国青年刚健自信、胸怀天下、担当有为,衷心拥护党的领导,奋力走在时代前列,展现出前所未有的昂扬风貌:追求远大理想,心中铭刻着对马克思主义的崇高信仰、对共产主义和中国特色社会主义的坚定信念;深植家国情怀,与国家同呼吸、与人民共命运,时刻彰显着鲜明的爱国主义精神气质;传承奋斗担当,先天下之忧而忧、后天下之乐而乐,勇做走在时代前列的奋进者、开拓者、奉献者。

历史清晰而深刻地昭示,没有中国共产党就没有朝气蓬勃的中国青年运动,矢志不渝跟党走是中国青年百年奋斗的最宝贵经验,深深融入血脉的红色基因是中国青年百年奋斗的最宝贵财富。

2021年7月1日,习近平总书记在庆祝中国共产党成立100周年大会上深情寄语:"新时代的中国青年要以实现中华民族伟大复兴为己任,增强做中国人的志气、骨气、底气,不负时代,不负韶华,不负党和人民的殷切期望!"

展望未来,民族复兴大业已经站在新的历史起点、踏上新的伟大征程。新时代中国青年迎来了实现抱负、施展才华的难得机遇,更肩负着建设社会主义现代化强国、实现中华民族伟大复兴中国梦的时代重任。

中国梦是历史的、现实的,也是未来的;是广大人民的,更是青年一代的。新时代中国青年必将以永不懈怠的精神状态、永不停滞的前进姿态,在接续奋斗中将中华民族伟大复兴的中国梦变为现实。

为充分展示新时代中国青年的风貌和担当,值此中国共产主义青年团成立 100 周年之际,特发布本白皮书。

一、新时代中国青年生逢盛世、共享机遇

时代造就青年，盛世成就青年。新时代的中国繁荣发展、充满希望，中华民族迎来了从站起来、富起来到强起来的伟大飞跃，实现中华民族伟大复兴进入了不可逆转的历史进程。新时代中国青年生逢中华民族发展的最好时期，拥有更优越的发展环境、更广阔的成长空间，面临着建功立业的难得人生际遇。

（一）拥有更高质量的发展条件

随着中国的经济实力、科技实力、综合国力不断迈上新台阶、取得新跨越，新时代中国青年的发展基础日益厚实，发展底气越来越足。

物质发展环境更为优越。青年高质量发展，物质丰裕是基础。中国创造了世所罕见的经济快速发展和社会长期稳定"两大奇迹"，2021年国内生产总值超过110万亿元、稳居世界第二。超过2500万贫困青年彻底摆脱贫困，中国青年共同迈向更高水平的小康生活。中国青年向往更有品质的美好生活，消费方式从大众化迈向个性化，消费需求从满足生存转向享受生活，从有衣穿到穿得

时尚、穿出个性,从吃饱饭到吃得丰富、吃出健康,从能出行到快捷通畅、平稳舒适。中国青年的生活水平实现了质的跃升,高质量发展有了更加丰盈、更为坚实的物质基础。

精神成长空间更为富足。青年高质量发展,离不开精神生活的多姿多彩。受益于图书馆、博物馆、文化馆、美术馆等惠及青年的公共文化设施的不断完善①,中国青年享受的公共文化服务水平显著提高,逐渐从"去哪儿都新鲜"转变为"去哪儿都习以为常",精神品位不断提升。随着图书、电视、电影、文艺演出等传统文化产业和数字创意、网络视听、数字出版、数字娱乐、线上演播等新兴文化产业迅猛发展,青年所需所盼的公共文化产品日渐丰富,逐渐从"有什么看什么"转变为"想看什么有什么",文化视野更加开阔。文化旅游、乡村旅游、红色旅游、国际旅游等各类旅游产品应有尽有,青年走出去看世界的需求得到更好满足,逐渐从"只在家门口转转"转变为"哪里都能去逛逛",见识阅历更加广博。不断扩展的精神文化生活空间,为中国青年追求更有高度、更有境界、更有品位的人生提供了更多可能。

在与互联网的相互塑造中成长。互联网深刻塑造了青年,青年也深刻影响了互联网。2020年底,中国6岁至18岁未成年人网民达1.8亿,未成年人互联网普及率达94.9%,城乡普及率差距从2018年的5.4个百分点缩小至0.3个百分点,互联网已经成为当代青少年不可或缺的生活方式、成长空间、"第六感官"。

---

① 截至2020年底,全国备案博物馆共5788家,"十三五"期间平均每2天就新增1家。

随着互联网的快速普及,越来越多的青年便捷地获取信息、交流思想、交友互动、购物消费,青年的学习、生活和工作方式发生深刻改变。在网络视频(短视频)、网络直播、网约车用户中,青年都是主体。中国青年日益成为网络空间主要的信息生产者、服务消费者、技术推动者,深刻影响了互联网发展潮流。面对纷繁复杂的网络信息,中国青年在网上积极弘扬正能量、展示新风尚,共同营造清朗网络空间。

单位: 万人

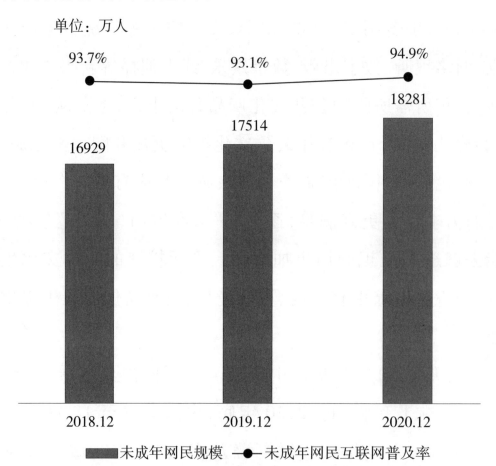

图1 2018年至2020年中国未成年人网民规模及普及率

（二）获得更多人生出彩机会

国家好,青年才会好。随着经济社会快速发展,新时代中国青年获得了更优越的发展机遇,实现人生出彩的舞台越来越宽阔。

教育机会更加均等。中国教育事业优先发展不断深化,中国青年享有更加平等、更高质量的教育机会。2021年,中国义务教育巩固率达95.4%;高中阶段毛入学率达91.4%;高等教育毛入学率达57.8%、在学总规模达4430万人,居世界第一,越来越多的青年打开了通往成功成才大门的重要路径。覆盖学前教育至研究生教育的学生资助政策体系建成且日趋完善,2020年资助资金总额超过2400亿元、资助学生近1.5亿人次,实现"三个全覆盖"①。义务教育阶段进城务工人员随迁子女、农村和贫困地区学生等群体受教育权益得到充分保障。2020年,85.8%的进城务工人员随迁子女在公办学校就读或享受政府购买学位服务;2012年至2021年,农村和贫困地区重点高校专项招生计划定向招生超过82万人,让更多的青年公平享有接受更好教育的机会,阻断贫困的代际传递。

职业选择丰富多元。中国青年职业选择日益市场化、多元化、自主化,不再只青睐传统意义上的"铁饭碗",非公有制经济组织和新社会组织逐渐成为青年就业的主要渠道。"非工即农"的就业选择

---

① 即学前教育、义务教育、高中阶段教育、本专科教育和研究生教育所有学段全覆盖,公办民办学校全覆盖,家庭经济困难学生全覆盖。

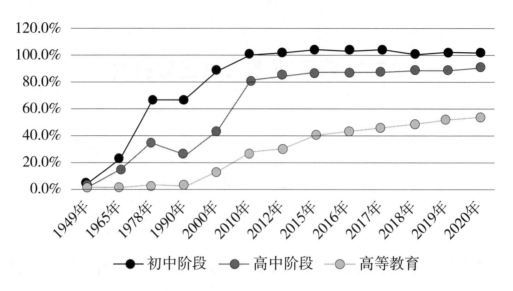

图2　1949年至2020年中国初中阶段、高中阶段、高等教育毛入学率

一去不返,第三产业成为吸纳青年就业的重要领域。2020年,第三产业就业占比47.7%,比十年前增长13.1个百分点。特别是近年来快速兴起的新产业、新业态,催生了电竞选手、网络主播、网络作家等大量新职业,集聚了快递小哥、外卖骑手等大量灵活就业青年,涌现了拥有多重身份和职业、多种工作和生活方式的"斜杠青年",充分体现了时代赋予青年的更多机遇、更多选择。

发展流动畅通自由。随着社会主义市场经济体制不断完善,市场主体活力持续提升,各类要素流动日益频繁,青年的发展渠道更加畅通、流动更加自由。在区域协调发展战略深入实施大背景下,中国青年逐渐由单向的"孔雀东南飞"转变为多向的"自由随心飞",在自己喜欢的城市寻找发展机会,在适合自己的地区拓展成长舞台。一批又一批农村青年走进城市,挥洒汗水、奋力拼搏、安家落户、实现梦想。2020年,外出农民工总数近1.7亿,其中多数为青年;青年常住人口城镇化率达71.1%、比十年前增加15.3个百分点、高于整体常住人口城镇化率7.2个百分点,更多青年通过城乡之间的发展流动更好融入城市生活、实现发展跃迁。

(三) 享受更全面的保障支持

青年的发展离不开国家的坚实保障。在社会公平正义不断彰显、人民发展权益得到有效维护的大背景下,新时代中国青年成长成才有了更良好的法治环境、更有力的政策支持、更可靠的社会保障、更温暖的组织关怀。

法治保障不断完善。随着全面依法治国深入推进,中国特色社会主义法治体系日益完善,为青年发展提供了坚实的保障。作为国家根本大法,宪法明确规定"国家培养青年、少年、儿童在品德、智力、体质等方面全面发展",为建立青年法治保障体系提供了根本遵循。青年发展涉及面广、系统性强,需要各个领域齐抓共管、共同发力。民法典赋予了青年各类民事权益,教育法、义务教育法、职业教育法、高等教育法、民办教育促进法、家庭教育促进法等全面构筑了保障青年受教育权的完备法治环境,就业促进法、劳动法、劳动合同法、社会保险法、科学技术进步法、人口与计划生育法、体育法、妇女权益保障法等充分保障了青年各领域发展权益,刑法、未成年人保护法、预防未成年人犯罪法、反家庭暴力法等共同构建了保护青少年合法权益的法律屏障。

政策保障日益完备。针对中国青年多元化发展需求,国家强化政策服务导向,健全完善政策体系。国民经济和社会发展"十三五"和"十四五"规划鲜明体现青年元素,科教兴国、人才强国、创新驱动发展、乡村振兴、健康中国等国家重大战略充分关注青年群体,青年发展得到越来越多的顶层设计支持。2017年4月,中共中央、国务院制定出台新中国历史上第一个国家级青年领域专项规划——《中长期青年发展规划(2016—2025年)》,为新时代中国青年发展提供根本政策指引。针对青年在毕业求职、创新创业、社会融入、婚恋交友、老人赡养、子女教育等方面的操心事、烦心事,党和政府高度重视,各项政策举措持续出台,青年发展型城市建设蓬勃开展,青年优先发展理念日益深入人心。目前,从中央到地方的青年工作机制基本建成,具有中国特色的青年发展政策体系初步形成。青年充分享受政策红利,实实在在感受到关爱就在身边、关怀就在眼前。

专栏1 《中长期青年发展规划(2016—2025年)》	
中长期青年发展规划(2016—2025年)	**总体目标** 到2020年,具有中国特色的青年发展政策体系和工作机制初步形成,广大青年思想政治素养和全面发展水平进一步提升,在决胜全面建成小康社会伟大实践中的生力军和突击队作用得到充分发挥。 到2025年,具有中国特色的青年发展政策体系和工作机制更加完善,广大青年思想政治素养和全面发展水平明显提升,不断成长为志存高远、德才并重、情理兼修、勇于开拓,堪当实现中华民族伟大复兴中国梦历史重任的有生力量。

发展领域	重点项目
青年思想道德	青年马克思主义者培养工程
青年教育	青年社会主义核心价值观培养工程
青年健康	青年体质健康提升工程
青年婚恋	青年就业见习计划
青年就业创业	青年文化精品工程
青年文化	青年网络文明发展工程
青年社会融入与社会参与	中国青年志愿者行动
维护青少年合法权益	青年民族团结进步促进工程
预防青少年违法犯罪	港澳台青少年交流工程
青年社会保障	青少年事务社会工作专业人才队伍建设工程

社会保障更加健全。中国建成世界上规模最大的社会保障体系,普惠型社会保障服务进一步发展。中国青年不仅能在步入社会之初就享受到社会保障的"遮风挡雨",也能在拼搏奋斗时免除各种"后顾之忧",生活得更舒心、工作得更安心、对未来更放心。政府出台一系列支持多渠道灵活就业的政策,逐步完善灵活就业社会保障,支持青年从事灵活就业。青年住房保障力度不断增强,更多大城市面向新市民、青年人加大保障性租赁住房供给,缓解青年住房难题。基本养老保险实现全国统筹,失业保险、工伤保险持续向青年职业劳动者扩大覆盖,青年社会保障水平不断迈上新台阶。

组织保障坚强有力。组织是青年成长的大熔炉,是青年发展的倍增器。作为中国共产党领导的先进青年的群团组织,中国共产主义青年团始终把维护青年发展权益放在重要位置,着力推动落实青年优先发展理念,充分发挥组织优势,大力调动社会资源,聚焦青年

"急难愁盼"突出问题开展政策倡导,千方百计为青年解决具体困难,为广大青年成长发展创造良好环境。作为中国共产党领导下的基本的人民团体之一,中华全国青年联合会始终坚持代表和维护各族各界青年的合法权益,引导青年积极健康地参与社会生活,努力为青年健康成长、奋发成才服务。作为中国共产党领导下的中国高等学校学生会、研究生会和中等学校学生会的联合组织,中华全国学生联合会依法依章程表达和维护青年学生的具体利益,通过开展健康有益、丰富多彩的课外活动和社会服务,努力为青年学生成长发展服务。

专栏2 希望工程

希望工程由共青团中央发起、中国青少年发展基金会实施,是以改善贫困地区基础教育设施、救助贫困地区失学少年重返校园为使命的社会公益事业。截至2021年底,全国希望工程累计接受捐款194.2亿元,资助家庭经济困难学生662.6万人,援建希望小学20878所。

近年来,希望工程秉承助学育人传统,推出助学兴教、健康守护、素质提升、紧急救助、铸魂育人"五大计划",探索实施"希望厨房"、红色研学营等公益项目,有力推动贫困地区教育事业发展、服务贫困家庭青少年成长。

2019年是希望工程实施30周年。习近平总书记寄语希望工程,高度评价希望工程在助力脱贫攻坚、促进教育发展、服务青少年成长、引领社会风尚等方面发挥的重要作用,强调把希望工程这项事业办得更好,努力为青少年提供新助力、播种新希望,让广大青少年充分感受到党的关怀和社会主义大家庭的温暖。

二、新时代中国青年素质过硬、全面发展

奋斗锤炼本领,磨砺增长才干。新时代中国青年积极主动学理论、学文化、学科学、学技能,思想素养、身体素质、精神品格、综合能力不断提升,努力成长为堪当民族复兴重任的时代新人。

(一)理想信念更为坚定

理想指引人生方向,信念决定事业成败。新时代中国青年把树立正确的理想、坚定的信念作为立身之本,努力成长为党、国家和人民所期盼的有志青年。

坚信中国道路。中国青年通过历史对比、国际比较、社会观察、亲身实践,深刻领悟党的领导、领袖领航、制度优势、人民力量的关键作用。2020年有关调查显示,绝大多数青年对中国特色社会主义道路由衷认同,对实现中华民族伟大复兴充满信心。用习近平新时代中国特色社会主义思想武装起来的中国青年,在展现国家发展成就的一系列生动事例、客观数字、亲身体验中,深切感受到"中国速度"、"中国奇迹"、"中国之治",做中国人的志气、骨气、底气进一步增强,为实现中华民族伟大复兴中国梦团结奋斗的思想基础更加牢固。

　　2007年启动的青年马克思主义者培养工程,旨在为党培养信仰坚定、能力突出、素质优良、作风过硬的青年政治骨干。2013年纳入中央马克思主义理论研究和建设工程。2017年列入《中长期青年发展规划(2016—2025年)》十大重点项目。2020年,共青团中央联合教育部、民政部、农业农村部、国务院国资委联合印发《关于深入实施青年马克思主义者培养工程的意见》。

　　目前,青年马克思主义者培养工程逐步构建起涵盖全国省(区、市)、市(地、州、盟)、县(市、区、旗)和高校、国有企业、农村、社会组织、少先队工作者各领域的工作体系,以理论学习、红色教育、实践锻炼为主要培养内容,在青年中着力培养造就一大批用马克思主义中国化最新成果武装的马克思主义者,引导青年成长为社会主义的合格建设者和可靠接班人。

　　高校班:突出对大学生骨干的政治训练和思想引领。

　　国企班:强化对国有企业青年骨干的政治锻造。

　　农村班:聚焦乡村振兴战略,培养更多"懂农业、爱农村、爱农民"的有志青年成长为乡村治理骨干力量。

　　社会组织班:突出对青年社会组织骨干的政治引领和价值引领。

　　少先队工作者班:切实增强少先队辅导员队伍政治素养。

　　截至2021年底,青年马克思主义者培养工程累计培养近300万人。

　　坚守价值追求。青年的价值取向决定了未来整个社会的价值取向。中国青年主动"扣好人生第一粒扣子",从英雄模范和时代楷模中感受道德风范,积极倡导富强、民主、文明、和谐,倡导自由、平等、公正、法治,倡导爱国、敬业、诚信、友善,成为社会主义核心价值观的实践者、推广者。一大批青年优秀人物成为全社会学习的榜样,1500余名中国青年五四奖章获奖者引社会风气之先,各级"优秀共青团员"发挥先锋模范作用,2万余名"向上向善好青年"展现青春正能量。面对社会思潮的交流交融交锋,中国青年有困惑、有迷惘,但有一条主线始终未变,就是对党和国家的赤诚热爱、对崇高价值理念的不懈追求。

坚定文化自信。文化是一个民族的精神和灵魂,高度的文化自信是实现民族复兴的重要基础。中国青年不断从中华优秀传统文化、革命文化、社会主义先进文化中汲取养分,特别注重从源远流长的中华文明中获取力量。2020年有关调查显示,超八成受访青年认为"青少年国学热"的原因是"国人开始重视传统文化的内在价值"。从热衷"洋品牌"到"国潮"火爆盛行,从青睐"喇叭裤"到"国服"引领风尚,从追捧"霹雳舞"到"只此青绿"红遍全国,中国青年对中华民族灿烂的文明发自内心地崇拜、从精神深处认同,传承中华文化基因更加自觉,民族自豪感显著增强,推动全社会形成浓厚的文化自信氛围。

(二) 身心素质向好向强

少年强、青年强则中国强,强健的体魄、阳光的心态是青年成长成才的重要前提。新时代中国青年素质过硬,首先就体现在身心素质更好更强,能够经得起风雨、受得住磨砺、扛得住摔打。

身体素质持续提升。在校园里,随着体育课时持续增加,更多青年学生既在课堂内"文明其精神",也在操场上"野蛮其体魄"。超过3700万名农村义务教育学生受惠于政府开展的学生营养改善计划,身体素质得到明显提升。2018年,14岁至19岁青年学生体质达标测试合格率达91.9%,优良率持续上升。在社区中,青年积极参加各种群众性体育运动,跑步、游泳、各项球类运动成为年轻人的运动时尚,体育健身场馆"人头攒动"。北京冬奥会激发了中国青年的冰雪运动热情,18岁至30岁青年成为参与冰雪运动的主力军,参与率达37.3%,为各年龄段最高。在竞技场上,奥运会、亚运会等国际赛事中始终活跃着中国青年争金夺银的身影,青年健儿大力弘扬中华体育精神和女排精神,向全世界诠释了"更快、更高、更强——更团结"的奥林匹克新格言,展示了中国青年强健有力的民族精神。中国青年关注体育、参与体育、享受体育,成为体育强国建设的积极开拓力量。

专栏4　农村义务教育学生营养改善计划

2011年,中国实施农村义务教育学生营养改善计划。中央财政按照每生每天3元的标准(2021年秋季学期起提高至5元)为农村义务教育阶段学生提供营养膳食补助。截至2020年底,28个省份的1732个县实施了营养改善计划,覆盖农村义务教育学校13.16万所,受益学生达3797.83万人。10年来,欠发达地区农村学生营养健康状况得到显著改善,身体素质明显提升。学生体质健康合格率从2012年的70.3%提高至86.7%,营养不良率、消瘦率大幅下降,身高、体重都有不同程度的增长,为青年身体素质持续提升打下良好基础。

心理素质自信达观。中国青年从身边做起、从小事做起,努力将牢固的理想信念、健康的价值认知、坚定的文化自信转化为良好的社会心态。虽然在就业、教育、住房、婚恋、养老等领域还面临不小压力,但在党和政府的关心关注和全社会的共同支持下,中国青年面对困难不消沉、面对压力愈坚韧,2021年有关调查显示,88.0%的受访青年认为自己可以做"情绪的主人"。对未来发展的信心斗志、对美好生活的向往追求占据着中国青年的主流,自信达观、积极向上是中

国青年的鲜明形象。

（三）知识素养不断提升

知识改变命运,教育改变人生。乘着教育事业优先发展的东风,新时代中国青年亲眼见证、亲身经历了教育事业取得的历史性成就,享受了更加公平、更高质量的教育,学习的主动性、自觉性进一步提高,科学文化素养迈上新台阶。

受教育水平大幅提升。在科教兴国、人才强国等国家战略支持下,亿万中国青年通过教育获得成长成才的机会,实现创造美好生活、彰显人生价值的愿望。2020 年,新增劳动力平均受教育年限达 13.8 年,比十年前提高 1.1 年;大学专科以上在职青年占同等文化程度就业总人口比例超过 50%,比在职青年占就业总人口比例高约 20 个百分点。提高学历层次、接受高质量教育,依然是中国青年改变命运、追梦逐梦、实现人生理想的主要方式。

专栏5　"挑战杯"全国大学生课外学术科技作品竞赛

"挑战杯"全国大学生课外学术科技作品竞赛是由共青团中央、中国科协、教育部、全国学联和地方政府共同主办,国内著名大学、新闻媒体联合发起的一项具有导向性、示范性和群众性的全国竞赛活动。自1989年首届竞赛举办以来,"挑战杯"竞赛始终坚持"崇尚科学、追求真知、勤奋学习、锐意创新、迎接挑战"的宗旨,在促进青年创新人才成长、深化高校素质教育、推动经济社会发展等方面发挥了积极作用,在广大高校乃至社会上产生了广泛而良好的影响。

热爱学习渐成风尚。越来越多的青年把学习作为一种生活乐趣、一种人生追求,学习提升的社会氛围愈加浓厚。有相当数量的青年在离开校园后选择继续深造、提升学历,2020年成人本专科在校生超过770万人,网络本专科在校生超过840万人。青年在职学习专业技能的热情空前高涨,调查显示,超过50%的社会青年参加过职业技能培训,工作之余"充充电"、"加加油"成为越来越多青年的共同选择。受益于网络媒体迅猛发展,数千万青年通过"慕课"(大型开放式网络课程)等方式选学课程、获取知识。

(四) 社会参与积极主动

社会是青年成长发展的重要课堂。新时代中国青年以更加自信的态度、更加主动的精神,适应社会、融入社会,参与社会发展进程,展现出积极的社会参与意识和能力,成为正能量的倡导者和践行者。

有序参与政治生活。中国青年追求政治进步,积极参与全过程人民民主实践。共产主义远大理想始终激励青年砥砺前行、奋发向上,青年加入中国共产党、中国共产主义青年团的意愿持续高涨。截至2021年6月,35岁及以下党员共2367.9万名,占党员总数的24.9%。中国共产党第十八次全国代表大会以来,每年新发展党员中35岁及以下党员占比均超过80%。截至2021年底,共青团员总数达7371.5万名。青年广泛参与各级人大、政协,积极履职尽责、参政议政,2019年县级人大、政协中青年代表、委员分别占10.9%、

13.7%。青年踊跃参与各类民主选举、民主决策、民主管理、民主监督,围绕经济社会发展重大问题建言献策,针对关系青年切身利益的实际问题充分行使民主权利、广泛开展协商、努力形成共识。

积极参与社会事务。近年来,越来越多的青年热情参与公益慈善、社区服务、生态保护、文化传播、养老助残等社会事务,不仅在很多有影响力的社会组织中发挥重要作用,还组建了一批以自愿成立、自主管理、自我服务为特征的社会组织。目前,全国有 7600 多个共青团指导的县级志愿服务、文艺体育类青年社会组织,带动成立青年活动团体 15 万余个,基本实现县域全覆盖。中国青年充分利用这些社会参与的重要渠道,在依法承接政府职能转移、开展行业自律、满足社会公众多样化服务需求、倡导文明健康生活方式、促进政府与社会沟通等方面发挥建设性作用,展现了强烈的参与意识和社会责任感。

三、新时代中国青年勇挑 重担、堪当大任

中国特色社会主义新时代,是青年大有可为,也必将大有作为的大时代。新时代中国青年争做经济高质量发展的积极推动者、社会主义民主政治建设的积极参与者、社会主义文化繁荣兴盛的积极创造者、社会文明进步的积极实践者、美丽中国的积极建设者,在实现第二个百年奋斗目标、建设社会主义现代化强国的新征程上努力拼搏、奋勇争先。

（一）在平凡岗位上奋斗奉献

新时代中国青年坚守"永久奋斗"光荣传统,把平凡的岗位作为成就人生的舞台,用艰辛努力推动社会发展、民族振兴、人民幸福,靠自己的双手打拼一个光明的中国。

无论是传统的"工农商学兵"、"科教文卫体",还是基于"互联网+"的新业态、新领域、新职业,青年在各行各业把平凡做成了不起、把不可能变成可能,将奋斗精神印刻在一个个普通岗位中。在工厂车间一线,青年工人苦练本领、精益求精,拧好每个螺丝、焊好每个接头,争当"青年岗位能手",让"中国制造"走向世界;在田间地头,青

年农民寒耕暑耘、精耕细作,用科学技术为粮食增产、为土地增效,努力把中国人的饭碗牢牢端在自己手中;在建筑工地,青年农民工不畏辛劳、日以继夜,用一砖一瓦筑造起一座座高楼大厦,将都市装点得更加美丽;在训练场上,青年健儿刻苦训练、顽强拼搏,以过硬的作风和惊人的毅力向世界顶峰发起冲锋,让五星红旗在国际赛场高高飘扬;在城市的大街小巷,快递小哥、外卖骑手风里来、雨里去,为千家万户传递幸福与温暖,他们用勤劳和汗水生动展现了中国青年"衣食无忧而不忘艰苦、岁月静好而不丢奋斗"的整体风貌,让青春在平凡岗位的奋斗中出彩闪光。

(二) 在急难险重任务中冲锋在前

新时代中国青年不畏难、不惧苦,危难之中显精神,关键时刻见真章,总能够在祖国和人民需要的时候挺身而出,自觉扛起责任,无私奉献,无畏向前,彰显青年一代应有的闯劲、锐气和担当。

在体现综合国力、弘扬民族志气的重大工程之中,在抗击重大自然灾害面前,在应对突发公共危机时刻,青年的身影始终挺立在最前沿。无论是西气东输、西电东送、南水北调、东数西算等战略工程现场,还是港珠澳大桥、北京大兴国际机场、"华龙一号"核电机组等标志性项目工地,"青年突击队"、"青年攻坚组"的旗帜处处飘扬。新冠肺炎疫情发生以来,青年不畏艰险、冲锋在前、舍生忘死,32万余支青年突击队、550余万名青年奋战在医疗救护、交通物流、项目建设等抗疫一线，为打赢疫情防控的人民战争、总体战、阻击战作出重大贡献。援鄂医疗队 2.86 万名护士中，"80后"、"90后"占 90%。在武汉火神山、雷神山医院建设工地上，占总数达 60% 的青年建设者组建 13 支青年突击队，靠钢铁般的意志和攻坚克难的勇气，拼搏在前、奉献在前，创造了令世人惊叹的建设奇迹，用事实证明中国青年面对困难挫折撑得住、关键时刻顶得住、风险挑战扛得住。

专栏6　青年突击队

1954 年，中国第一支青年突击队由 18 名团员青年在北京发起成立。60 多年来，在党的领导下，在共青团的组织和倡导下，一批又一批青年突击队成立，在日常生产建设、创新攻关前沿、抢险救灾一线等经济社会改革发展稳定中发挥了积极作用。青年突击队成为中国社会主义建设中的一项创举以及共青团围绕中心、服务大局的重要体现。

青年突击队以企业、机关事业单位、县（市、区）、乡镇（街道）、村（社区）、高校等团组织为主组建，以共青团员为政治骨干、以青年为主体。企业青年突击队，重点围绕生产经营、工程建设、创新创效、安全生产等完成攻坚任务，坚持科学管理，弘扬工匠精神；机关事业单位青年突击队，重点聚焦政务服务、商业服务、社会服务等领域完成攻坚任务，弘扬职业文明、展示职业形象；城市青年突击队，重点面向基层社会治理领域，在文明城市创建、突发事件响应、扶危济困、矛盾纠纷化解等方面完成工作任务；农村青年突击队，重点服务乡村振兴战略实施，围绕农产品产销、种养技术推广、基础设施建设、人居环境整治等方面进行攻坚；高校青年突击队，注重发挥高校学生专业特长，围绕学校部署的有关工作、积极助力学校所在地等完成攻坚任务；其他领域青年突击队，结合突击攻坚任务的内容特点，组织相关青年群体骨干开展有针对性的工作。

随着青年突击队工作的深化开展和持续改进，共青团员的模范带头作用在"急、难、险、重、新"等任务面前更好地彰显，广大青年在经济社会发展中为国家和人民奋斗拼搏的自觉性、坚定性进一步提升。

（三）在基层一线经受磨砺

新时代中国青年把基层作为最好的课堂，把实践作为最好的老师，将个人奋斗的"小目标"融入党和国家事业的"大蓝图"，将自己对中国梦的追求化作一件件身边实事，在磨砺中长才干、壮筋骨。

在农村为乡亲们排忧解难，在社区为邻里们倾心服务，在边疆为祖国巡逻戍边……越来越多的青年深入基层、投身现代化建设最需要的地方，在复杂艰苦环境中成就人生。2021年，中共中央、国务院表彰的1981名全国脱贫攻坚先进个人和1501个先进集体中，就有许多青年先进典型。1800多名同志将生命定格在了脱贫攻坚征程上，其中很多是年轻的面孔。在乡村振兴战略实施中，青年领办专业合作社、推广现代农业科技、壮大农村新产业新业态，带头移风易俗、改善农村人居环境、倡导文明乡风，带动农民增收致富，助力农村焕发新貌。截至2021年，47万名"三支一扶"人员参加基层支教、支农、支医和帮扶乡村振兴（扶贫），数百万青年学生参与"三下乡"社会实践活动，为脱贫攻坚和乡村振兴提供新助力。

（四）在创新创业中走在前列

新时代中国青年富有想象力和创造力，思想解放、开拓进取，勇于参与日益激烈的国际竞争,成为创新创业的有生力量。

受益于党和国家的好政策,在经济、社会、科技、文化等领域,青年以聪明才智贡献国家、服务人民,奋力走在创新创业创优的前列。在国家创新驱动发展战略的引领和"揭榜挂帅"、"赛马"等制度的激励推动下,一批具有国际竞争力的青年科技人才脱颖而出,在"天宫"、"蛟龙"、"天眼"、"悟空"、"墨子"、"天问"、"嫦娥"等重大科技攻关任务中担重任、挑大梁,北斗卫星团队核心人员平均年龄36岁,量子科学团队平均年龄35岁,中国天眼FAST研发团队平均年龄仅30岁。在工程技术创新一线,每年超过300万名理工科高校毕业生走出校门,为中国工程师队伍提供源源不断的有生力量,他们用扎实的学识、过硬的技术,持续创造难得的"工程师红利",有力提升了中国的发展动力和国际竞争力。在国家持续出台创业扶持政策的大背景下,青年积极投身大众创业、万众创新热潮,踊跃参加"创青春"中国青年创新创业大赛、"中国国际互联网+"大学生创新创业大赛等创业交流展示活动,用智慧才干开创自己的事业。2014年以来,在新登记注册的市场主体中,大学生创业者超过500万人。在信息技术服务业、文化体育娱乐业、科技应用服务业等以创新创意为关键竞争力的行业中,青年占比均超过50%,一大批由青年领衔的"独角兽企业"、"瞪羚企业"喷涌而出。中国青年自觉将人生追求同国家发展进步紧密结合起来,在创新创业中展现才华、服务社会。

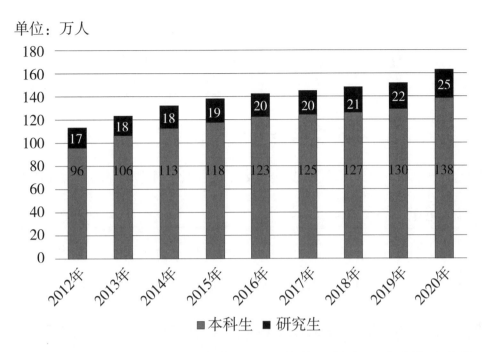

单位：万人

图3　2012年至2020年中国高等学校工科专业本科、研究生毕业生数

专栏7　中国青年创业发展报告（2021）

　　2021年12月，《中国青年创业发展报告（2021）》由中国青年创业就业基金会与相关研究团队联合发布。

　　《报告》显示，创业在中国整体蓬勃发展，不仅创业规模大、创投活跃，创业质量、创业生态也逐步向好，19岁至23岁青年成为创业主体。

　　《报告》从创业环境、企业家精神、创业结果三个维度出发，构建了包括17个具体指标的中国青年创业发展指数，评选出50座青年创业友好型城市。结果显示，2015年至2020年，中国青年创业发展指数整体由100升至167.5，北京、上海、广州位列2020年创业友好型城市前三名，一线城市、发达省会城市及东部发达地级市的创业发展指数排名居前。东部地区城市在青年创业发展排名前50名城市中的比例为60%，东部经济发达地区在创业发展领域居领先地位。从创业结果看，创业活动活跃地区集中在核心城市内，长三角地区区位优势明显。江苏、上海、北京、广东等成为优质科技创新型企业的聚集地。

　　《报告》从创业者的基础特征、创业资金、创业驱动力、创业现状、面临困难等五个方面描绘了中国创业青年群像，并为进一步促进青年创业发展提出意见建议。

（五）在社会文明建设中引风气之先

新时代中国青年顺应社会发展潮流，适应国家治理体系和治理能力现代化要求，在社会文明建设中引领时代新风，争当正能量的倡导者、新风尚的践行者。

无论在城镇还是乡村、企业还是学校，青年都自觉把正确的道德认知、自觉的道德养成、积极的道德实践紧密结合起来，带头倡导向上向善社会风气、塑造社会文明新风尚。在城乡社区建设中，越来越多的青年投身社区治理和服务体系建设，主动参加"社区青春行动"，加强实践锻炼、提升服务贡献。在各行各业，青年秉承"敬业、协作、创优、奉献"的理念，踊跃创建"青年文明号"，大力弘扬新时代职业文明，展现新时代职业形象。广大青年运动员弘扬体育道德风尚，以良好的赛风赛纪和文明礼仪，获得竞技成绩和精神文明双丰收。1993 年"中国青年志愿者行动"启动以来，志愿服务成为青年参与社会治理、履行社会责任的一面旗帜，成为青年在奉献人民、服务社会中锻炼成长的重要途径。截至 2021 年底，全国志愿服务信息系统中 14 岁至 35 岁的注册志愿者已超过 9000 万人，他们活跃在社区建设、大型赛事、环境保护、扶贫开发、卫生健康、应急救援、文化传承等各个领域，弘扬"奉献、友爱、互助、进步"的志愿精神，在全社会形成团结互助、平等友爱、共同前进的新风尚。中国青年志愿者扶贫接力计划研究生支教团、大学生志愿服务"西部计划"连续 18 年派遣 41 万余名研究生、大学毕业生,到中西部 2100 多个县(市区旗)开展扶贫支教、卫生医疗等志愿服务。青年始终是大型赛会志愿服务的主体力量,给千家万户乃至全世界留下深刻印象。

专栏8 青年文明号

1994 年起,共青团中央在全国启动创建青年文明号活动,近 30 年来,共开展评定表彰 20 届次,累计评选全国级青年文明号 2 万余个,各省份(行业)累计评选省级青年文明号 10 万余个,青年文明号成为精神文明建设特别是职业文明建设领域的一道绚丽风景线。

进入新时代,青年文明号活动秉承"敬业、协作、创优、奉献"的理念,面向各行业一线青年,主要在政务服务、商业服务、社会服务等"窗口"行业和单位开展,以实施科学管理、人本管理、自我管理和开展岗位创新创效创优活动为基本手段,致力于弘扬职业文明、引导岗位建功、建设先进集体、培育青年人才,是一项具有群众性、实践性、品牌性的精神文明创建活动,是广大青年为经济社会发展大局贡献智慧和力量的重要载体。

专栏9 中国青年志愿者行动

自 1993 年共青团中央发起实施"中国青年志愿者行动"以来,在社会各界大力支持下,中国青年志愿者行动在全国广泛开展,"奉献、友爱、互助、进步"的志愿精神深入人心,志愿服务组织网络日趋健全、服务领域不断拓展,志愿者队伍持续壮大,工作机制逐步完善,在服务社会、教育青年、传播文明等方面的积极作用日益增强。

截至 2021 年,全部省(区、市)和新疆生产建设兵团、95% 的地市、69% 的县区和 2000 多所高校建立了青年志愿者协会。研究生支教团、大学生志愿服务"西部计划"成为中国青年志愿者的亮丽品牌,700 多名海外服务的青年志愿者迈出国门播撒友谊。599 万多名青年志愿者长期结对关爱留守儿童和残疾青少年,490 多万名青年志愿者参与汶川地震、玉树地震等抗震救灾。数以百万计的青年志愿者在北京夏季和冬季奥运会、上海世博会、G20 杭州峰会等大型赛会和重要活动提供细致周到的志愿服务。

四、新时代中国青年胸怀世界、展现担当

青年是国家的未来,也是世界的未来。新时代中国青年既有家国情怀,也有人类关怀,秉承中华文化崇尚的四海一家、天下为公理念,积极学习借鉴各国有益经验和文明成果,与世界各国青年共同推动构建人类命运共同体,共同弘扬和平、发展、公平、正义、民主、自由的全人类共同价值,携手创造人类更加美好的未来。

(一)更加开放自信地融入世界

随着中国对外开放的大门越开越大,新时代中国青年以前所未有的深度和广度认识世界、融入世界,在对外交流合作中更加理性包容、自信自强。

"走出去"的道路越来越宽。通过留学、务工、旅游、考察等方式,中国青年以极大的热情和包容的心态,全方位、深层次了解世界、融入世界、拥抱世界,学习借鉴其他国家的有益经验和文明成果。出国留学是中国青年了解世界的重要途径。1978 年,中国选派出国留学人员仅 800 余名;2019 年,超过 70 万人出国深造,40 多年来各类出国留学人员累计超过 650 万人;1978 年回国留学人员仅 248 人,

2019 年超过 58 万人学成回国,40 多年来回国留学人员累计达 420 余万人。与此同时,大批中国青年通过旅游、考察、商务、劳务等方式走出国门、感知世界,2019 年国内居民出境达 1.7 亿人次,中国青年认识世界的渠道更加广阔、国际视野不断拓展。

表 1 1978 年至 2019 年中国出国留学人员、
学成回国留学人员发展情况

年份	出国留学人员数 (人)	学成回国留学人员数 (人)
1978	860	248
1980	2124	1223
1985	7144	3880
1990	19352	2099
1995	21934	5090
2000	38989	9121
2005	118515	34987
2010	284700	134800
2015	523700	409100
2016	544500	432500
2017	608400	480900
2018	662100	519400
2019	703500	580300

沟通合作的"朋友圈"越来越大。在各种国际舞台上,中国青年讲述中国故事、参与全球青年事务治理,在双多边框架下积极交流互动、促进合作共赢。中国青年参与双边交流机制更加广泛深入,与各有关国家青年走得越来越近、友谊越来越深。在"中国青年全球伙

伴行动"框架下,中国与 100 多个国际组织及外国政府青年机构、政党和非政府青年组织建立交流合作关系。在中俄、中美、中欧、中印、中日等中外人文交流机制框架下,中国青年在教育、科学、文化、艺术、体育、媒体等领域对外互动合作活跃。中国青年不仅与周边国家和广大发展中国家青年伙伴开展亮点纷呈的人文交流,还通过创新创业、经贸往来、技术交流等方式实现互惠互利。中国青年更加主动地加入国际组织、参加国际会议、参与全球治理,树立了更加亮丽的国际形象。在联合国和其他国际组织中,数百名中国青年为世界和平与发展事业付出辛劳、作出贡献;在联合国青年论坛、联合国教科文组织青年会议和相关多边机制框架下,在亚洲青年理事会等国际性青年组织中,中国青年更加自信地发出中国声音、阐述中国观点,成为沟通中外友好的青年使者。

(二)展现构建人类命运共同体的青春担当

新时代中国青年深刻地认识到,每个民族、每个国家的前途命运都紧紧联系在一起,应该风雨同舟、守望相助,努力把共同的地球家园建成一个命运与共的大家庭。

在心与心的交流对话中汇聚青春共识。中国青年积极倡导、努力践行构建人类命运共同体理念,围绕脱贫减贫、气候变化、抗疫合作等主题,征集世界各国青年故事、传播世界各国青年声音、凝聚世界各国青年共识。2020 年,在联合国有关机构、世界卫生组织共同举办的应对新冠肺炎疫情网络会议上,中国青年代表向全世界介绍参与抗疫志愿服务的感人故事、分享科学应对疫情的经验做法。在上海合作组织、金砖国家、G20 等国际机制青年领域合作文件的制定过程中,中国青年积极贡献智慧、提出主张,为保障世界各国青年的生存权、发展权、受保护权、参与权贡献智慧。在 2022 年北京冬奥会、冬残奥会上,各国青年运动员和青年志愿者,超越语言的障碍、文化的差异,用笑容播撒温暖、用拥抱传递友谊、用心灵汇聚力量,共同搭建起"一起向未来"的桥梁,以青春特有的方式向全世界传递了构建人类命运共同体的理念。

专栏 10   国际青年发展指数报告 2021

2021 年 12 月,中国青少年研究中心、中国国际青年交流中心、清华大学青少年德育研究中心、北京大学中国国情研究中心联合课题组发布《国际青年发展指数报告2021》,通过多维度、多层次的评估,立体综合呈现各国青年发展现状、特点、趋势和存在问题,促进各国青年发展交流互鉴。

《报告》共选取 85 个国家进行测算。从总体排名看,新加坡、挪威、比利时排前三位;从地域分布看,前十名中有 4 个亚洲国家、5 个欧洲国家、1 个大洋洲国家;从发展程度看,前十名中有 8 个发达国家、2 个发展中国家。

《报告》显示,中国总体排名处于前 30%(第 23 位),高于人均 GDP 和人类发展指数(HDI)的世界排名。在"公共参与"和"健康与生活"一级指标中,中国排名均处于前15%(第 9、12 位),高于总体排名和不少发达国家排名。这一结果充分展现了中国青年发展取得的巨大成就。

在手拉手的并肩前行中绘就美好图景。推动构建人类命运共同体,中国青年铭于心,更笃于行。中国青年积极投身"一带一路"建设,践行共商共建共享理念。几十万名海外中资机构青年员工在异

国他乡辛勤工作,为当地经济社会发展作出贡献;开展志愿服务、慈善捐赠、文化交流,增进与所在国青年之间的友谊与合作。以青年为主体的国际中文教师志愿者在100多个国家服务,帮助各国青年学习中华文化。"中国青年志愿者海外服务计划"累计派出超过700名青年志愿者,在亚洲、非洲、拉丁美洲的20多个国家,开展医疗卫生、农业技术、土木工程、工业技术、经济管理、社会发展等方面服务。中国军队青年官兵积极参加联合国维和行动,胸怀人间大爱,恪守维和使命责任,秉持人道主义精神,为世界和平与发展注入更多正能量。截至2020年,4万余人次中国军人为和平出征,16名中国军人在维和行动中牺牲、平均年龄不到30岁。中国青年用行动向世人证明,只要世界各国人民同心同向、携手共进,人类命运共同体的前景必将更加美好。

（三）中国青年的全球行动倡议

人类已经进入互联互通的新时代,各国利益休戚相关、命运紧密相连。当今世界面临越来越突出的治理赤字、信任赤字、和平赤字、发展赤字,混乱、撕裂、不公愈演愈烈。百年变局和世纪疫情叠加,给世界经济发展和民生改善带来严重挑战。和平还是战争,光明还是黑暗,人类在进步和倒退的十字路口面临着重要抉择。时代呼唤全世界青年团结一心,加强彼此了解、相互取长补短,用欣赏、互鉴、共享的观点看待世界,携手构建人类命运共同体。为此,中国青年向全世界青年倡议：

——坚持向美向上向善的价值追求。立正心、明大德、行大道，崇德向善、追求美好，热爱生活、奉献社会，在一点一滴中弘扬真善美、传播正能量。

——展现朝气蓬勃的精神风貌。自信自强、昂扬向上，不断自我提升、自我超越，努力做最好的自己，实现青春梦想和人生价值。倡导健康生活，锻炼强健体魄，涵养阳光心态，保持青春活力。

——为国家发展进步奋斗担当。以主人翁的姿态，刻苦学习本领、发挥聪明才智、大胆创新创造，始终保持拼搏向上、奋斗进取的精神，始终走在时代最前列，担负起国家发展进步的历史责任。

——为世界和平发展贡献智慧力量。胸怀世界、胸怀未来，秉持全人类共同价值，顺应时代潮流和历史大势，站在历史正确的一边、人类进步的一边，维护世界和平，促进共同发展，弘扬公平正义，捍卫民主自由，为建设繁荣美好的世界作出积极贡献。

中国青年真诚希望世界和平稳定、发展繁荣，真诚希望每个国家和地区都能为青年发展提供良好条件，真诚希望全世界青年能够携起手来，为建设一个持久和平、普遍安全、共同繁荣、开放包容、清洁美丽的世界贡献智慧力量、展现青春担当。

结　束　语

青年一代有理想、有本领、有担当,国家就有前途,民族就有希望。中国的未来属于青年,世界的未来也属于青年。

未来的中国青年,必将"以青春之我,创建青春之家庭,青春之国家,青春之民族,青春之人类,青春之地球,青春之宇宙",在实现民族复兴的伟大实践中放飞青春梦想。

未来的中国,必将在一代又一代青年的接续奋斗中,实现物质文明、政治文明、精神文明、社会文明、生态文明的全面提升。中国人民将享有更加幸福安康的生活,中华民族将以更加昂扬的姿态屹立于世界民族之林,伟大的中国梦一定能够变成现实。

未来的世界,关系到每一名青年的前途命运,更取决于每一名青年的拼搏奋斗。只要各国青年团结起来、同向同行,坚持平等协商、开放创新、同舟共济、坚守正义,就一定能远离战火硝烟、倾轧斗争,真正建设一个和平发展、亲如一家的"地球村",共同开创共赢共享、发展繁荣、健康安全、互尊互鉴的美好未来,实现全人类的共同梦想。

中国青年愿同世界各国青年一道,为推动构建人类命运共同体、建设更加美好的世界贡献智慧和力量。

台湾问题与新时代中国统一事业

（2022 年 8 月）

中华人民共和国 国务院台湾事务办公室
国务院新闻办公室

前　言

解决台湾问题、实现祖国完全统一，是全体中华儿女的共同愿望，是实现中华民族伟大复兴的必然要求，是中国共产党矢志不渝的历史任务。中国共产党、中国政府和中国人民为此进行了长期不懈的努力。

中共十八大以来，中国特色社会主义进入新时代。在以习近平同志为核心的中共中央坚强领导下，中国共产党和中国政府积极推进对台工作理论和实践创新，牢牢把握两岸关系主导权和主动权，有力维护台海和平稳定，扎实推进祖国统一进程。但一个时期以来，台湾民进党当局加紧进行"台独"分裂活动，一些外部势力极力搞"以台制华"，企图阻挡中国实现完全统一和中华民族迈向伟大复兴。

中国共产党团结带领全国各族人民长期奋斗，如期全面建成小康社会、实现第一个百年奋斗目标，开启全面建设社会主义现代化国家、向第二个百年奋斗目标进军新征程。中华民族迎来了从站起来、富起来到强起来的伟大飞跃，实现中华民族伟大复兴进入了不可逆转的历史进程。这是中国统一大业新的历史方位。

中国政府于1993年8月、2000年2月分别发表了《台湾问题与中国的统一》、《一个中国的原则与台湾问题》白皮书，全面系统阐述了解决台湾问题的基本方针和有关政策。为进一步重申台湾是中国的一部分的事实和现状,展现中国共产党和中国人民追求祖国统一的坚定意志和坚强决心,阐述中国共产党和中国政府在新时代推进实现祖国统一的立场和政策,特发布本白皮书。

一、台湾是中国的一部分
不容置疑也不容改变

台湾自古属于中国的历史经纬清晰、法理事实清楚。不断有新的考古发现和研究证明海峡两岸深厚的历史和文化联系。大量的史书和文献记载了中国人民早期开发台湾的情景。公元 230 年,三国时期吴人沈莹所著《临海水土志》留下了关于台湾最早的记述。隋朝政府曾三次派兵到时称"流求"的台湾。宋元以后,中国历代中央政府开始在澎湖、台湾设治,实施行政管辖。1624 年,荷兰殖民者侵占台湾南部。1662 年,民族英雄郑成功驱逐荷兰殖民者收复台湾。清朝政府逐步在台湾扩增行政机构,1684 年设立台湾府,隶属福建省管辖;1885 年改设台湾为行省,是当时中国第 20 个行省。

1894 年 7 月,日本发动侵略中国的甲午战争,次年 4 月迫使战败的清朝政府割让台湾及澎湖列岛。抗日战争时期,中国共产党人明确提出收复台湾的主张。1937 年 5 月 15 日,毛泽东同志会见美国记者尼姆·韦尔斯时表示:"中国的抗战是要求得最后的胜利,这个胜利的范围,不限于山海关,不限于东北,还要包括台湾的解放。"

1941 年 12 月 9 日,中国政府发布对日宣战布告,宣告"所有一切条约、协定、合同,有涉及中日间之关系者,一律废止",并宣布将收回台湾、澎湖列岛。1943 年 12 月 1 日,中美英三国政府发表《开罗宣言》宣布,三国之宗旨在使日本所窃取于中国之领土,例如东北、台湾、澎湖列岛等,归还中国。1945 年 7 月 26 日,中美英三国共同签署、后来苏联参加的《波茨坦公告》,重申"开罗宣言之条件必将实施"。同年 9 月,日本签署《日本投降条款》,承诺"忠诚履行波茨坦公告各项规定之义务"。10 月 25 日,中国政府宣告"恢复对台湾行使主权",并在台北举行"中国战区台湾省受降仪式"。由此,通过一系列具有国际法律效力的文件,中国从法律和事实上收复了台湾。

1949 年 10 月 1 日,中华人民共和国中央人民政府宣告成立,取代中华民国政府成为代表全中国的唯一合法政府。这是在中国这一国际法主体没有发生变化情况下的政权更替,中国的主权和固有领土疆域没有改变,中华人民共和国政府理所当然地完全享有和行使中国的主权,其中包括对台湾的主权。由于中国内战延续和外部势力干涉,海峡两岸陷入长期政治对立的特殊状态,但中国的主权和领土从未分割也决不允许分割,台湾是中国领土的一部分的地位从未改变也决不允许改变。

1971 年 10 月,第 26 届联合国大会通过第 2758 号决议,决定:"恢复中华人民共和国的一切权利,承认她的政府的代表为中国在联合国组织的唯一合法代表并立即把蒋介石的代表从它在联合国组织及其所属一切机构中所非法占据的席位上驱逐出去。"这一决议不仅从政治上、法律上和程序上彻底解决了包括台湾在内全中国在联合国的代表权问题,而且明确了中国在联合国的席位只有一个,不存在"两个中国"、"一中一台"的问题。随后,联合国相关专门机构以正式决议等方式,恢复中华人民共和国享有的合法席位,驱逐台湾当局的"代表",如1972年5月第25届世界卫生大会通过第25.1号决议。联合国秘书处法律事务办公室官方法律意见明确指出,"台湾作为中国的一个省没有独立地位","台湾当局不享有任何形式的政府地位"。实践中,联合国对台湾使用的称谓是"台湾,中国的省(Taiwan,Province of China)"①。

联大第2758号决议是体现一个中国原则的政治文件,国际实践充分证实其法律效力,不容曲解。台湾没有任何根据、理由或权利参加联合国及其他只有主权国家才能参加的国际组织。近年来,以美国为首的个别国家一些势力与"台独"分裂势力沆瀣一气,妄称该决议没有处理"台湾的代表权问题",炒作非法无效的"旧金山和约"②,无视《开罗宣言》、《波茨坦公告》在内的一系列国际法律文件,再度鼓吹"台湾地位未定",宣称支持台湾"有意义地参与联合国体系",其实质是企图改变台湾是中国的一部分的地位,制造"两个中国"、"一中一台",实现其"以台制华"的政治目的。这些行径歪曲联大第2758号决议,违反国际法,严重背弃有关国家对中国作出的政治承

---

① 详见《联合国司法年鉴2010》(United Nations Juridical Yearbook 2010)第516页。

② 1951年9月4日至8日,美国纠集一些国家,在排斥中华人民共和国、苏联的情况下,在美国旧金山召开所谓"对日和会",签署包含"日本放弃对台湾、澎湖列岛之所有权利和请求权"等内容的"旧金山和约"。该"和约"违反1942年中美英苏等26国签署的《联合国家宣言》规定,违反《联合国宪章》和国际法基本原则,对台湾主权归属等任何涉及中国作为非缔约国的领土和主权权利的处置也都是非法、无效的。中国政府从一开始就郑重声明,"旧金山和约"由于没有中华人民共和国参加准备、拟制和签订,中国政府认为是非法无效的,绝不承认。苏联、波兰、捷克斯洛伐克、朝鲜、蒙古、越南等国家也拒绝承认"和约"效力。

诺,侵犯中国的主权和尊严,践踏国际关系基本准则。对此,中国政府已经表明了反对和谴责的严正立场。

一个中国原则是国际社会的普遍共识,是遵守国际关系基本准则的应有之义。目前,全世界有包括美国在内的181个国家,在一个中国原则的基础上与中国建立了外交关系。1978年12月发表的《中美建交公报》声明:"美利坚合众国政府承认中国的立场,即只有一个中国,台湾是中国的一部分";"美利坚合众国承认中华人民共和国政府是中国的唯一合法政府。在此范围内,美国人民将同台湾人民保持文化、商务和其他非官方关系"。

1982年12月,中华人民共和国第五届全国人民代表大会第五次会议通过《中华人民共和国宪法》,规定:"台湾是中华人民共和国的神圣领土的一部分。完成统一祖国的大业是包括台湾同胞在内的全中国人民的神圣职责。"2005年3月,第十届全国人民代表大会第三次会议通过《反分裂国家法》,规定:"世界上只有一个中国,大陆和台湾同属一个中国,中国的主权和领土完整不容分割。维护国家主权和领土完整是包括台湾同胞在内的全中国人民的共同义务。""台湾是中国的一部分。国家绝不允许'台独'分裂势力以任何名义、任何方式把台湾从中国分裂出去。"2015年7月,第十二届全国人民代表大会常务委员会第十五次会议通过《中华人民共和国国家安全法》,规定:"中国的主权和领土完整不容侵犯和分割。维护国家主权、统一和领土完整是包括港澳同胞和台湾同胞在内的全中国人民的共同义务。"

世界上只有一个中国，台湾是中国的一部分的历史事实和法理事实不容置疑，台湾从来不是一个国家而是中国的一部分的地位不容改变。任何歪曲事实、否定和挑战一个中国原则的行径都将以失败告终。

二、中国共产党坚定不移
推进祖国完全统一

中国共产党始终致力于为中国人民谋幸福、为中华民族谋复兴。在成立初期,中国共产党就把争取台湾摆脱殖民统治回归祖国大家庭、实现包括台湾同胞在内的民族解放作为奋斗目标,付出了巨大努力。

中国共产党始终把解决台湾问题、实现祖国完全统一作为矢志不渝的历史任务,团结带领两岸同胞,推动台海形势从紧张对峙走向缓和改善、进而走上和平发展道路,两岸关系不断取得突破性进展。

新中国成立以后,以毛泽东同志为主要代表的中国共产党人,提出和平解决台湾问题的重要思想、基本原则和政策主张;进行了解放台湾的准备和斗争,粉碎了台湾当局"反攻大陆"的图谋,挫败了各种制造"两个中国"、"一中一台"的图谋;促成联合国恢复了中华人民共和国的合法席位和一切权利,争取了世界上绝大多数国家接受一个中国原则,为实现和平统一创造了重要条件。中共中央还通过适当渠道与台湾当局高层人士接触,为寻求和平解决台湾问题而积极努力。

中共十一届三中全会以后,以邓小平同志为主要代表的中国共产党人,从国家和民族的根本利益出发,在实现中美建交的时代条件下,在争取和平解决台湾问题思想的基础上,确立了争取祖国和平统一的大政方针,创造性地提出了"一个国家,两种制度"的科学构想,并首先运用于解决香港问题、澳门问题;主动缓和两岸军事对峙状态,推动打破两岸长期隔绝状态,开启两岸民间交流合作的大门,使两岸关系进入新的历史阶段。

中共十三届四中全会以后,以江泽民同志为主要代表的中国共产党人,提出发展两岸关系、推进祖国和平统一进程的八项主张[①];推动两岸双方达成体现一个中国原则的"九二共识",开启两岸协商谈判,实现两岸授权团体负责人首次会谈,持续扩大两岸各领域交流合作;坚决开展反对李登辉分裂祖国活动的斗争,沉重打击"台独"分裂势力;实现香港、澳门顺利回归祖国,实行"一国两制",对解决台湾问题产生积极影响。

中共十六大以后,以胡锦涛同志为主要代表的中国共产党人,提出两岸关系和平发展重要思想;针对岛内"台独"分裂活动猖獗制定实施《反分裂国家法》,举行中国共产党和中国国民党两党主要领导人60年来首次会谈,坚决挫败陈水扁"法理台独"图谋;开辟两岸关系和平发展新局面,推动两岸制度化协商谈判取得丰硕成果,实现两岸全面直接双向"三通",签署实施《海峡两岸经济合作框架协议》,两岸关系面貌发生深刻变化。

---

① 1995年1月30日,时任中共中央总书记、国家主席江泽民发表题为《为促进祖国统一大业的完成而继续奋斗》的讲话,提出发展两岸关系、推进祖国和平统一进程的八项主张,强调"坚持一个中国的原则,是实现和平统一的基础和前提"、"我们不承诺放弃使用武力,决不是针对台湾同胞,而是针对外国势力干涉中国统一和搞'台湾独立'的图谋的"等。详见《江泽民文选》第一卷,人民出版社2006年8月第1版,第418至423页。

中共十八大以来,以习近平同志为主要代表的中国共产党人,全面把握两岸关系时代变化,丰富和发展国家统一理论和对台方针政策,推动两岸关系朝着正确方向发展,形成新时代中国共产党解决台湾问题的总体方略,提供了新时代做好对台工作的根本遵循和行动纲领。2017年10月,中共十九大确立了坚持"一国两制"和推进祖国统一的基本方略,强调:"绝不允许任何人、任何组织、任何政党、在任何时候、以任何形式、把任何一块中国领土从中国分裂出去!"2019年1月,习近平总书记在《告台湾同胞书》发表40周年纪念会上发表重要讲话,郑重提出了新时代推动两岸关系和平发展、推进祖国和平统一进程的重大政策主张:携手推动民族复兴,实现和平统一目标;探索"两制"台湾方案,丰富和平统一实践;坚持一个中国原则,维护和平统一前景;深化两岸融合发展,夯实和平统一基础;实现同胞心灵契合,增进和平统一认同。中国共产党和中国政府采取一系列引领两岸关系发展、促进祖国和平统一的重大举措:

——推动实现1949年以来两岸领导人首次会晤、直接对话沟通,将两岸交流互动提升到新高度,为两岸关系发展翻开了新篇章、开辟了新空间,成为两岸关系发展道路上一座新的里程碑。双方两岸事务主管部门在共同政治基础上建立常态化联系沟通机制,两部门负责人实现互访、开通热线。

——坚持一个中国原则和"九二共识",推进两岸政党党际交流,与台湾有关政党、团体和人士就两岸关系与民族未来开展对话协商,深入交换意见,达成多项共识并发表共同倡议,与台湾社会各界共同努力探索"两制"台湾方案。

——践行"两岸一家亲"理念,以两岸同胞福祉为依归,推动两岸关系和平发展、融合发展,完善促进两岸交流合作、保障台湾同胞福祉的制度安排和政策措施,实行卡式台胞证,实现福建向金门供水,制发台湾居民居住证,逐步为台湾同胞在大陆学习、创业、就业、生活提供同等待遇,持续率先同台湾同胞分享大陆发展机遇。

——团结广大台湾同胞,排除"台独"分裂势力干扰阻挠,推动两岸各领域交流合作和人员往来走深走实。克服新冠肺炎疫情影响,坚持举办海峡论坛等一系列两岸交流活动,保持了两岸同胞交流合作的发展态势。

——坚定捍卫国家主权和领土完整,坚决反对"台独"分裂和外部势力干涉,有力维护台海和平稳定和中华民族根本利益。依法打击"台独"顽固分子,有力震慑"台独"分裂势力。妥善处理台湾对外交往问题,巩固发展国际社会坚持一个中国原则的格局。

在中国共产党的引领推动下,70多年来特别是两岸隔绝状态打破以来,两岸关系获得长足发展。两岸交流合作日益广泛,互动往来日益密切,给两岸同胞特别是台湾同胞带来实实在在的好处,充分说明两岸和则两利、合则双赢。1978年两岸贸易额仅有4600万美元,2021年增长至3283.4亿美元,增长了7000多倍;大陆连续21年成为台湾最大出口市场,每年为台湾带来大量顺差;大陆是台商岛外投资的第一大目的地,截至2021年底,台商投资大陆项目共计123781

个、实际投资额 713.4 亿美元①。1987 年两岸人员往来不足 5 万人次，2019 年约 900 万人次。近 3 年来受疫情影响，线上交流成为两岸同胞沟通互动的主要形式，参与及可及人数屡创新高。

中国共产党始终是中国人民和中华民族的主心骨，是民族复兴、国家统一的坚强领导核心。中国共产党为解决台湾问题、实现祖国完全统一不懈奋斗的历程充分表明：必须坚持一个中国原则，绝不允许任何人任何势力把台湾从祖国分裂出去；必须坚持为包括台湾同胞在内的全体中国人民谋幸福，始终致力于实现两岸同胞对美好生活的向往；必须坚持解放思想、实事求是、守正创新，把握民族根本利益和国家核心利益，制定实施对台方针政策；必须坚持敢于斗争、善于斗争，同一切损害中国主权和领土完整、企图阻挡祖国统一的势力进行坚决斗争；必须坚持大团结大联合，广泛调动一切有利于反"独"促统的积极因素，共同推进祖国统一进程。

---

① 这里不含经第三地的转投资。

三、祖国完全统一进程不可阻挡

当前，在国内国际两个大局都发生深刻复杂变化的时代背景下，推进祖国完全统一面临着新的形势。中国共产党和中国政府有驾驭复杂局面、战胜风险挑战的综合实力和必胜信心，完全有能力推动祖国统一大业阔步前进。

（一）实现祖国完全统一是中华民族
伟大复兴的必然要求

在中华民族五千多年的发展进程中，追求统一、反对分裂始终是全民族的主流价值观，这一价值观早已深深融入整个中华民族的精神血脉。近代以后，由于西方列强入侵和封建统治腐败，中国逐步成为半殖民地半封建社会，国家蒙辱、人民蒙难、文明蒙尘，中华民族遭受了前所未有的劫难。台湾被日本霸占半个世纪的历史，是中华民族近代屈辱的缩影，给两岸同胞留下了刻心之痛。一水之隔、咫尺天涯，两岸迄今尚未完全统一是历史遗留给中华民族的创伤。两岸同胞应该共同努力，谋求国家统一，抚平历史创伤。

实现中华民族伟大复兴，是近代以来中国人民和中华民族最伟大的梦想。实现祖国完全统一，才能使两岸同胞彻底摆脱内战的阴霾,共创共享台海永久和平;才能避免台湾再次被外国侵占的危险,打掉外部势力遏制中国的图谋,维护国家主权、安全、发展利益;才能清除"台独"分裂的隐患,稳固台湾作为中国的一部分的地位,推进中华民族伟大复兴;才能更好地凝聚两岸同胞力量建设共同家园,增进两岸同胞利益福祉,创造中国人民和中华民族更加幸福美好的未来。正如中国伟大的革命先行者孙中山先生所言:"'统一'是中国全体国民的希望。能够统一,全国人民便享福;不能统一,便要受害。"

中华民族在探寻民族复兴强盛之道的过程中饱经苦难沧桑。"统则强、分必乱",这是一条历史规律。实现祖国完全统一,是中华民族的历史和文化所决定的,也是中华民族伟大复兴的时和势所决定的。我们比历史上任何时期都更接近、更有信心和能力实现中华民族伟大复兴的目标,也更接近、更有信心和能力实现祖国完全统一的目标。台湾问题因民族弱乱而产生,必将随着民族复兴而解决。全体中华儿女团结奋斗,就一定能在同心实现中华民族伟大复兴进程中完成祖国统一大业。

(二) 国家发展进步引领两岸关系发展方向

决定两岸关系走向、实现祖国完全统一的关键因素是国家的发展进步。国家发展进步特别是40多年来改革开放和现代化建设所取得的伟大成就,深刻影响着解决台湾问题、实现祖国完全统一的历史进程。无论何党何派在台湾掌权,都无法改变两岸关系向前发展的总体趋势和祖国统一的历史大势。

根据国际货币基金组织的统计[①],1980 年,大陆生产总值约 3030 亿美元,台湾生产总值约 423 亿美元,大陆是台湾的 7.2 倍;2021 年,大陆生产总值约 174580 亿美元,台湾生产总值约 7895 亿美元,大陆是台湾的 22.1 倍。国家发展进步特别是经济实力、科技实力、国防实力持续增强,不仅有效遏制了"台独"分裂活动和外部势力干涉,更为两岸交流合作提供了广阔空间、带来了巨大机遇。越来越多的台湾同胞特别是台湾青年来大陆学习、创业、就业、生活,促进了两岸社会各界交往交流交融,加深了两岸同胞利益和情感联系,增进了两岸同胞文化、民族和国家认同,有力牵引着两岸关系沿着统一的正确方向不断前行。

中国共产党团结带领中国人民已经踏上了全面建设社会主义现代化国家的新征程。大陆坚持中国特色社会主义道路,治理效能提升,经济长期向好,物质基础雄厚,人力资源丰厚,市场空间广阔,发展韧性强大,社会大局稳定,继续发展具有多方面优势和条件,并持续转化为推进统一的动力。立足新发展阶段,贯彻新发展理念,构建新发展格局,推动高质量发展,将使大陆综合实力和国际影响力持续提升,大陆对台湾社会的影响力、吸引力不断扩大,我们解决台湾问题的基础更雄厚、能力更强大,必将有力推动祖国统一进程。

---

① 根据 2022 年 4 月国际货币基金组织"世界经济展望数据库"的统计。

（三）"台独"分裂势力抗拒统一不会得逞

台湾自古是中国的神圣领土。所谓"台湾独立"，是企图把台湾从中国分割出去，是分裂国家的严重罪行，损害两岸同胞共同利益和中华民族根本利益，是走不通的绝路。

民进党当局坚持"台独"分裂立场，勾连外部势力不断进行谋"独"挑衅。他们拒不接受一个中国原则，歪曲否定"九二共识"，妄称"中华民国与中华人民共和国互不隶属"，公然抛出"新两国论"；在岛内推行"去中国化"、"渐进台独"，纵容"急独"势力鼓噪推动"修宪修法"，欺骗台湾民众，煽动仇视大陆，阻挠破坏两岸交流合作和融合发展，加紧"以武谋独"、"以武拒统"；勾结外部势力，在国际上竭力制造"两个中国"、"一中一台"。民进党当局的谋"独"行径导致两岸关系紧张，危害台海和平稳定，破坏和平统一前景、挤压和平统一空间，是争取和平统一进程中必须清除的障碍。

台湾是包括2300万台湾同胞在内的全体中国人民的台湾，中国人民捍卫国家主权和领土完整、维护中华民族根本利益的决心不可动摇、意志坚如磐石，这是挫败一切"台独"分裂图谋的根本力量。100多年前中国积贫积弱，台湾被外国侵占。70多年前中国打败侵略者，收复了台湾。现在的中国，跃升为世界第二大经济体，政治、经济、文化、科技、军事等实力大幅增强，更不可能再让台湾从中国分裂出去。搞"台独"分裂抗拒统一，根本过不了中华民族的历史和文化这一关,也根本过不了 14 亿多中国人民的决心和意志这一关,是绝对不可能得逞的。

(四)外部势力阻碍中国完全统一必遭失败

外部势力干涉是推进中国统一进程的突出障碍。美国一些势力出于霸权心态和冷战思维,将中国视为最主要战略对手和最严峻的长期挑战,竭力进行围堵打压,变本加厉推行"以台制华"。美国声称"奉行一个中国政策,不支持'台独'",但美国一些势力在实际行动上却背道而驰。他们虚化、掏空一个中国原则,加强与台湾地区官方往来,不断策动对台军售,加深美台军事勾连,助台拓展所谓"国际空间",拉拢其他国家插手台湾问题,不时炮制损害中国主权的涉台议案。他们颠倒黑白、混淆是非,一方面怂恿"台独"分裂势力制造两岸关系紧张动荡,另一方面却无端指责大陆"施压"、"胁迫"、"单方面改变现状",为"台独"分裂势力撑腰打气,给中国实现和平统一制造障碍。

《联合国宪章》规定的尊重国家主权和领土完整、不干涉别国内政等重要原则,是现代国际法和国际关系的基石。维护国家统一和领土完整,是每个主权国家的神圣权利,中国政府理所当然可以采取一切必要手段解决台湾问题、实现国家统一,不容外部势力干涉。美国的一些反华势力以所谓"自由、民主、人权"和"维护以规则为基础的国际秩序"为幌子,刻意歪曲台湾问题纯属中国内政的性质,企图否定中国政府维护国家主权和领土完整的正当性与合理性。这充分暴露了他们搞"以台制华"、阻挠中国统一的政治图谋，必须予以彻底揭露和严正谴责。

外部势力打"台湾牌"，是把台湾当作遏制中国发展进步、阻挠中华民族伟大复兴的棋子，牺牲的是台湾同胞的利益福祉和光明前途，绝不是为了台湾同胞好。他们纵容鼓动"台独"分裂势力滋事挑衅，加剧两岸对抗和台海形势紧张，破坏亚太地区和平稳定，既违逆求和平、促发展、谋共赢的时代潮流，也违背国际社会期待和世界人民意愿。新中国成立之初，在百废待兴、百业待举的情况下，中国共产党和中国政府紧紧依靠人民，以"钢少气多"力克"钢多气少"，赢得抗美援朝战争伟大胜利，捍卫了新中国安全，彰显了新中国大国地位，展现了我们不畏强暴、反抗强权的铮铮铁骨。中国坚定不移走和平发展道路，同时决不会在任何外来干涉的压力面前退缩，决不会容忍国家主权、安全、发展利益受到任何损害。"挟洋谋独"没有出路，"以台制华"注定失败。

要安宁、要发展、要过好日子，是台湾同胞的普遍心声，创造美好生活是两岸同胞的共同追求。在中国共产党的坚强领导下，中国人民和中华民族迎来从站起来、富起来到强起来的伟大飞跃，一穷二白、人口众多的祖国大陆全面建成小康社会，我们更有条件、更有信心、更有能力完成祖国统一大业，让两岸同胞都过上更好的日子。祖国统一的历史车轮滚滚向前，任何人任何势力都无法阻挡。

四、在新时代新征程上
推进祖国统一

在民族复兴的新征程上,中国共产党和中国政府统筹中华民族伟大复兴战略全局和世界百年未有之大变局,深入贯彻新时代中国共产党解决台湾问题的总体方略和对台大政方针,扎实推动两岸关系和平发展、融合发展,坚定推进祖国统一进程。

(一) 坚持"和平统一、一国两制"基本方针

以和平方式实现祖国统一,最符合包括台湾同胞在内的中华民族整体利益,最有利于中国的长期稳定发展,是中国共产党和中国政府解决台湾问题的第一选择。尽管几十年来遇到困难和阻力,但我们仍然坚持不懈地争取和平统一,这体现了我们对民族大义、同胞福祉与两岸和平的珍视和维护。

"一国两制"是中国共产党和中国政府为实现和平统一作出的重要制度安排,是中国特色社会主义的一个伟大创举。"和平统一、一国两制"是我们解决台湾问题的基本方针,也是实现国家统一的最佳方式,体现了海纳百川、有容乃大的中华智慧,既充分考虑台湾现实情况,又有利于统一后台湾长治久安。我们主张,和平统一后,

台湾可以实行不同于祖国大陆的社会制度,依法实行高度自治,两种社会制度长期共存、共同发展。"一国"是实行"两制"的前提和基础,"两制"从属和派生于"一国"并统一于"一国"之内。我们将继续团结台湾同胞,积极探索"两制"台湾方案,丰富和平统一实践。"一国两制"在台湾的具体实现形式会充分考虑台湾现实情况,会充分吸收两岸各界意见和建议,会充分照顾到台湾同胞利益和感情。

"一国两制"提出以来,台湾一些政治势力曲解误导,民进党及其当局不遗余力地造谣抹黑,造成部分台湾同胞的偏颇认知。事实是,香港、澳门回归祖国后,重新纳入国家治理体系,走上了同祖国内地优势互补、共同发展的宽广道路,"一国两制"实践取得举世公认的成功。同时,一个时期内,受各种内外复杂因素影响,"反中乱港"活动猖獗,香港局势一度出现严峻局面。中国共产党和中国政府审时度势,采取一系列标本兼治的举措,坚持和完善"一国两制"制度体系,推动香港局势实现由乱到治的重大转折,进入由治及兴的新阶段,为推进依法治港治澳、促进"一国两制"实践行稳致远打下了坚实基础。

实现两岸和平统一,必须面对大陆和台湾社会制度与意识形态不同这一基本问题。"一国两制"正是为解决这个问题而提出的最具包容性的方案。这是一个和平的方案、民主的方案、善意的方案、共赢的方案。两岸制度不同,不是统一的障碍,更不是分裂的借口。我们相信,随着时间的推移,"一国两制"将被广大台湾同胞重新认识;在两岸同胞共同致力实现和平统一的过程中,"两制"台湾方案的空间和内涵将得到充分展现。

和平统一,是平等协商、共议统一。两岸长期存在的政治分歧问题是影响两岸关系行稳致远的总根子,总不能一代一代传下去。两岸协商谈判可以有步骤、分阶段进行,方式可灵活多样。我们愿意在一个中国原则和"九二共识"的基础上,同台湾各党派、团体和人士就解决两岸政治分歧问题开展对话沟通,广泛交换意见。我们也愿意继续推动由两岸各政党、各界别推举的代表性人士开展民主协商,共商推动两岸关系和平发展、融合发展和祖国和平统一的大计。

(二) 努力推动两岸关系和平发展、融合发展

两岸关系和平发展、融合发展是通向和平统一的重要途径,是造福两岸同胞的康庄大道,需要凝聚两岸同胞力量共同推进。我们要在两岸关系和平发展进程中深化两岸融合发展,密切两岸交流合作,拉紧两岸情感纽带和利益联结,增强两岸同胞对中华文化和中华民族的认同,铸牢两岸命运共同体意识,厚植祖国和平统一的基础。

突出以通促融、以惠促融、以情促融,勇于探索海峡两岸融合发展新路,率先在福建建设海峡两岸融合发展示范区。持续推进两岸应通尽通,不断提升两岸经贸合作畅通、基础设施联通、能源资源互通、行业标准共通。推动两岸文化教育、医疗卫生合作,社会保障和公共资源共享,支持两岸邻近或条件相当地区基本公共服务均等化、普惠化、便捷化。积极推进两岸经济合作制度化,打造两岸共同市

场,壮大中华民族经济。

完善保障台湾同胞福祉和在大陆享受同等待遇的制度和政策,依法维护台湾同胞正当权益。支持台胞台企参与"一带一路"建设、国家区域重大战略和区域协调发展战略,融入新发展格局,参与高质量发展,让台湾同胞分享更多发展机遇,参与国家经济社会发展进程。

排除干扰、克服障碍,不断扩大两岸各领域交流合作。推动两岸同胞共同传承和创新发展中华优秀传统文化,加强两岸基层民众和青少年交流,吸引更多台胞特别是台湾青年来大陆学习、创业、就业、生活,使两岸同胞加深相互理解,增进互信认同,逐步实现心灵契合。

(三)坚决粉碎"台独"分裂和外来干涉图谋

搞"台独"分裂只会将台湾推入灾难深渊,给台湾同胞带来深重祸害。维护包括台湾同胞在内的中华民族整体利益,必须坚决反对"台独"分裂、促进祖国和平统一。我们愿意为和平统一创造广阔空间,但绝不为各种形式的"台独"分裂活动留下任何空间。中国人的事要由中国人来决定。台湾问题是中国的内政,事关中国核心利益和中国人民民族感情,不容任何外来干涉。任何利用台湾问题干涉中国内政、阻挠中国统一进程的图谋和行径,都将遭到包括台湾同胞在内的全体中国人民的坚决反对。任何人都不要低估中国人民捍卫国家主权和领土完整的坚强决心、坚定意志、强大能力。

我们愿继续以最大诚意、尽最大努力争取和平统一。我们不承诺放弃使用武力,保留采取一切必要措施的选项,针对的是外部势力干涉和极少数"台独"分裂分子及其分裂活动,绝非针对台湾同胞,非和平方式将是不得已情况下做出的最后选择。如果"台独"分裂势力或外部干涉势力挑衅逼迫,甚至突破红线,我们将不得不采取断然措施。始终坚持做好以非和平方式及其他必要措施应对外部势力干涉和"台独"重大事变的充分准备,目的是从根本上维护祖国和平统一的前景、推进祖国和平统一的进程。

当前,美国一些势力图谋"以台制华",处心积虑打"台湾牌",刺激"台独"分裂势力冒险挑衅,不仅严重危害台海和平稳定,妨碍中国政府争取和平统一的努力,也严重影响中美关系健康稳定发展。如果任其发展下去,必将导致台海形势紧张持续升级,给中美关系造成颠覆性的巨大风险,并严重损害美国自身利益。美国应该恪守一个中国原则,慎重妥善处理涉台问题,停止说一套做一套,以实际行动履行不支持"台独"的承诺。

(四) 团结台湾同胞共谋民族复兴和国家统一

国家统一是中华民族走向伟大复兴的历史必然。台湾前途在于国家统一,台湾同胞福祉系于民族复兴。实现中华民族伟大复兴,与两岸同胞前途命运息息相关。民族强盛,是两岸同胞之福;民族弱乱,是两岸同胞之祸。民族复兴、国家强盛,两岸同胞才能过上富足美好的生活。实现中华民族伟大复兴需要两岸同胞共同奋斗,实现祖国完全统一同样需要两岸同胞携手努力。

由于受到"台独"思想毒害,也由于两岸政治分歧问题尚未得到解决,一些台湾同胞对两岸关系性质和国家认同问题认识出现偏差,对祖国统一心存疑惧。台湾同胞是我们的骨肉天亲,两岸同胞是血浓于水的一家人。我们愿意保持足够的耐心和包容心,创造条件加强两岸交流交往,不断加深广大台湾同胞对祖国大陆的了解,逐步减少他们的误解和疑虑,进而走出受"台独"煽惑的历史误区。

我们将团结广大台湾同胞共创祖国统一、民族复兴的光荣伟业。希望广大台湾同胞坚定站在历史正确的一边,做堂堂正正的中国人,认真思考台湾在民族复兴中的地位和作用,深明大义、奉义而行,坚决反对"台独"分裂和外部势力干涉,积极参与到推进祖国和平统一的正义事业中来。

五、实现祖国和平统一的
光明前景

按照"一国两制"实现两岸和平统一,将给中国发展进步和中华民族伟大复兴奠定新的基础,将给台湾经济社会发展创造巨大机遇,将给广大台湾同胞带来实实在在的好处。

(一)台湾发展空间将更为广阔

台湾经济发展水平较高,产业特色明显,对外贸易发达,两岸经济互补性强。统一后,两岸经济合作机制、制度更加完善,台湾经济将以大陆市场为广阔腹地,发展空间更大,竞争力更强,产业链供应链更加稳定通畅,创新活力更加生机勃勃。长期困扰台湾经济发展和民生改善的众多难题,可以在两岸融合发展、应通尽通中得到解决。台湾财政收入尽可用于改善民生,多为老百姓做实事、办好事、解难事。

台湾的文化创造力将得到充分发扬,两岸同胞共同传承中华文化、弘扬民族精神,台湾地域文化在中华文化根脉的滋养中更加枝繁叶茂、焕发光彩。

（二）台湾同胞切身利益将得到充分保障

在确保国家主权、安全、发展利益的前提下，台湾可以作为特别行政区实行高度自治。台湾同胞的社会制度和生活方式等将得到充分尊重，台湾同胞的私人财产、宗教信仰、合法权益将得到充分保障。所有拥护祖国统一、民族复兴的台湾同胞将在台湾真正当家作主，参与祖国建设，尽享发展红利。有强大祖国做依靠，台湾同胞在国际上腰杆会更硬、底气会更足，更加安全、更有尊严。

（三）两岸同胞共享民族复兴的伟大荣光

台湾同胞崇敬祖先、爱土爱乡、勤劳勇敢、自强不息，具有光荣的爱国主义传统。两岸同胞发挥聪明才智，携手共创美好未来潜力巨大。统一后，两岸同胞可以弥合因长期没有统一而造成的隔阂，增进一家人的同胞亲情，更加紧密地团结起来；可以发挥各自优势，实现互利互补，携手共谋发展；可以共同促进中华民族的繁荣昌盛，让中华民族以更加昂扬的姿态屹立于世界民族之林。

两岸同胞血脉相连、命运与共。统一后，中国的国际影响力、感召力、塑造力将进一步增强，中华民族的自尊心、自信心、自豪感将进一步提升。台湾同胞将同大陆同胞一道，共享一个伟大国家的尊严和荣耀，以做堂堂正正的中国人而骄傲和自豪。两岸同胞共同探索实施"两制"台湾方案,共同发展完善"一国两制"制度体系,确保台湾长治久安。

（四） 有利于亚太地区及全世界和平与发展

实现两岸和平统一,不仅是中华民族和中国人民之福,也是国际社会和世界人民之福。中国的统一,不会损害任何国家的正当利益包括其在台湾的经济利益,只会给各国带来更多发展机遇,只会给亚太地区和世界繁荣稳定注入更多正能量,只会为构建人类命运共同体、为世界和平发展和人类进步事业作出更大贡献。

统一后,有关国家可以继续同台湾发展经济、文化关系。经中国中央政府批准,外国可以在台湾设立领事机构或其他官方、半官方机构,国际组织和机构可以在台湾设立办事机构,有关国际公约可以在台湾适用,有关国际会议可以在台湾举办。

结 束 语

　　具有五千多年文明史的中华民族创造了震古烁今的灿烂文化，对人类社会发展进步作出了重大贡献。在经历了近代以来从屈辱走向奋起、从落伍走向崛起的百年沧桑之后，中华民族迎来了大发展大作为的时代，迈出了走向伟大复兴的铿锵步伐。

　　在新时代新征程上，中国共产党和中国政府将继续团结带领两岸同胞顺应历史大势，勇担时代责任，把前途命运牢牢掌握在自己手中，为实现祖国完全统一和中华民族伟大复兴而努力奋斗。

　　前进道路不可能一马平川，但只要包括两岸同胞在内的所有中华儿女同心同德、团结奋斗，就一定能够粉碎任何形式的"台独"分裂和外来干涉图谋，就一定能够汇聚起促进祖国统一和民族复兴的磅礴伟力。祖国完全统一的历史任务一定要实现，也一定能够实现！

新时代的中国北斗

（2022 年 11 月）

中华人民共和国
国务院新闻办公室

前　言

北斗卫星导航系统（以下简称北斗系统）是中国着眼于国家安全和经济社会发展需要，自主建设、独立运行的卫星导航系统。经过多年发展，北斗系统已成为面向全球用户提供全天候、全天时、高精度定位、导航与授时服务的重要新型基础设施。

党的十八大以来，北斗系统进入快速发展的新时代。2020年7月31日，习近平总书记向世界宣布北斗三号全球卫星导航系统正式开通，标志着北斗系统进入全球化发展新阶段。从改革开放新时期到中国发展进入新时代，从北斗一号到北斗三号，从双星定位到全球组网，从覆盖亚太到服务全球，北斗系统与国家发展同频共振，与民族复兴同向同行。

新时代的中国北斗，既造福中国人民，也造福世界各国人民。北斗系统秉持"中国的北斗、世界的北斗、一流的北斗"发展理念，在全球范围内实现广泛应用，赋能各行各业，融入基础设施，进入大众应用领域，深刻改变着人们的生产生活方式，成为经济社会发展的时空基石，为卫星导航系统更好服务全球、造福人类贡献了中国智慧和力量。

新时代的中国北斗，展现了中国实现高水平科技自立自强的志气和骨气，展现了中国人民独立自主、自力更生、艰苦奋斗、攻坚克难的精神和意志,展现了中国特色社会主义集中力量办大事的制度优势,展现了胸怀天下、立己达人的中国担当。

为介绍新时代中国北斗发展成就和未来愿景,分享中国北斗发展理念和实践经验,特发布本白皮书。

一、北斗发展进入新时代

进入新时代，伴随着中国发展取得历史性成就、发生历史性变革，中国北斗走上高质量发展之路，机制体系、速度规模等不断实现新突破、迈上新台阶，创造了中国北斗耀苍穹的奇迹。

（一）走出自主发展的中国道路

中国立足国情国力，坚持自主创新、分步建设、渐进发展，不断完善北斗系统，走出一条从无到有、从有到优、从有源到无源、从区域到全球的中国特色卫星导航系统建设道路。

实施"三步走"发展战略。1994年，中国开始研制发展独立自主的卫星导航系统，至2000年底建成北斗一号系统，采用有源定位体制服务中国，成为世界上第三个拥有卫星导航系统的国家。2012年，建成北斗二号系统，面向亚太地区提供无源定位服务。2020年，北斗三号系统正式建成开通，面向全球提供卫星导航服务，标志着北斗系统"三步走"发展战略圆满完成。

向全球时代加速迈进。2012年12月，北斗二号系统建成并提供服务，这是北斗系统发展的新起点。2015年3月，首颗北斗三号系统试验卫星发射。2017年11月，完成北斗三号系统首批2颗中圆地球轨道卫星在轨部署,北斗系统全球组网按下快进键。2018 年 12 月,完成 19 颗卫星基本星座部署。2020 年 6 月,由 24 颗中圆地球轨道卫星、3 颗地球静止轨道卫星和 3 颗倾斜地球同步轨道卫星组成的完整星座完成部署。2020 年 7 月,北斗三号系统正式开通全球服务,"中国的北斗"真正成为"世界的北斗"。

(二) 更好服务全球、造福人类

新时代的中国北斗,以更好服务全球、造福人类为宗旨,进一步提高多种技术手段融合水平,不断提升多样化、特色化服务能力,大力推动北斗应用产业发展,全方位加强国际交流合作,更好满足经济社会发展和人民美好生活需要,更好实现共享共赢。

——开放兼容。免费提供公开的卫星导航服务,持续提升全球公共服务能力。积极开展国际合作与交流,倡导和加强多系统兼容共用。

——创新超越。坚持创新驱动发展战略,实现创新引领,提升自主发展能力。持续推动系统升级换代,融合新一代通信、低轨增强等新兴技术,推动与非卫星导航技术融合发展。

——优质服务。确保系统连续稳定运行,发挥特色服务优势,为全球用户提供优质的卫星导航服务。完善标准、政策法规、知识产权、宣传推广等体系环境建设,优化北斗产业生态。

——共享共赢。深化北斗系统应用推广,推进北斗产业高质量发展,融入千行百业,赋能生产生活。与世界共享中国卫星导航系统建设发展成果,实现互利互赢。

（三）铸就新时代北斗精神

在面对未知的艰辛探索中,中国北斗建设者披荆斩棘、接续奋斗,培育了"自主创新、开放融合、万众一心、追求卓越"的新时代北斗精神,生动诠释了以爱国主义为核心的民族精神和以改革创新为核心的时代精神,丰富了中国共产党人的精神谱系。

自主创新是中国北斗的核心竞争力。北斗系统始终坚持自主创新、自主设计、自主建造、自主可控,把关键核心技术牢牢掌握在自己手中,这是中国北斗应对各种挑战、战胜各种困难的主动选择。

开放融合是中国北斗的世界胸襟。北斗系统顺应开放的时代大势和融合的发展潮流,践行"让各国人民共享发展机遇和成果"的承诺,展现了登高望远的格局和美美与共的胸襟。

万众一心是中国北斗的成功密码。北斗系统是全体北斗建设者同舟共济、合作奉献的结果,是全国上下支持、各方力量协作的结果,生动诠释了中华民族团结拼搏的优良传统和中国人民深沉的家国情怀。

追求卓越是中国北斗的永恒目标。北斗系统对标世界一流,"要做就做最好",实现工程技术卓越、运行服务卓越、工程实施管理卓越,成为新时代中国的一个闪亮品牌。

（四）展望北斗发展新愿景

面向未来,中国将建设技术更先进、功能更强大、服务更优质的北斗系统,建成更加泛在、更加融合、更加智能的综合时空体系,提供高弹性、高智能、高精度、高安全的定位导航授时服务,更好惠及民生福祉、服务人类发展进步。

建强北斗卫星导航系统,建成中国特色北斗系统智能运维管理体系,突出短报文、地基增强、星基增强、国际搜救等特色服务优势,不断提升服务性能、拓展服务功能,形成全球动态分米级高精度定位导航和完好性保障能力,向全球用户提供高质量服务。

推动北斗系统规模应用市场化、产业化、国际化发展,提供更加优质、更加多样的公共服务产品,进一步挖掘市场潜力、丰富应用场景、扩大应用规模,构建新机制,培育新生态,完善产业体系,加强国际产业合作,打造更加完整、更富韧性的产业链,让北斗系统发展成果更好惠及各国人民。

构建国家综合定位导航授时体系,发展多种导航手段,实现前沿技术交叉创新、多种手段聚能增效、多源信息融合共享,推动服务向水下、室内、深空延伸,提供基准统一、覆盖无缝、弹性智能、安全可信、便捷高效的综合时空信息服务,推动构建人类命运共同体,建设更加美好的世界。

二、跻身世界一流的中国北斗

中国北斗的建设发展,始终锚定世界一流目标,坚持创新引领、追求卓越,不断实现自我超越。中国的北斗,技术先进、设计领先、功能强大,是世界一流的全球卫星导航系统。

(一) 核心技术自主研发

中国从自身实际出发,因应世界卫星导航发展趋势,从星座构型、技术体制、服务功能等方面创新系统设计,攻克混合星座、星间链路、信号体制设计等多项核心关键技术,在全球范围实现一流能力。

创新星座构型。首创中高轨混合异构星座,高轨卫星单星覆盖区域大、抗遮挡能力强,中轨卫星星座全球运行、全球覆盖,是实现全球服务的核心,各轨道卫星优势互补,既能实现全球覆盖,又能加强区域能力。

构建星间链路。首次通过星间链路实现卫星与卫星之间、卫星与地面之间一体化组网运行,实现星间高精度测量和数据传输,基于国内布站条件提供全球运行服务。

优化信号体制。突破调制方式、多路复用、信道编码等关键技术,率先实现全星座三频服务,实现导航定位功能与通信数传功能、基本导航信息与差分增强信息的融合设计,信号测距精度、抗干扰和抗多径等性能达到世界一流水平,实现与其他卫星导航系统的兼容共用并支持多样化特色服务。

（二）系统组成创新引领

北斗系统由空间段、地面段和用户段组成。其中,空间段由中圆地球轨道、地球静止轨道、倾斜地球同步轨道等三种轨道共30颗卫星组成;地面段由运控系统、测控系统、星间链路运行管理系统,以及国际搜救、短报文通信、星基增强和地基增强等多种服务平台组成;用户段由兼容其他卫星导航系统的各类终端及应用系统组成。

北斗系统星间星地一体组网,是中国首个实现全球组网运行的航天系统,显著提升了中国航天科研生产能力,有力推动中国宇航技术跨越式发展。

组批生产能力卓越。创新星地产品研制和星箭制造,研制运载火箭上面级、导航卫星专用平台,实现星箭批量生产、密集发射、快速组网,以两年半时间18箭30星的中国速度完成全球星座部署,创造世界导航卫星组网新纪录。

关键器件自主可控。实现宇航级存储器、星载处理器、大功率微波开关、行波管放大器、固态放大器等器部件国产化研制,北斗系统核心器部件100%自主可控,为北斗系统广泛应用奠定了坚实基础。

（三）系统服务优质多样

北斗系统服务性能优异、功能强大，可提供多种服务，满足用户多样化需求。其中，向全球用户提供定位导航授时、国际搜救、全球短报文通信等三种全球服务；向亚太地区提供区域短报文通信、星基增强、精密单点定位、地基增强等四种区域服务。

定位导航授时服务。通过 30 颗卫星，免费向全球用户提供服务，全球范围水平定位精度优于 9 米、垂直定位精度优于 10 米，测速精度优于 0.2 米/秒、授时精度优于 20 纳秒。

国际搜救服务。通过 6 颗中圆地球轨道卫星，旨在向全球用户提供符合国际标准的遇险报警公益服务。创新设计返向链路，为求救者提供遇险搜救请求确认服务。

全球短报文通信服务。北斗系统是世界上首个具备全球短报文通信服务能力的卫星导航系统，通过 14 颗中圆地球轨道卫星，为特定用户提供全球随遇接入服务，最大单次报文长度 560 比特（40 个汉字）。

区域短报文通信服务。北斗系统是世界上首个面向授权用户提供区域短报文通信服务的卫星导航系统，通过 3 颗地球静止轨道卫星，为中国及周边地区用户提供数据传输服务，最大单次报文长度 14000 比特（1000 个汉字），具备文字、图片、语音等传输能力。

星基增强服务。创新集成设计星基增强服务，通过 3 颗地球静止轨道卫星,旨在向中国及周边地区用户提供符合国际标准的 I 类精密进近服务,支持单频及双频多星座两种增强服务模式,可为交通运输领域提供安全保障。

精密单点定位服务。创新集成设计精密单点定位服务,通过 3 颗地球静止轨道卫星,免费向中国及周边地区用户提供定位精度水平优于 30 厘米、高程优于 60 厘米,收敛时间优于 30 分钟的高精度定位增强服务。

地基增强服务。建成地面站全国一张网,向行业和大众用户提供实时米级、分米级、厘米级和事后毫米级高精度定位增强服务。

三、提高系统运行管理水平

作为负责任的航天大国,中国不断提高北斗系统运行管理水平,保障系统连续稳定运行、保持系统性能稳步提升、保证系统信息公开透明,确保系统持续、健康、快速发展,提供高稳定、高可靠、高安全、高质量的时空信息服务。

(一) 保障系统稳定运行

稳定运行是卫星导航系统的生命线。中国北斗坚持系统思维,构建以齐抓共管多方联保为组织特色、星地星间全网管控为系统特色、软硬协同智能运维为技术特色的中国特色北斗系统运行管理体系,融"常态保障、平稳过渡、监测评估、智能运维"为一体,为系统连续稳定运行提供了基本保障。

强化常态保障。完善多方联合保障、运行状态会商、设备巡检维护等制度机制,建立协同顺畅、信息共享、决策高效的工作流程,不断提升常态化运行管理保障能力。

确保平稳过渡。从空间段、地面段、用户段等方面,有序实施从北斗二号向北斗三号的平稳过渡,保障用户无需更换设备,以最小代价享受系统升级服务。

加强监测评估。统筹优化北斗系统全球连续监测评估资源配置,对系统星座状态、信号精度、信号质量和服务性能等进行全方位、常态化监测评估,及时准确掌握系统运行服务状态。

提升运维水平。充分利用大数据、人工智能、云计算等新技术,构建北斗系统数据资源池,促进系统运行、监测评估、空间环境等多源数据融通,实现信息按需共享,提升系统智能化运行管理水平。

(二)提升系统服务性能

更高精度、更稳运行是北斗系统的不懈追求。中国北斗坚持稳中求进,在系统状态、时空基准、应用场景等方面持续用力,推动系统服务能力不断提升、服务场域不断拓展、服务品质不断升级。

升级系统状态。实施地面设备升级改造,按需更新在轨卫星软件,动态优化星地处理模型和算法,持续加强星间星地一体化网络运行能力,不断提升空间信号精度与质量,实现服务性能稳中有升。

建强时空基准。建立与维持北斗系统高精度时间基准,持续开展与其他卫星导航系统时差监测,在导航电文中播发,加强与其他卫星导航系统时间系统互操作。北斗坐标系统与国际大地参考框架保持对齐,加强与其他卫星导航系统坐标系统互操作。

拓展服务场域。开展多手段导航能力建设,实现弹性定位导航授时服务功能。开展北斗地月空间服务应用探索和试验,推动北斗服务向深空延展。突破导航通信融合系列关键技术,提升复杂环境和人类活动密集区服务能力。

（三）发布系统动态信息

发布系统信息是卫星导航系统提升用户感知度和信赖度的基本途径。中国北斗坚持公开透明,建设发布平台,完善发布机制,动态发布权威准确的系统信息,向全球用户提供负责任的服务。

建设多渠道信息发布平台。通过北斗官方网站（www.beidou.gov.cn）、监测评估网站（www.csno-tarc.cn 和 www.igmas.org）、官方微信公众号（beidousystem）等渠道平台,发布系统建设运行、应用推广、国际合作、政策法规等相关信息。

发布系统服务文件。更新发布北斗公开服务信号接口控制文件,定义北斗系统卫星与用户终端之间的接口关系,规范信号结构、基本特性、测距码、导航电文等内容,为全球研发北斗应用产品提供输入。更新发布公开服务性能规范,明确北斗系统公开服务覆盖范围和性能指标。

发布系统状态信息。及时发布卫星发射入网、在轨测试、监测评估结果以及卫星退役退网等系统状态信息。在采取可能影响用户服务的计划操作之前,适时向国内外用户发布通告。

四、推动应用产业可持续发展

新时代的中国北斗,坚持在发展中应用、在应用中发展,不断夯实产品基础、拓展应用领域、完善产业生态,持续推广北斗规模化应用,推动北斗应用深度融入国民经济发展全局,促进北斗应用产业健康发展,为经济社会发展注入强大动力。

(一)制定实施产业发展战略

中国北斗坚持以用促建、建用并举,体系化设计北斗应用产业发展,工程化推进北斗行业和区域应用,不断深化北斗系统推广应用,推动北斗产业高质量发展。

创新谋划应用产业总体思路。面对新时代、新形势、新要求,坚持以抓生态保障、抓共性基础、推应用产业为重心的总体思路,凝聚各方力量,形成齐抓共管、合力推动新局面。

加强产业发展规划设计。编制实施《全面加强北斗系统产业化应用发展总体方案》、北斗产业发展专项规划,各行业、各地区陆续出台实施北斗产业专项计划、专项行动,持续完善产业创新体系、融合应用体系、产业生态体系、全球服务体系。

实施北斗产业化重大工程。按照统筹集约、突出重点、分类推进的原则,聚焦保安全、促创新、强产业,发挥重大工程的战略牵引作用,加快形成以市场为主导、企业为主体的北斗产业发展格局。

（二） 夯实产业发展根基

中国北斗聚焦应用基础设施、应用基础产品和应用基础软件,加强应用基础平台建设,加大应用技术研发支持力度,不断夯实北斗应用产业发展根基。

完善应用基础设施。全面打造国际搜救、短报文通信、星基增强、地基增强等北斗特色服务平台,加强北斗特色服务与多种通信手段融合,拓展应用广度深度,为用户提供更加高效便捷的服务。

研发应用基础产品。研制芯片、模块、天线等系列基础产品,实现北斗基础产品亿级量产规模。研发卫星导航与惯性导航、移动通信、视觉导航等多种手段融合的基础产品,增强应用弹性。

研发应用基础软件。加大自主研发力度,加强定位解算、模型开发、数据分析、设计仿真等共性基础技术软件化和工具化,推动应用基础软件可用好用。

（三） 优化产业发展生态

中国北斗围绕标准规范、知识产权、检测认证、产业评估等,成体系打造要素完备、创新活跃、良性健康的产业生态,实现供应链、产业链、创新链、政策链共振耦合，推动应用产业集群发展。

推进标准化建设。充分发挥标准的基础性、引领性作用，更新发布北斗卫星导航标准体系，加快北斗应用标准制（修）订。持续推动形成包括团体标准、行业标准、国家标准和国际标准在内的相互衔接、覆盖全面、科学合理的应用标准体系，推动产业优化升级。

加强知识产权保护。提升北斗卫星导航领域专利审查质量和效率，为北斗系统的专利布局提供支撑。激发北斗创新应用主体在知识产权创造、运用、保护、管理方面的动力和活力，提升中国卫星导航专利基础储备和应用转化能力。

完善产品检测认证体系。强化北斗卫星导航产品检测认证顶层设计，构建检测认证公共服务网络平台，开展重点行业和领域北斗产品检测认证，提升产品质量水平，确保应用安全可靠。

构建产业评估体系。面向重点行业、关键领域、主要区域、大众应用和国际应用，健全应用信息反馈机制，建立北斗应用产业评估机制，保障产业健康可持续发展。

提高产业发展协作水平。鼓励北斗产业联盟建设，加强产学研用协同合作，加强与市场需求对接。发挥相关行业协会、学会的政企桥梁纽带作用，促进交流合作和行业自律。

打造产业集群。推动重点区域、重点城市结合国家战略和自身特点，全面布局北斗产业应用，巩固区域发展特色优势，形成以研发机构、骨干企业、特色园区为主体的北斗产业集群。

（四）做强产业发展业态

中国北斗广泛应用于经济社会发展各行业各领域，与大数据、物联网、人工智能等新兴技术深度融合，催生"北斗+"和"+北斗"新业态，支撑经济社会数字化转型和提质增效，让人民生活更便捷、更精彩。

示范引领带动。瞄准具有较大应用规模、社会效益和经济效益显著的重要行业，结合国家发展战略，实施行业和区域示范应用，形成综合应用解决方案，带动北斗规模化应用。

融入关键领域。快速融入影响国计民生、社会公益，涉及国家安全、公共安全和经济安全的重要领域，实现应用更可靠、安全有保障。

赋能各行各业。深度融入信息基础设施、融合基础设施、创新基础设施等新型基础设施建设，广泛进入交通、能源、农业、通信、气象、自然资源、生态环境、应急减灾等重点行业，实现降本增效。

走进千家万户。广泛进入大众消费、共享经济和民生领域，通过智能手机、车载终端、穿戴设备等应用产品，全面服务于绿色出行、外卖送餐、健康养老、儿童关爱、医疗教育等人民生活衣食住行方方面面。

专栏 北斗应用产业快速发展

2021 年,中国卫星导航与位置服务产业总体产值达到约 4700 亿元人民币。

产品制造方面,北斗芯片、模块等系列关键技术持续取得突破,产品出货量快速增长。截至 2021 年底,具有北斗定位功能的终端产品社会总保有量超过 10 亿台/套。

行业服务方面,北斗系统广泛应用于各行各业,产生显著经济和社会效益。截至 2021 年底,超过 780 万辆道路营运车辆安装使用北斗系统,近 8000 台各型号北斗终端在铁路领域应用推广,基于北斗系统的农机自动驾驶系统超过 10 万台/套,医疗健康、防疫消杀、远程监控、线上服务等下游运营服务环节产值近 2000 亿元。

大众应用方面,以智能手机和智能穿戴式设备为代表的北斗大众领域应用获得全面突破,包括智能手机器件供应商在内的国际主流芯片厂商产品广泛支持北斗。2021 年国内智能手机出货量中支持北斗的已达 3.24 亿部,占国内智能手机总出货量的 94.5%。

五、提升现代化治理水平

新时代的中国北斗,坚持制度创新、机制创新、发展创新,完善政策法规,优化组织管理,厚植人才优势,以改革创新驱动科技创新,充分发挥有效市场和有为政府作用,不断提升现代化治理水平。

(一)创新组织管理体制机制

中国立足北斗系统建设发展需求,科学统筹、优化机制,充分发挥国家制度优势,集中力量办大事,把政府、市场、社会等各方面力量汇聚起来,形成北斗事业发展强大合力。

创新工程建设组织管理。充分发挥北斗系统工程建设领导机构作用,构建多部门协同、责任清晰、分工明确、分级实施的组织管理体系,创建工程、应用、国际合作"三位一体"协同推进机制,确保北斗工程建设管理运行顺畅、协调高效、规范有序。

建立统筹协调机制。加强基础设施建设、应用推广、国际合作、卫星频率轨道资源管理、知识产权保护、标准制定、人才队伍建设等方面的系统谋划和协调推进,构建全联动、大协调工作新格局。

（二）以制度创新驱动科技创新

中国深入实施创新驱动发展战略，坚持科技创新与制度创新"双轮驱动"，建立健全卫星导航科技创新动力机制，加快推进科技创新。

建立原始集成协同创新机制。秉承自主创新、开放交流的发展原则，培育卫星导航科技原始创新发源地，超前部署战略性、基础性、前瞻性科学技术研究，构建先进的技术攻关体系和产品研发体系。适应北斗与新一代信息技术深度融合发展要求，分阶段组织、增量式发展、多功能集成，建立跨学科、跨专业、跨领域协同创新机制，汇聚创新资源和要素，激发创新发展的聚变效应。

完善竞争择优的激励机制。以公开透明、公平竞争、互学互鉴为原则，创建多家参与、产品比测、综合评估、动态择优的竞争机制，既保持竞争压力，又充分调动各方积极性，实现高质量、高效益、低成本、可持续发展。

完善科研生产组织体系。强化数字工程等新技术引领，构建智能化试验验证评估体系。优化"研制、测评、改进、再验证"迭代演进科研生产流程，创建适应多星、多箭、多站同期研发、组批生产新模式，提升星地一体快速组网能力。

（三）推进卫星导航法治建设

中国统筹发展与安全、统筹当前和长远、统筹国内法治与涉外法治，全方位构建中国卫星导航法治体系，积极参与卫星导航全球治理，为北斗系统持续健康发展营造良好内外环境。

加快推进卫星导航立法。研究制定《中华人民共和国卫星导航条例》，规范和加强卫星导航活动管理，健全卫星导航系统建设、运行服务、应用管理、国际合作、安全保障等配套制度，不断完善卫星导航法律制度体系。

持续优化营商环境。坚持市场化、法治化、国际化原则，规范卫星导航市场秩序，持续净化市场环境，保护市场主体权益，优化政府服务，营造稳定、公平、透明、可预期的营商环境，激发市场活力和发展动力。

规范卫星导航活动。根据空间物体登记规定，及时准确完整报送北斗卫星信息。依法办理相关无线电频率使用许可、空间无线电执照和卫星地球站执照。依法保护北斗系统频谱使用，严禁生产、销售或使用卫星导航非法干扰设备，依法查处非法干扰行为。

参与卫星导航全球治理。践行共商共建共享的全球治理观，在全球卫星导航系统国际委员会（ICG）框架下处理卫星导航国际事务，参与卫星导航国际规则制定，推动卫星导航国际秩序朝着更加公正合理的方向发展。

（四）厚植发展人才优势

人才是发展和创新的第一资源。中国北斗坚持用事业培养人才、团结人才、引领人才、成就人才，不断壮大人才队伍、发挥人才优势，为卫星导航事业发展注入不竭动力。

建强人才队伍。完善定位导航授时相关领域人才培养体系，健全人才培养、交流和激励机制，构建人才培养平台，推动建设国家重点实验室，壮大跨学科、复合型、国际化人才队伍。

促进学术繁荣。面向定位导航授时前沿技术和产业发展需求，深化定位导航授时基础理论和应用研究，加强定位导航授时学术交流，多措并举提升科技创新能力和水平。

推进科普教育。持续推动科普教育基地建设，注重打造体验式科普场景，开展科普活动，出版科普读物，丰富科普内容，促进定位导航授时知识大众化、普及化，激发全民探索科学、探索时空的热情。

六、助力构建人类命运共同体

卫星导航是全人类的共同财富。中国坚持开放融合、协调合作、兼容互补、成果共享，积极开展北斗系统国际合作，推进北斗应用国际化进程，让北斗系统更好服务全球、造福人类，助力构建人类命运共同体。

（一）促进多系统兼容共用

中国积极倡导和持续促进卫星导航系统间兼容与互操作，积极开展频率轨位协调与磋商，共同提高卫星导航系统服务水平，为全球用户提供更加优质多样、安全可靠的服务。

倡导兼容与互操作合作。持续推进北斗系统与其他卫星导航系统、星基增强系统的兼容与互操作，促进卫星导航系统兼容共用，实现资源共享、优势互补、技术进步。建立卫星导航多双边合作机制，持续开展兼容与互操作协调，与其他国家就卫星导航系统和星基增强系统开展合作与交流，促进各卫星导航系统的共同发展。

开展频率轨位协调与磋商。遵循国际电信联盟规则，维护卫星网络申报协调国际秩序，通过多双边友好协商开展卫星导航频率轨位协调与磋商。积极参与国际组织主导的技术和标准研究制定，与相关国家共同维护、使用和拓展卫星导航频率轨位资源。

（二）广泛开展国际合作交流

中国深化国际合作机制，共拓国际合作渠道，打造国际合作平台，建立国际合作窗口，持续扩大北斗系统国际"朋友圈"，不断提升卫星导航全球应用水平。

深度参与卫星导航国际事务。参加联合国框架下系列活动，举办全球卫星导航系统国际委员会大会，参与议题研究，研提合作建议，发起合作倡议，共商共促世界卫星导航事业发展。

开展多双边合作交流。与东盟、阿盟等区域组织和非洲、拉美等地区的国家开展合作与交流，举办北斗/GNSS合作论坛，发布应用场景，推介解决方案，提高国际应用水平。

深化测试评估合作。联合开展北斗及其他全球卫星导航系统定位导航授时、短报文通信、国际搜救等服务性能测试评估，发布测试评估报告，增进用户对卫星导航系统状态和服务性能的了解，增强用户信心，提高合作水平。

搭建国际教育培训平台。持续开展卫星导航相关专业国际学生学历教育，特别是硕士及博士生教育。依托联合国空间科技教育亚太区域中心（中国）、北斗/GNSS中心、北斗国际交流培训中心等平台，积极开展卫星导航培训，为国际社会特别是发展中国家培养卫星导航人才，促进国际卫星导航能力建设。

广泛开展国际学术交流。做强中国卫星导航年会和北斗规模应用国际峰会等交流平台,持续提升国际影响力。积极参加国际卫星导航领域学术交流活动,促进国际卫星导航技术进步。

(三) 推进加入国际标准体系

中国持续推动北斗系统进入国际标准组织、行业和专业应用等标准组织,使北斗系统更好服务全球用户与相关行业发展。

国际民航领域标准。北斗系统相关技术指标通过国际民航组织验证,满足国际民航领域标准要求,具备为全球民用航空用户提供定位导航授时服务的能力。

国际海事领域标准。北斗系统成为世界无线电导航系统重要组成部分,取得面向海事应用的国际合法地位。北斗船载接收设备检测标准正式发布,为国际海事设备制造商提供设计、生产和检测依据。北斗短报文通信服务加入国际海事组织全球海上遇险与安全系统稳步推进。

国际搜救领域标准。发布搜救卫星应急示位标国际标准。推动北斗返向链路纳入全球搜救卫星系统组织标准,开展返向链路国际兼容共用协调。

国际移动通信领域标准。国际移动通信第三代合作伙伴计划制定发布支持北斗信号的技术标准、性能标准和一致性测试标准,为2G、3G、4G、5G移动通信系统和终端使用北斗网络辅助定位和高精度定位功能提供重要支持。

国际数据交换标准。推动北斗进入高精度差分服务、通用数据交换格式、定位信息输出协议等接收机国际通用数据标准。

（四）推动发展成果惠及全球

中国不断推进北斗产品、服务和产业国际应用的深度和广度,加速北斗规模应用国际化进程,助力全球经济社会发展和民生改善,增进世界人民福祉。

提升北斗产品国际贡献。推动芯片、模块、终端等北斗产品加速融入国际产业体系,对接国际需求、对标国际水准、发挥特色优势,融入本地产业,服务转型升级,促进经济社会发展。

促进北斗服务海外落地。建立卫星导航国际应用服务体系,合作共建卫星导航服务平台,联合推动国际搜救、短报文通信、星基增强、地基增强等特色服务国际应用,满足国际用户多样化应用需求。

深化应用产业国际合作。开展卫星导航应用技术研发和产业合作,建立海外北斗应用产业促进中心,培育卫星导航产业基础。加大与东盟、阿盟、非盟、拉共体等区域组织合作力度,发布智慧城市、公共安全、精准农业、数字交通、防灾减灾等北斗应用解决方案,在亚洲、非洲、拉美等地区重点示范应用。

结　束　语

探索宇宙时空,是中华民族的千年梦想。从夜观"北斗"到建用"北斗",从仰望星空到经纬时空,中国北斗未来可期、大有可为。中国将坚定不移走自主创新之路,以下一代北斗系统为核心,建设更加泛在、更加融合、更加智能的综合时空体系,书写人类时空文明新篇章。

宇宙广袤,容得下各国共同开发利用;星海浩瀚,需要全人类合作探索。中国愿同各国共享北斗系统建设发展成果,共促世界卫星导航事业蓬勃发展,携手迈向更加广阔的星辰大海,为构建人类命运共同体、建设更加美好的世界作出新的更大贡献。

携手构建网络空间命运共同体

（2022 年 11 月）

中华人民共和国
国务院新闻办公室

前　言

互联网是人类社会发展的重要成果,是人类文明向信息时代演进的关键标志。随着新一轮科技革命和产业变革加速推进,互联网让世界变成了"地球村",国际社会越来越成为你中有我、我中有你的命运共同体。发展好、运用好、治理好互联网,让互联网更好造福人类,是国际社会的共同责任。

中国全功能接入国际互联网以来,始终致力于推动互联网发展和治理。党的十八大以来,以习近平同志为核心的党中央,坚持以人民为中心的发展思想,高度重视互联网、大力发展互联网、积极运用互联网、有效治理互联网,中国网信事业取得历史性成就,亿万人民在共享互联网发展成果上拥有更多获得感,为构建和平、安全、开放、合作、有序的网络空间作出积极贡献。

随着互联网的快速发展,网络空间治理面临的问题日益突出。习近平总书记提出构建网络空间命运共同体重要理念,深入阐释了全球互联网发展治理一系列重大原则和主张。构建网络空间命运共同体重要理念,顺应信息时代发展潮流和人类社会发展大势,回应网络空间风险挑战,彰显了中国共产党为人类谋进步、为世界谋大同的情怀,表达了中国同世界各国加强互联网发展和治理合作的真诚愿望。新时代的中国网络空间国际合作,在构建网络空间命运共同体的愿景下，不断取得新成绩、实现新突破、展现新气象。

为介绍新时代中国互联网发展和治理理念与实践，分享中国推动构建网络空间命运共同体的积极成果，展望网络空间国际合作前景，特发布此白皮书。

一、构建网络空间命运共同体是
信息时代的必然选择

互联互通是网络空间的基本属性,共享共治是互联网发展的共同愿景。随着全球信息技术高速发展,互联网已渗透到人类生产生活的方方面面,同时,人类在网络空间也日益面临发展和安全方面的问题和挑战,需要携起手来,共同应对。

(一)网络空间命运共同体是人类命运
共同体的重要组成部分

当前,世界百年未有之大变局加速演进,新一轮科技革命和产业变革深入发展。同时,世纪疫情影响深远,逆全球化思潮抬头,单边主义、保护主义明显上升,世界经济复苏乏力,局部冲突和动荡频发,全球性问题加剧,世界进入新的动荡变革期。互联网领域发展不平衡、规则不健全、秩序不合理等问题日益凸显,网络霸权主义对世界和平与发展构成新的威胁。个别国家将互联网作为维护霸权的工具,滥用信息技术干涉别国内政,从事大规模网络窃密和监控活动,网络空间冲突对抗风险上升。一些国家搞"小圈子""脱钩断链",制造网络空间的分裂与对抗,网络空间安全面临的形势日益复杂。网络空间治理呼唤更加公平、合理、有效的解决方案,全球性威胁和挑战需要强有力的全球性应对。

作为全球最大的发展中国家和网民数量最多的国家,中国顺应信息时代发展趋势,坚持以人民为中心的发展思想,秉持共商共建共享的全球治理观,推动构建网络空间命运共同体。网络空间命运共同体坚持多边参与、多方参与,尊重网络主权,发扬伙伴精神,坚持大家的事由大家商量着办,推动国际社会深化务实合作,共同应对风险挑战。构建网络空间命运共同体,这一理念符合信息时代的发展规律、符合世界人民的需求与期待,为全球在尊重网络主权的基础上,推进网络空间发展和治理体系变革贡献了中国方案。

网络空间命运共同体是人类命运共同体的重要组成部分,是人类命运共同体理念在网络空间的具体体现。网络空间命运共同体所包含的关于发展、安全、治理、普惠等方面的理念主张,与人类命运共同体理念既一脉相承,又充分体现了网络空间的客观规律和鲜明特征。同时,推动构建网络空间命运共同体,将为构建人类命运共同体提供充沛的数字化动力,构筑坚实的安全屏障,凝聚更广泛的合作共识。

(二) 构建发展、安全、责任、利益共同体

构建网络空间命运共同体,坚持共商共建共享的全球治理观,推动构建多边、民主、透明的国际互联网治理体系,努力实现网络空间

创新发展、安全有序、平等尊重、开放共享的目标,做到发展共同推进、安全共同维护、治理共同参与、成果共同分享,把网络空间建设成为造福全人类的发展共同体、安全共同体、责任共同体、利益共同体。

构建发展共同体。随着新一代信息通信技术加速融合创新,数字化、网络化、智能化在经济社会各领域加速渗透,深刻改变人们的生产方式和生活方式。同时,不同国家和地区在互联网普及、基础设施建设、技术创新创造、数字经济发展、数字素养与技能等方面的发展水平不平衡,影响和限制世界各国特别是发展中国家的信息化建设和数字化转型。构建发展共同体,就是采取更加积极、包容、协调、普惠的政策,推动全球信息基础设施加快普及,为广大发展中国家提供用得上、用得起、用得好的网络服务。充分发挥数字经济在全球经济发展中的引擎作用,积极推进数字产业化发展和产业数字化转型。

构建安全共同体。安全是发展的前提,一个安全稳定繁荣的网络空间,对世界各国都具有重大意义。网络安全是全球性挑战,没有哪个国家能够置身事外、独善其身,维护网络安全是国际社会的共同责任。构建安全共同体,就是倡导开放合作的网络安全理念,坚持安全与发展并重、鼓励与规范并举。加强关键信息基础设施保护和数据安全国际合作,维护信息技术中立和产业全球化,共同遏制信息技术滥用。进一步增强战略互信,及时共享网络威胁信息,有效协调处置重大网络安全事件,合作打击网络恐怖主义和网络犯罪,共同维护网络空间和平与安全。

构建责任共同体。网络空间是人类共同的活动空间,网络空间前途命运应由世界各国共同掌握。构建责任共同体,就是坚持多边参与、多方参与,积极推进全球互联网治理体系改革和建设。发挥联合国在网络空间国际治理中的主渠道作用,发挥政府、国际组织、互联网企业、技术社群、社会组织、公民个人等各主体作用,建立相互信任、协调有序的合作。完善对话协商机制,共同研究制定网络空间治理规范,更加平衡地反映各方利益关切特别是广大发展中国家利益,使治理体系更公正合理。

构建利益共同体。互联网发展治理成果应由世界各国共同分享,确保不同国家、不同民族、不同人群平等享有互联网发展红利。构建利益共同体,就是坚持以人为本,推动科技向善,提升数字经济包容性。加大政策支持,帮助中小微企业利用新一代信息技术促进产品、服务、流程、组织和商业模式的创新,让中小微企业更多从数字经济发展中分享机遇。注重对弱势群体的网络保护,加强网络伦理和网络文明建设,推动网络文化健康发展,培育良好网络生态。在全球范围内促进普惠式发展,提升广大发展中国家网络发展能力,弥合数字鸿沟,共享互联网发展成果,助力《联合国 2030 年可持续发展议程》有效落实。

(三) 构建网络空间命运共同体的基本原则

构建网络空间命运共同体,坚持以下基本原则:

尊重网络主权。《联合国宪章》确立的主权平等原则是当代国际关系的基本准则,同样适用于网络空间。网络主权是国家主权在网络空间的自然延伸,应尊重各国自主选择网络发展道路、治理模式和平等参与网络空间国际治理的权利。各国有权根据本国国情,借鉴国际经验,制定有关网络空间的公共政策和法律法规。任何国家都不搞网络霸权,不利用网络干涉他国内政,不从事、纵容或支持危害他国国家安全的网络活动,不侵害他国关键信息基础设施。

维护和平安全。实现网络空间的安全稳定,事关人类的共同福祉。各国应坚持以对话解决争端、以协商化解分歧,统筹应对传统和非传统安全威胁,确保网络空间的和平与安全。各国应反对网络空间敌对行动和侵略行径,防止网络空间军备竞赛,防范网络空间军事冲突,防范和反对利用网络空间进行的恐怖、淫秽、贩毒、洗钱、赌博等犯罪活动。各方应摒弃冷战思维、零和博弈、双重标准,以合作谋和平,致力于在共同安全中实现自身安全。

促进开放合作。开放是开展网络空间国际合作的前提,也是构建网络空间命运共同体的重要条件。各国应秉持开放理念,奉行开放政策,丰富开放内涵,提高开放水平,共同推动互联网健康发展。积极搭建双边、区域和国际合作平台,强化资源优势互补,维护全球协同一致的创新体系,促进不同制度、不同民族和不同文化在网络空间包容性发展。反对将网络安全问题政治化。反对贸易保护主义。反对狭隘的、封闭的小集团主义,反对分裂互联网,反对利用自身优势损害别国信息通信技术产品和服务供应链安全。

构建良好秩序。网络空间同现实社会一样,既提倡自由,也保持秩序。自由是秩序的目的,秩序是自由的保障。既尊重网民交流思想、表达意愿的权利,也依法构建良好网络秩序。网络空间不是"法外之地"。网络空间是虚拟的,但运用网络空间的主体是现实的,都应遵守法律,明确各方权利义务。坚持依法管网、依法办网、依法上网,让互联网在法治轨道上健康运行。加强网络伦理、网络文明建设,发挥道德教化引导作用,用人类文明优秀成果滋润网络空间、涵养网络生态。

二、中国的互联网发展治理实践

中国的互联网,是开放合作的互联网、有秩序的互联网、正能量充沛的互联网,是造福人民的互联网。中国立足新发展阶段、贯彻新发展理念、构建新发展格局,建设网络强国、数字中国,在激发数字经济活力、推进数字生态建设、营造清朗网络空间、防范网络安全风险等方面不断取得新的成效,为高质量发展提供了有力服务、支撑和保障,为构建网络空间命运共同体提供了坚实基础。

(一) 数字经济蓬勃发展

中国大力推进信息基础设施建设和互联网普及应用,依靠信息技术创新驱动,不断催生新产业新业态新模式,加快发展数字经济,促进数字经济和实体经济深度融合,用新动能推动新发展。据研究机构测算,截至 2021 年,中国数字经济规模达到 45.5 万亿元,占国内生产总值比重为 39.8%,数字经济已成为推动经济增长的主要引擎之一。数字经济规模连续多年位居全球第二。

信息基础设施建设规模日益扩大。截至 2022 年 6 月,中国网民规模达 10.51 亿,互联网普及率提升到 74.4%。截至 2022 年 6 月,中国累计建成开通 5G 基站 185.4 万个,5G 移动电话用户数达 4.55 亿,建成全球规模最大5G网络,成为5G标准和技术的全球引领者之一。独立组网率先实现规模商用,积极开展5G技术创新及开发建设的国际合作,为全球5G应用普及作出重要贡献。骨干网、城域网和LTE网络完成互联网协议第六版(IPv6)升级改造,主要互联网网站和应用IPv6支持度显著提升。截至2022年7月,中国IPv6活跃用户数达6.97亿。

北斗三号全球卫星导航系统建成开通。2020年7月,北斗三号全球卫星导航系统正式开通,向全球提供服务。2021年,中国卫星导航与位置服务总体产业规模达到4690亿元。截至2021年底,具有北斗定位功能的终端产品社会总保有量超过10亿台/套,超过790万辆道路营运车辆、10万台/套农机自动驾驶系统安装使用北斗系统,医疗健康、远程监控、线上服务等下游运营服务环节产值近2000亿元,北斗产业体系基本形成,经济和社会效益显著。

数字技术创新应用持续深化。中国大力培育人工智能、物联网、下一代通信网络等新技术新应用,推动经济社会各领域从数字化、网络化向智能化加速跃升,进入创新型国家行列。大数据产业快速发展,"十三五"时期产业规模年均复合增长率超过30%。2021年,中国规模以上互联网和相关服务企业完成业务收入15500亿元,同比增长21.2%。智慧工业、智慧交通、智慧健康、智慧能源等领域成为产业物联网连接数快速增长的领域。

工业互联网发展进入快车道。制造业数字化转型持续深化,截至2022年2月,规模以上工业企业关键工序数控化率达55.3%,数字化研发工具的普及率达 74.7%。制定《工业互联网发展行动计划（2018—2020 年）》，实施工业互联网创新发展工程，带动总投资近 700 亿元，遴选 4 个国家级工业互联网产业示范基地和 258 个试点示范项目。《工业互联网创新发展行动计划（2021—2023 年）》正在推进。通过兼容的工业互联网基础设施，有力推动企业、人、设备、物品之间的互联互通。

农业数字化转型稳步推进。5G、物联网、大数据、人工智能等数字技术在农业生产经营中融合应用，智慧农业、智慧农机关键技术攻关和创新应用研究不断加强。致力于打造农业物联网试点示范，实施智慧水利工程，积极推动水利公共基础设施的数字化管理与智慧化改造，推动农业农村大数据应用，建立农业全产业链信息服务体系。建成世界第二大物种资源数据库和信息系统，开发了"金种子育种平台"，推广农业装备数字化管理服务。

数字化水平和能力不断提升。电子商务持续繁荣。2021 年中国实物商品网上零售额 10.8 万亿元，同比增长 12%，占社会消费品零售总额比重达 24.5%。2021 年，中国跨境电商进出口规模达到 1.92 万亿元，同比增长 18.6%。第三方支付交易规模持续扩大。服务业商业模式不断创新，互联网医疗、在线教育、远程办公等为服务业数字化按下了快进键。数字服务跨境支付能力不断增强。2021年，中国可数字化交付的服务贸易规模达 2.33 万亿元，同比增长 14.4%。

（二）数字技术惠民便民

中国互联网的发展不仅有广度、有深度，更有温度。中国坚持以人为本，积极推进互联网用于教育、医疗、扶贫等公共服务事业，提高数字技术服务水平，推动数字普惠包容，提升不同群体的数字素养和技能，加快落实《联合国 2030 年可持续发展议程》。

互联网助力精准扶贫取得积极成效。实施《网络扶贫行动计划》，充分发挥互联网在助推脱贫攻坚中的重要作用，实施网络覆盖、农村电商、网络扶智、信息服务、网络公益等五大工程，助力打赢脱贫攻坚战。中国历史性彻底解决了贫困地区不通网的难题，截至 2020 年底，贫困村通光纤比例达 98% 以上，面向贫困地区精准降费惠及超过 1200 万户贫困群众。中国农村网络零售额 2021 年达 2.05 万亿元，同比增长 11.3%，全国建设县级电商公共服务和物流配送中心 2400 多个，村级电商服务站点超过 14.8 万个。网络扶贫信息服务体系基本建立，截至 2020 年底，全国共建设运营益农信息社 45.4 万个，远程医疗实现国家级贫困县县级医院全覆盖，基础金融服务覆盖行政村比例达 99.2%。截至 2020 年底，贫困地区农副产品网络销售平台实现 832 个国家级贫困县全覆盖，上架农副产品 9 万多个，平台交易额突破 99.7 亿元。中国社会扶贫网累计注册用户 6534 万人，累计发布需求信息 737 万条，成功对接 584 万条。

教育信息化水平持续提升。聚焦信息网络、平台体系、数字资源、智慧校园、创新应用、可信安全等方面,加快推进教育新型基础设施建设,构建高质量教育支撑体系。完成学校联网攻坚行动,截至 2021 年底,中小学互联网接入率达到 100%,出口带宽 100M 以上的学校比例达到 99.95%,接入无线网的学校数超过 21 万所,99.5%的中小学拥有多媒体教室。实施国家教育数字化战略行动。2022 年 3 月,国家智慧教育公共服务平台正式上线,整合集成国家中小学智慧教育平台、国家职业教育智慧教育平台、国家高等教育智慧教育平台等资源服务平台和国家 24365 大学生就业服务平台。平台已连接 52.9 万所学校,面向 1844 万教师、2.91 亿在校生及广大社会学习者,汇集了基础教育课程资源 3.4 万条、职业教育在线精品课 6628 门、高等教育优质课程 2.7 万门。

针对不同群体的信息化服务保障日趋健全。加强信息无障碍建设,帮助老年人、残疾人等共享数字生活。采取多项措施,为残疾人信息交流无障碍创造条件。围绕老年人日常生活涉及的出行、就医、消费、文娱、办事等七类高频事项和服务场景,制定具体举措,切实解决老年人运用智能技术的困难。利用互联网,切实保障妇女在健康、教育、环境等方面的权益。针对未成年人,加强网络保护,取得显著成效。

　　中国充分发挥互联网在助推脱贫攻坚中的重要作用,制定《网络扶贫行动计划》,统筹推进网络扶贫工作。《行动计划》包括五大工程:一是实施网络覆盖工程,包括推进贫困地区网络覆盖,加快实用移动终端研发和应用,开发网络扶贫移动应用程序,推动民族语言语音、视频技术研发。二是实施农村电商工程,包括大力发展农村电子商务,建立扶贫网络博览会,推动互联网金融服务向贫困地区延伸。三是实施网络扶智工程,包括开展网络远程教育,加强干部群众培训工作,支持大学生村官和大学生返乡开展网络创业创新。四是实施信息服务工程,包括构建统一的扶贫开发大数据平台,搭建一县一平台,完善一乡(镇)一节点,培养一村一带头人,开通一户一终端,建立一户一档案,形成一支网络扶贫队伍,构筑贫困地区民生保障网络系统。五是实施网络公益工程,包括开展网络公益扶贫系列活动,推动网络公益扶贫行动,实施贫困地区结对帮扶计划,打造网络公益扶贫品牌项目。

（三）网络空间法治体系不断完善

　　中国始终把依法治网作为加强数字生态建设、构建规范有序网络环境的基础性手段,坚定不移推进依法管网、依法办网、依法上网,推动互联网在法治轨道上健康运行。

　　健全网络法律体系。制定出台《中华人民共和国电子商务法》、《中华人民共和国电子签名法》、《中华人民共和国网络安全法》(以下简称《网络安全法》)、《中华人民共和国数据安全法》(以下简称《数据安全法》)、《中华人民共和国个人信息保护法》(以下简称《个人信息保护法》)等基础性、综合性、全局性法律,中国网络立法的"四梁八柱"基本构建,基本形成以宪法为根本,以法律、行政法规、部门规章和地方性法规规章为依托,以传统立法为基础,以网络内容建设与管理、信息化发展和网络安全等网络专门立法为主干的网络法律体系。

严格网络执法。建立健全网络执法协调机制,严厉打击电信网络诈骗、网络赌博、网络传销、网络谣言、网络暴力等违法犯罪行为。深入推进个人信息保护、网络信息内容管理、网络安全和数据安全保护等领域执法。不断提升网络执法的针对性、时效性和震慑力,有效遏制网络违法乱象,网络空间日益规范有序。

创新网络司法。坚持司法改革与信息化建设统筹推进,积极利用信息技术,推动司法网络化、阳光化改革,推出智慧法院、智慧检务等服务,健全在线诉讼规则,推动互联网法院"网上案件网上审理"的新型审理机制不断成熟。

开展网络普法。始终将普法守法作为加强法治的基础性工作,不断加强互联网普法宣传教育。结合国家宪法日、全民国家安全教育日、国家网络安全宣传周、知识产权宣传周等重要节点,大力开展《中华人民共和国宪法》和《网络安全法》《数据安全法》《个人信息保护法》等法律法规知识普及。通过以案说法、以案释法等形式,有效提高全民特别是青少年网络法治意识和网络素养,推动形成全网全社会尊法学法守法用法的良好氛围。

(四) 网上内容丰富多彩

网上正能量强劲、主旋律高昂,马克思主义中国化时代化最新成果深入人心,社会主义核心价值观引领网上文化建设,互联网日益成为文化繁荣的新载体、亿万民众精神生活的新家园,成为凝聚共识的新空间、汇聚正能量的新场域。世界也通过互联网这个窗口进一步认识真实、立体、全面的中国。

网络正能量遒劲充沛。网上主流思想舆论不断巩固壮大,积极健康的优质网络内容不断增加,共产党好、社会主义好、改革开放好、伟大祖国好、各族人民好的时代主旋律在互联网上高亢响亮,先进文化和时代精神充盈网络空间,中国互联网充满向上向善的正能量。中国互联网既开放自由又和谐有序,10亿多中国网民通过网络了解天下大事、表达交流观点、参与国家和社会治理,凝聚起团结奋斗、共向未来的强大共识和力量。

网络文化多元多样。网络视听、网络文学、网络音乐、网络互动娱乐等不断发展,产生海量网络文化内容,为人们提供了丰富的精神食粮。数字图书馆、"云端博物馆"、网上剧场、"云展览"、线上演唱会、VR旅游等,让人们足不出户就能享受高品质文化盛宴。多元网络文化催生众多新型文化业态。

网络传播形态迭代更新。大数据、云计算、人工智能、VR、AR等信息技术突飞猛进,推动网络传播方法手段、载体渠道不断创新,传播主渠道更加移动化、表达方式更加大众化、传播形式更加多样化,技术先进、样态新颖的融媒体产品持续涌现,好声音成为中国网络空间"最强音",传播得更快更广更远、更加深入人心。

（五）网络空间日益清朗

网络空间是亿万网民共同的精神家园。网络空间天朗气清、生态良好，符合人民利益。网络空间乌烟瘴气、生态恶化，不符合人民利益。中国汇聚向上向善能量，营造文明健康、风清气正的网络生态，持续推动网络空间日益清朗。

推进"清朗"系列专项行动。聚焦群众反映强烈的网络生态乱象，深入推进"清朗"系列专项行动。深入推进"饭圈"乱象治理，强化规范管理，严厉打击违法违规行为，着力遏制网上"饭圈"乱象。聚焦网络直播、短视频等领域，重点治理"色、丑、怪、假、俗、赌"等违法违规内容呈现乱象，有力规范平台功能运行失范等顽疾。持续开展网络水军、网络账号运营等乱象治理，严防反弹反复，有效遏制了网络乱象滋生蔓延，持续塑造和净化了网络生态。

加强网络文明建设。规范网上内容生产、信息发布和传播流程，规范互联网公益事业管理，举办中国网络文明大会，开展网络文明创建活动，用积极健康、向上向善的网络文化滋养人心、引导社会。充分发挥政府、平台、社会组织、网民等主体作用，共同推进文明办网、文明用网、文明上网，共享网络文明成果，构建网上网下同心圆。

（六）互联网平台运营不断规范

近年来，中国平台经济蓬勃发展，各种新业态、新模式层出不穷，对推动经济社会高质量发展、满足人民日益增长的美好生活需要发挥了重要作用。同时，平台垄断、算法滥用等给市场公平竞争和消费者权益造成了不利影响。中国积极构建与平台经济相适应的法律体系，完善促进企业发展和规范运营的监管机制，营造良好数字生态环境，促进平台经济公平竞争、有序发展。

开展反垄断审查和监管。制定《国务院反垄断委员会关于平台经济领域的反垄断指南》《网络交易监督管理办法》等政策法规，为平台经济健康运行提供明确规则指引。针对互联网平台"二选一""大数据杀熟""屏蔽网址链接"等影响市场公平竞争、侵犯消费者和劳动者合法权益等问题，实施反垄断调查和行政处罚，有效保护中小微企业、劳动者、消费者等市场主体权益。

加强新技术新应用治理。不断完善适应人工智能、大数据、云计算等新技术新应用的制度规则，对区块链、算法推荐服务等加强管理，依法规制算法滥用、非法处理个人信息等行为，推动各类新技术新应用更好地服务社会、造福人民。

推动互联网行业自律。中国网络社会组织和行业组织充分发挥作用，制定发布行业自律公约，加强社会责任建设，引导督促互联网企业规范平台经营活动，主动承担社会责任，自觉接受社会监督，共同营造诚信经营、良性互动、公平竞争的健康市场秩序。

（七）网络空间安全有效保障

加强网络安全顶层设计,《网络安全法》《数据安全法》《个人信息保护法》等法律框架基本形成,网络安全保障能力不断提升,全社会网络安全防线进一步筑牢。

强化关键信息基础设施安全保护。制定出台《关键信息基础设施安全保护条例》,坚持综合协调、分工负责、依法保护,充分发挥政府及社会各方面的作用,加强风险评估和安全检测,强化监测预警能力,积极推动建立网络安全信息共享机制,及时发现安全风险,尽早开展研判分析和应急响应,采取多种措施共同保护关键信息基础设施安全。

促进网络空间规范发展。坚持促进发展和依法管理相统一,积极鼓励平台在引领技术创新、激发经济活力、促进信息惠民等方面发挥更大作用。同时,防范一些平台利用数据、技术、市场、资本等优势无序竞争,全面营造公平竞争、包容发展、开放创新的市场环境。

推动网络安全教育、技术、产业融合发展。增设网络空间安全一级学科,实施一流网络安全学院建设示范项目,设立网络安全专项基金,国内有 60 余所高校设立网络安全学院,200 余所高校设立网络安全本科专业。网络安全产业生态不断完善,技术产业体系基本形成,网络安全产品细分领域和技术方向持续拓展外延。建成国家网络安全人才与创新基地,建设国家网络安全产业园区、国家网络安全教育技术产业融合发展试验区,推动形成相互促进的良性生态。

　　加强个人信息保护。不断完善个人信息保护法律制度,出台《个人信息保护法》,着力解决个人信息被过度收集、违法获取、非法买卖等突出问题,为个人信息权益保护提供了全方位、系统化的法律依据。加强对移动互联网应用程序违法违规收集使用个人信息等行为的治理,严厉打击违法违规活动,保护公民个人隐私安全。

　　提高数据安全保障能力。积极应对经济社会数字化转型带来的数据安全挑战,制定《数据安全法》,构建起数据安全管理基本法律框架,建立健全数据分类分级保护、风险监测预警和应急处置、数据安全审查、数据跨境流动安全管理等数据安全管理基本制度,持续提升数据安全保护能力,有效防范和化解数据安全风险。

　　打击网络犯罪和网络恐怖主义。依法严厉打击网络违法犯罪行为,切断网络犯罪利益链条,维护网民在网络空间的合法权益。连续开展打击网络犯罪"净网"专项行动,持续推进专项治理,依法严厉打击黑客攻击、电信网络诈骗、网络侵权盗版等网络犯罪,不断压缩涉网犯罪活动空间,净化网络空间环境。中国坚决执行联合国安理会有关决议,坚决打击恐怖组织利用网络策划、实施恐怖活动,持续依法开展打击网上暴恐音视频专项行动,持续做好反恐宣传教育工作,着力构筑政府为主导、互联网企业为主体、社会组织和公众共同参与的网络反恐体系。

三、构建网络空间命运
共同体的中国贡献

中国不断深化网络空间国际交流合作,秉持共商共建共享理念,加强双边、区域和国际对话与合作,致力于与国际社会各方建立广泛的合作伙伴关系,深化数字经济国际合作,共同维护网络空间安全,积极参与全球互联网治理体系改革和建设,促进互联网普惠包容发展,与国际社会携手推动构建网络空间命运共同体。

(一)不断拓展数字经济合作

中国积极参与数字经济国际合作,大力推进信息基础设施建设,促进全球数字经济与实体经济融合发展,携手推进全球数字治理合作,为全球数字经济发展作出了积极贡献。

1.携手推进全球信息基础设施建设

中国同国际社会一道,积极推进全球信息基础设施建设,推动互联网普及应用,努力提升全球数字互联互通水平。

为全球光缆海缆等建设贡献力量。中国企业支持多国信息通信基础设施建设项目,为发展中国家打开了数字化信息高速通道。通过光纤和基站助力开展信息通信基础设施建设,提高相关国家光通信覆盖率,推动了当地信息通信产业的跨越式发展,大幅提高了网络速度,降低了通信成本。

促进互联网普及应用。开展国家顶级域名系统服务平台海外节点建设,覆盖全球五大洲,面向全球用户提供不间断的、稳定的国家域名解析服务。推广 IPv6 技术应用。为企业通信技术、信息技术、云计算和大数据技术的深度融合转型构筑全球"IPv6+"网络底座,助力数字丝路建设,创新"IPv6+"应用,"云间高速"项目首次在国际云互联目标网络使用 SRv6 技术,接入海内外多种公有云、私有云,实现端到端跨域部署、业务分钟级开通,已经应用于欧亚非 10 多个国家和地区。

北斗成为全球重要时空基础设施。推动北斗相关产品及服务惠及全球,北斗相关产品已出口至全球一半以上国家和地区。与阿盟、东盟、中亚、非洲等地区国家和区域组织持续开展卫星导航合作与交流。建立卫星导航双边合作机制,开展卫星导航系统兼容与互操作协调。推动北斗系统进入国际标准化组织、行业和专业应用等标准组织,使北斗系统更好服务于全球用户和相关产业发展。

助力提升全球数字互联互通水平。大力推进 5G 网络建设,积极开展 5G 技术创新及开发建设的国际合作。中国企业支持南非建成非洲首个 5G 商用网络和 5G 实验室。中国积极支持共建"一带一路"国家公路、铁路、港口、桥梁、通信管网等骨干通道建设,助力打造"六廊六路多国多港"互联互通大格局,不断提升智慧港口、智能化铁路等基础设施互联互通数字化水平。将"智慧港口"建设作为港口高质量发展的新动能,加强互联网、大数据、人工智能等新技术与港口各领域深度融合,有效提升港口服务效率、口岸通关效率,实现主要单证"全程无纸化"。

2.数字技术助力全球经济发展

中国积极发挥数字技术对经济发展的放大、叠加、倍增作用,持续深化全球电子商务发展合作,助推全球数字产业化和产业数字化进程,倡导与各国一道推进数字化和绿色化协同转型。

"丝路电商"合作成果丰硕。自 2016 年以来,中国与五大洲 23 个国家建立双边电子商务合作机制,建立中国—中东欧国家、中国—中亚五国电子商务合作对话机制,通过政企对话、联合研究、能力建设等推动多层次交流合作,营造良好发展环境,构建数字合作格局。电子商务企业加速"出海",带动跨境物流、移动支付等各领域实现全球发展。积极参与世界贸易组织、二十国集团、亚太经合组织、金砖国家、上合组织等多边和区域贸易机制下的电子商务议题讨论,与自贸伙伴共同构建高水平数字经济规则。电子商务国际规则构建取得突破,区域全面经济伙伴关系协定电子商务章节成为目前覆盖区域最广、内容全面、水平较高的电子商务国际规则。

云计算、人工智能等新技术创新应用发展。2020 年,中国云计算积极为非洲、中东、东南亚国家以及共建"一带一路"国家提供云服务支持。以世界微生物数据中心为平台,有效利用云服务平台等资源,建立起来自 51 个国家、141 个合作伙伴参加的全球微生物数据信息化合作网络,牵头建立全球微生物菌种保藏目录,促进全球微生物数据资源的有效利用。协助泰国共同打造泰国 5G 智能示范工厂，赋能"5G+"工业应用创新。积极同以色列等国家开展交流合作，提升农业数字化水平。在亚太经合组织提出合作倡议，助力亚太地区数字化、绿色化协同转型发展。2015 年 5 月，中国与联合国教科文组织合作在青岛举办国际教育信息化大会。通过成果文件《青岛宣言》，在国际社会推动教育信息化方面发挥了重要作用。2019 年 5 月，中国与联合国教科文组织合作在北京举办国际人工智能与教育大会，通过成果文件《北京共识》，形成了全球对智能时代教育发展的共同愿景。2020 年至 2021 年，双方继续合作举办国际人工智能与教育会议，为全球教育数字化贡献中国力量。

专栏3　"丝路电商"云上大讲堂

　　2020 年，为应对新冠肺炎疫情带来的冲击，中国创新"丝路电商"能力建设合作，采用线上直播方式，面向伙伴国政府、商协会和企业推出"丝路电商"云上大讲堂，内容涉及法律法规、实操技能和创新实践等方面。"丝路电商"云上大讲堂已举办拉美农产品出口专场、上合组织国家专场等 51 场直播讲座，累计参训人数超过 6000 人次，在线观看超过 10 万人次。

　　"丝路电商"云上大讲堂搭建了共同提升数字素养的新平台，受到广泛好评，取得积极成效。在 2021 年第三届"双品网购节"的"丝路电商"专场活动中，"丝路电商"伙伴国商品日均网络零售额比活动前增长 20.9%，其中十多个伙伴国重点产品实现销售额翻倍，卢旺达咖啡、阿根廷果蔬汁、智利红酒等成为网红产品。2022 年"上合组织国家特色商品电商直播活动"中，乌兹别克斯坦 8 款产品成为"国别爆款"。2022 年"第四届双品网购节暨非洲好物网购节"期间，来自主要电商平台上的 20 余个非洲国家的重点产品销售额同比均显著增长，其中 18 个国家的特色产品销售额同比增长超过 50%。"丝路电商"云上大讲堂为共享数字经济发展红利，促进全球民心相通开创了有效新模式。

3. 积极参与数字经济治理合作

中国积极参与国际和区域性多边机制下的数字经济治理合作，推动发起多个倡议、宣言，提出多项符合大多数国家利益和诉求的提案，加强同专业性国际组织合作，为全球数字经济治理贡献力量。

推进亚太经合组织数字经济合作进程。2014 年，中国作为亚太经合组织东道主首次将互联网经济引入亚太经合组织合作框架，发起并推动通过《促进互联网经济合作倡议》。2019 年，亚太经合组织数字经济指导组成立后，中国积极推动全面平衡落实《APEC 互联网和数字经济路线图》。2020 年以来，中国先后提出"运用数字技术助力新冠肺炎疫情防控和经济复苏""优化数字营商环境　激活市场主体活力""后疫情时代加强数字能力建设，弥合数字鸿沟"等倡议，均获亚太经合组织协商一致通过。

积极参与二十国集团框架下数字经济合作。2016 年，二十国集团领导人第十一次峰会在中国举行，在中国推动下，会议首次将"数字经济"列为二十国集团创新增长蓝图中的一项重要议题，并通过了《二十国集团数字经济发展与合作倡议》，这是全球首个由多国领导人共同签署的数字经济政策文件，此后，数字经济成为二十国集团核心议题之一。近年来，中国积极参加二十国集团数字经济部长会议和数字经济任务组相关磋商，推动数字经济任务组升级为工作组，推动数字经济发展成果惠及世界人民。

不断拓展金砖国家数字经济交流合作。2017 年，金砖国家领导人第九次会晤在中国举行，会上通过的《金砖国家领导人厦门宣言》，明确提出将深化信息通信技术、电子商务、互联网空间领域的务实合作。2019年，金砖国家未来网络研究院中国分院正式在深圳揭牌成立。2022年金砖国家领导人第十四次会晤通过了《金砖国家数字经济伙伴关系框架》。举办了金砖国家数字经济对话会等重要活动，开启了金砖国家数字经济合作新进程。

深化同东盟数字经济合作。2020年，中国和东盟举办以"集智聚力共战疫　互利共赢同发展"为主题的中国—东盟数字经济合作年，举行网络事务对话，第二十三次中国—东盟领导人会议发表《中国—东盟关于建立数字经济合作伙伴关系的倡议》，同意进一步加深数字经济领域合作。

积极推动世贸组织数字经济合作。2017年，中国正式宣布加入世贸组织"电子商务发展之友"，协同发展中成员共同支持世贸组织电子商务议题磋商。2019年，中国与美国、欧盟、俄罗斯、巴西、新加坡、尼日利亚、缅甸等76个世贸组织成员共同发表《关于电子商务的联合声明》，启动与贸易有关的电子商务议题谈判。2022年，中国与其他世贸组织成员共同发表《电子商务工作计划》部长决定，支持电子传输免征关税，助力全球数字经济发展。

积极开展同世界经济论坛和全球移动通信系统协会的合作。支持全球移动通信系统协会自2015年以来在上海举办多届世界移动大会。全球移动通信系统协会连续多年参与协办世界互联网大会，深化了与中国在网信领域特别是移动互联网新技术新应用领域的合作。

为拓展数字经济领域的合作,2017年12月3日,在第四届世界互联网大会上,中国、老挝、沙特、塞尔维亚、泰国、土耳其、阿联酋等国家相关部门共同发起《"一带一路"数字经济国际合作倡议》。《倡议》指出,数字经济是全球经济增长日益重要的驱动力,作为支持"一带一路"倡议的相关国家,各国将本着互联互通、创新发展、开放合作、和谐包容、互利共赢的原则,通过加强政策沟通、设施联通、贸易畅通、资金融通和民心相通,致力于实现互联互通的"数字丝绸之路",打造互利共赢的利益共同体和共同发展繁荣的命运共同体。《倡议》提出了15个方面的合作意向,主要包括扩大宽带接入,提高宽带质量;促进数字化转型;促进电子商务合作;支持互联网创业创新;促进中小微企业发展;加强数字化技能培训;促进信息通信技术领域的投资;推动城市间的数字经济合作;提高数字包容性;鼓励培育透明的数字经济政策;推进国际标准化合作;增强信心和信任;鼓励促进合作并尊重自主发展道路;鼓励共建和平、安全、开放、合作、有序的网络空间;鼓励建立多层次交流机制。

（二）持续深化网络安全合作

维护网络安全是国际社会的共同责任。中国积极履行国际责任,深化网络安全应急响应国际合作,与国际社会携手提高数据安全和个人信息保护合作水平,共同打击网络犯罪和网络恐怖主义。

1. 深化网络安全领域合作伙伴关系

中国积极推动金砖国家网络安全领域合作。2017年,金砖五国达成《金砖国家网络安全务实合作路线图》。2022年,金砖国家网络安全工作组第八次会议一致通过"《金砖国家网络安全务实合作路线图》进展报告",总结了过去五年工作组落实"路线图"的经验和进展,并就未来合作方向达成重要共识。深度参与上海合作组织网络安全进程。2021 年,上合组织信息安全专家组一致通过《上合组织成员国保障国际信息安全 2022—2023 年合作计划》。2021 年,中国与印度尼西亚签署《关于发展网络安全能力建设和技术合作的谅解备忘录》。2022 年,中国与泰国签署《关于网络安全合作的谅解备忘录》。

积极开展网络安全应急响应领域的国际合作。中国国家计算机网络应急技术处理协调中心与全球主要国家级计算机应急响应组织、政府部门、国际组织和联盟、互联网服务提供商、域名注册机构、学术机构以及其他互联网相关公司和组织开展交流。截至 2021 年,已与 81 个国家和地区的 274 个计算机应急响应组织建立了"CNCERT 国际合作伙伴"关系,与其中 33 个组织签订网络安全合作备忘录。建立"中国—东盟网络安全交流培训中心",共同提升网络安全能力。

2. 提高数据安全和个人信息保护合作水平

中国坚持以开放包容的态度推动全球数据安全治理、加强个人信息保护合作。始终坚持科学平衡数据安全保护和数据有序流动之间的关系,在保障个人信息和重要数据安全的前提下,与世界各国开展交流合作,共同探索反映国际社会共同关切、符合国际社会共同利益的数据安全和个人信息保护规则。2020 年 9 月,中国发布《全球数据安全倡议》,为制定全球数据安全规则提供了蓝本。2021 年 3 月,中国同阿拉伯国家联盟秘书处发表《中阿数据安全合作倡议》,彰显了中阿在数字治理领域的高度共识。2022 年 6 月,"中国+中亚五国"外长第三次会晤通过《"中国+中亚五国"数据安全合作倡议》,标志着发展中国家在携手推进全球数字治理方面迈出了重要一步。中国支持联合国大会及人权理事会有关隐私权保护问题的讨论,推动网络空间确立个人隐私保护原则,推动各国采取措施制止利用网络侵害个人隐私的行为。

3.共同打击网络犯罪和网络恐怖主义

中国一贯支持打击网络犯罪国际合作,支持在联合国框架下制订全球性公约。中国推动联合国网络犯罪政府间专家组于2011年至2021年召开7次会议,为通过关于启动制订联合国打击网络犯罪全球性公约相关决议作出重要贡献。中国在上海合作组织框架下参与签署了《上海合作组织成员国元首阿斯塔纳宣言》《上海合作组织成员国元首关于共同打击国际恐怖主义的声明》等重要文件,共同打击包括网络恐怖主义在内的恐怖主义、分裂主义和极端主义。中国主办和积极参与金砖国家反恐工作组系列会议,就打击网络恐怖主义介绍中国具体实践,提出金砖国家加强网络反恐合作交流建议。

(三) 积极参与网络空间治理

网络空间是人类共同的活动空间,需要世界各国共同建设,共同治理。中国积极参与全球互联网治理机制,搭建起世界互联网大会等国际交流平台,加强同各国在网络空间的交流合作,推动全球互联网治理体系改革和建设。

1.积极参与全球互联网治理

中国坚定维护以联合国为核心的国际体系、以国际法为基础的国际秩序、以《联合国宪章》宗旨和原则为基础的国际关系基本准则，并在此基础上，制定各方普遍接受的网络空间国际规则。

中国始终恪守《联合国宪章》确立的主权平等、不得使用或威胁使用武力、和平解决争端等原则，尊重各国自主选择网络发展道路、网络管理模式、互联网公共政策和平等参与网络空间国际治理的权利。中国始终认为，国家不分大小、强弱、贫富，都是平等成员，都有权平等参与国际规则与秩序建构，确保网络空间未来发展由各国人民共同掌握。2020 年 9 月，《中国关于联合国成立 75 周年立场文件》发布，呼吁国际社会要在相互尊重、平等互利基础上，加强对话合作，把网络空间用于促进经济社会发展、国际和平与稳定和人类福祉，反对网络战和网络军备竞赛，共同建立和平、安全、开放、合作、有序的网络空间。

积极参与联合国网络空间治理进程。中国与上海合作组织其他成员国向联大提交"信息安全国际行为准则"，并于 2015 年提交更新案文，成为国际上第一份系统阐述网络空间行为规范的文件。中国建设性参与联合国信息安全开放式工作组与政府专家组，推动联合国信息安全开放式工作组与政府专家组成功达成最终报告，为网络空间国际规则的制定与网络安全全球治理机制建设奠定了基础。中国深度参与联合国互联网治理论坛，中国代表积极参与联合国互联网治理论坛领导小组、多利益相关方咨询专家组，连续多年在联合国互联网治理论坛主办开放论坛、研讨会等活动，与来自全球政界、商界、学界及非政府组织代表开展广泛交流讨论。

不断拓展与联合国专门机构的网络事务合作。国际电信联盟和世界知识产权组织连续多年担任世界互联网大会协办单位。2019年7月,中国与世界知识产权组织签署合作备忘录,并向世界知识产权组织仲裁与调解中心正式授权,在域名规则制定以及域名争议解决领域开展广泛合作。中国积极参与联合国教科文组织《人工智能伦理建议书》制定工作。2019年底,联合国教科文组织二类中心国际高等教育创新中心与4所中国高校以及11所亚太、非洲地区的高等院校和9家合作企业共同发起设立了国际网络教育学院,通过开放的网络平台促进发展中国家高校与教师数字化转型。

积极参与全球互联网组织事务。积极参与互联网名称和数字地址分配机构等平台或组织活动。支持互联网名称和数字地址分配机构治理机制改革,增强发展中国家代表性,推进互联网基础资源管理国际化进程。积极参与国际互联网协会、互联网工程任务组、互联网架构委员会活动,促进社群交流,推进产品研发和应用实践,深度参与相关标准、规则制定,发挥建设性作用。

2. 广泛开展国际交流与合作

中国秉持相互尊重、平等相待的原则,加强同世界各国在网络空间的交流合作,以共进为目的,以共赢为目标,走出一条互信共治之路。

2017年3月,中国发布首份《网络空间国际合作战略》,就推动网络空间国际交流合作,首次全面系统提出中国主张,向世界发出了中国致力于网络空间和平发展、合作共赢的积极信号。

深化中俄网信领域的高水平合作。在中俄新时代全面战略协作伙伴关系框架下,贯彻落实两国元首合作共识,不断推动中俄网信合作深化发展。2015年,签署《中华人民共和国政府和俄罗斯联邦政府关于在保障国际信息安全领域合作协定》,为两国信息安全领域合作规划方向。2021年,在《中俄睦邻友好合作条约》签署20周年之际,中俄发布联合声明,双方重申将巩固国际信息安全领域的双、多边合作,继续推动构建以防止信息空间冲突、鼓励和平使用信息技术为原则的全球国际信息安全体系。2016年以来,共同举办五届中俄网络媒体论坛,加强两国新媒体合作交流。通过中俄信息安全磋商机制不断深化信息安全领域协调合作。

坚持以开放包容的态度推进中欧网信合作。举办中欧数字领域高层对话,围绕加强数字领域合作,就通信技术标准、人工智能等进行务实和建设性讨论。与欧盟委员会共同成立中欧数字经济和网络安全专家工作组,先后召开四次会议。2012年建立中欧网络工作组机制,目前已召开八次会议,双方在工作组框架下不断加强网络领域对话合作。与英、德、法等国开展双边网络事务对话。深化同欧洲智库交流对话。与德国联合主办"2019中德互联网经济对话",共同发布《2019中德互联网经济对话成果文件》。与英国联合主办多届中英互联网圆桌会议,在数字经济、网络安全、儿童在线保护、数据和人工智能等领域达成多项合作共识。

加强与周边和广大发展中国家网信合作。中国—东盟信息港论坛连续成功举办,持续推动中国与东盟国家数字领域合作,建立中国—东盟网络事务对话机制。建立中日韩三方网络磋商机制。

与韩国联合主办中韩互联网圆桌会议。举办中非互联网发展与合作论坛,发布"中非携手构建网络空间命运共同体倡议",提出了"中非数字创新伙伴计划"。中国—南非新媒体圆桌会议、中坦(坦桑尼亚)网络文化交流会、中肯(肯尼亚)数字经济合作发展研讨会等活动加强了中非在新媒体、网络文化、数字经济等领域交流合作。举办多届网上丝绸之路大会,在信息基础设施、跨境电子商务、智慧城市等领域与阿拉伯国家开展务实合作。举办中古(古巴)互联网圆桌论坛、中巴(巴西)互联网治理研讨会,围绕信息时代互联网的发展与治理开展对话交流。与亚非国家开展网络法治对话。2015年4月,亚洲—非洲法律协商组织("亚非法协")第54届年会在北京举行。在中方建议下,"亚非法协"决定设立"网络空间国际法工作组"。工作组围绕相关议题深入开展讨论。

专栏5　中非互联网发展与合作论坛

2021年8月24日,以"共谋发展,共享安全,携手构建网络空间命运共同体"为主题的中非互联网发展与合作论坛以视频连线方式举办。塞内加尔、卢旺达、刚果(金)、尼日利亚、坦桑尼亚、科特迪瓦等14个非洲国家和非盟委员会的约100名代表在线出席。

论坛期间,中方发起"中非携手构建网络空间命运共同体倡议",欢迎广大非洲国家支持和参与,并提出愿同非方共同制定并实施"中非数字创新伙伴计划",共同设计未来三年数字领域务实合作举措,并纳入中非合作论坛新一届会议成果文件。非洲代表予以积极回应,表示愿以本次论坛为契机,进一步加强中非之间的互利合作,推动非洲数字经济的发展,携手维护网络空间安全,推动构建网络空间命运共同体。

论坛期间,中国国家计算机网络应急技术处理协调中心与贝宁计算机安全事件应急响应中心签署了合作备忘录。

以平等和相互尊重的态度与美国开展对话交流。中国致力于在尊重彼此核心关切、妥善管控分歧的基础上,与美国开展互联网领域对话交流,为包括美国在内的世界各国企业在华发展创造良好市场环境,推进中美网信领域的合作。但一段时间以来,美国采取错误对华政策,致使中美关系遭遇严重困难,美政府还持续实施网络攻击和网络窃密活动。中国将坚持独立自主,坚定不移地维护在网络空间的国家主权、安全、发展利益。

3.搭建世界互联网大会交流平台

2014年以来,中国连续八年在浙江乌镇举办世界互联网大会,搭建中国与世界互联互通的国际平台和国际互联网共享共治的中国平台。各国政府、国际组织、互联网企业、智库、行业协会、技术社群等各界代表应邀参会交流,共商世界互联网发展大计。大会不断创新办会模式、丰富活动形式,分论坛、"携手构建网络空间命运共同体精品案例"发布展示、世界互联网领先科技成果发布、"互联网之光"博览会和"直通乌镇"全球互联网大赛等受到广泛关注。

大会组委会先后发布《携手构建网络空间命运共同体》概念文件、《携手构建网络空间命运共同体行动倡议》,举办案例发布展示活动,深入阐释落实构建网络空间命运共同体理念。大会组委会每年发布《世界互联网发展报告》《中国互联网发展报告》蓝皮书,全面分析世界与中国互联网发展态势,为全球互联网发展与治理提供思想借鉴与智力支撑。大会高级别专家咨询委员会发布的《乌镇展望》,向国际社会阐释大会对网络空间现实发展和未来前景的规划思路。

八年来,大会的成功举办极大促进了各国互联网领域紧密联系与深入交流,有力推动了构建网络空间命运共同体的中国经验、中国方案、中国智慧日益从理念共识走向具体实践,进一步激发了世界各国人民共同构建网络空间命运共同体的信心和热情,推动全球互联网治理体系向着更加公正合理的方向迈进。

近年来,国际各方建议将世界互联网大会打造成为国际组织,更好助力全球互联网发展治理。在多家单位共同发起下,世界互联网大会国际组织于2022年7月在北京成立,宗旨是搭建全球互联网共商共建共享平台,推动国际社会顺应数字化、网络化、智能化趋势,共迎安全挑战,共谋发展福祉,携手构建网络空间命运共同体。

专栏6　携手构建网络空间命运共同体行动倡议

2020年11月18日,世界互联网大会组委会发布《携手构建网络空间命运共同体行动倡议》,呼吁各国政府、国际组织、互联网企业、技术社群、社会组织和公民个人坚持共商共建共享的全球治理观,秉持"发展共同推进、安全共同维护、治理共同参与、成果共同分享"的理念,把网络空间建设成为造福全人类的发展共同体、安全共同体、责任共同体、利益共同体。

行动倡议共20项,包括四方面内容:采取更加积极、包容、协调、普惠的政策,加快全球信息基础设施建设,推动数字经济创新发展,提升公共服务水平;倡导开放合作的网络安全理念,坚持安全与发展并重,共同维护网络空间和平与安全;坚持多边参与、多方参与,加强对话协商,推动构建更加公正合理的全球互联网治理体系;坚持以人为本、科技向善,缩小数字鸿沟,实现共同繁荣。

（四）促进全球普惠包容发展

中国坚持以人为本、科技向善，积极响应国际社会需求，携手推动落实《联合国 2030 年可持续发展议程》，共同致力于弥合数字鸿沟，推动网络文化交流与文明互鉴，加强对弱势群体的支持和帮助，促进互联网发展成果惠及不同国家和地区的人民。

1. 积极开展网络扶贫国际合作

中国始终把自身命运与世界各国人民命运紧密相连，致力于做国际减贫事业的倡导者、推动者和贡献者，在利用网络消除自身贫困的同时，采取多种技术手段帮助发展中国家提高最贫困地区居民以及人口密度低的地区居民的宽带接入，努力为最不发达国家提供普遍和可负担得起的互联网接入，以消除因网络设施缺乏所导致的贫困。2021 年 6 月，中国以线上线下相结合方式举办亚太经合组织数字减贫研讨会，为亚太地区消除贫困事业作出了积极贡献。中国企业提出的解决方案，可以将简单小巧的基站放置在一根木杆上，而且自带电源、功耗很低，快速、低成本地为发展中国家偏远地区提供移动通信服务。为非洲国家信息产业现代化项目提供融资支持，提升了信息通信服务现代化程度，助力当地扶贫事业发展。此外，还为非洲提供跨网络多业务服务，助力偏远地区网络建设，为全人类的减贫事业作出了重要贡献。

2. 助力提升数字公共服务水平

中国积极研发数字公共产品,提升数字公共服务合作水平。中阿电子图书馆项目以共建数字图书馆的形式,面向中国、阿盟各国提供中文和阿拉伯文自由切换浏览的数字资源和文化服务。充分利用网络信息技术建设国际合作教育"云上样板区"。联合日本、英国、西班牙、泰国等国教育机构、社会团体,共同发起"中文联盟",为国际中文教育事业搭建教学服务及信息交流平台。新冠肺炎疫情在全球暴发以来,中国研发的疫情预测信息平台、防疫外呼机器人在助力相关国家疫情防控中发挥了积极作用。2020 年 10 月,与东盟国家联合举办"中国—东盟数字经济抗疫政企合作论坛"。向相关国家捐赠远程视频会议系统,提供远程医疗系统、人工智能辅助新冠诊疗、5G 无人驾驶汽车等技术设备及解决方案。

3. 推动网络文化交流与文明互鉴

打造网上文化交流平台,促进文明交流互鉴。2020 年 6 月,上线"中国联合展台在线平台",集信息发布、展览展示、版权交易、互动交流等于一体,成为各国视听机构、视听节目和技术设备展示交流平台。构建多语种的"丝绸之路数字遗产与旅游信息服务平台",以图片、音视频等推介丝绸之路沿线国家 1500 处世界遗产与旅游资源,充分展现科学、美学、历史、文化和艺术价值。2020 年 9 月,中国举办"全球博物馆珍藏展示在线接力"项目,来自五大洲 15 个国家的 16 家国家级博物馆参与。2021 年 5 月,联合法国相关博物馆举办

"敦煌学的跨时空交流与数字保护探索"线上研讨会,共同探索法藏敦煌文物的数字化保护与传播的新方向、新模式、新方案,以推进敦煌文物的数字化呈现和传播。

四、构建更加紧密的网络空间命运共同体的中国主张

互联网是人类的共同家园，让这个家园更繁荣、更干净、更安全，是国际社会的共同责任。中国将一如既往立足本国国情，坚持以人为本、开放合作、互利共赢，与各方一道携手推动构建网络空间命运共同体，让互联网的发展成果更好地造福全人类。

（一）坚持尊重网络主权

中国倡导尊重各国网络主权，尊重各国自主选择网络发展道路、网络管理模式、互联网公共政策和平等参与网络空间国际治理的权利。坚决反对一切形式的霸权主义和强权政治，反对干涉别国内政，反对搞双重标准，不从事纵容或支持危害他国国家安全的网络活动。中国倡导《联合国宪章》确立的主权平等原则适用于网络空间，在国家主权基础上构建公正合理的网络空间国际秩序。

（二）维护网络空间和平、安全、稳定

网络空间互联互通，各国利益深度交融，网络空间和平、安全、稳

定是世界各国人民共同的诉求。中国主张，各国政府应遵守《联合国宪章》的宗旨与原则，和平利用网络，以和平方式解决争端。中国反对以牺牲别国安全谋求自身所谓绝对安全，反对一切形式的网络空间军备竞赛。中国坚持国家不分大小、强弱、贫富一律平等，对网络安全问题的关切都应得到关注和保障，倡导各国和平利用网络空间促进经济社会发展，开展全球、双边、多边、多方等各层级的合作与对话，共同维护网络空间和平与稳定。

（三）营造开放、公平、公正、非歧视的数字发展环境

全球数字经济是开放和紧密相连的整体，"筑墙设垒"、"脱钩断链"只会伤己伤人，合作共赢才是唯一正道。营造开放、公平、公正、非歧视的数字发展环境，是加强全球数字经济合作的需要，有利于促进全球经济复苏和发展。中国反对将技术问题政治化，反对滥用国家力量，违反市场经济原则和国际贸易规则，不择手段打压遏制他国企业。中国倡导，各国政府应积极维护全球信息技术产品和服务的供应链开放、安全、稳定，加强新一代信息技术协同研发，积极融入全球创新网络。各国政府、国际组织、企业、智库等应携起手来，共同探讨制定反映各方意愿、尊重各方利益的数字治理国际规则，推动数字经济健康有序发展。

（四） 加强关键信息基础设施保护国际合作

关键信息基础设施是信息时代各国经济社会正常运行的重要基础,有效应对关键信息基础设施安全风险是国际社会的共同责任。中国坚决反对利用信息技术破坏他国关键信息基础设施或窃取重要数据,搞你输我赢的零和博弈。国际社会应倡导开放合作的网络安全理念,反对网络监听和网络攻击,各国政府和相关机构应加强在预警防范、信息共享、应急响应等方面的合作,积极开展关键信息基础设施保护的经验交流。

（五） 维护互联网基础资源管理体系安全稳定

互联网基础资源管理体系是互联网运行的基石。应确保承载互联网核心资源管理体系的机构运作更加可信,不因任何一国的司法管辖而对其他国家的顶级域名构成威胁。中国主张,保障各国使用互联网基础资源的可用性和可靠性,推动国际社会共同管理和公平分配互联网基础资源,让包括域名系统在内的互联网核心资源技术系统更加安全、稳定和富有韧性,确保其不因任何政治或人为因素而导致服务中断或终止。中国倡导各国政府、行业组织、企业等共同努力,加快推广和普及 IPv6 技术和应用。

（六）合作打击网络犯罪和网络恐怖主义

网络空间不应成为各国角力的战场,更不能成为违法犯罪的温床。当前,网络犯罪和网络恐怖主义已经成为全球公害,国际合作是打击网络犯罪和网络恐怖主义的必由之路。中国倡导各国政府共同努力,根据相关法律和国际公约坚决打击各类网络犯罪行为;倡导对网络犯罪开展生态化、链条化打击整治,健全打击网络犯罪和网络恐怖主义执法司法协作机制。中国支持并积极参与联合国打击网络犯罪全球性公约谈判,探讨制定网络空间国际反恐公约。愿与各国政府有效协调立法和实践,合力应对网络犯罪和网络恐怖主义威胁。

（七）促进数据安全治理和开发利用

数据作为新型生产要素,是数字化、网络化、智能化的基础,已快速融入生产、分配、流通、消费和社会服务管理等各个环节,深刻改变着生产方式、生活方式和社会治理方式。中国支持数据流动和数据开发利用,促进数据开放共享。愿与各国政府、国际组织、企业、智库等各方积极开展数据安全治理、数据开发利用等领域的交流合作,在双边和多边合作框架下推动相关国际规则和标准的制定,不断提升不同数据保护通行规则之间的互操作性,促进数据跨境安全、自由流动。

（八）构建更加公正合理的网络空间治理体系

网络空间具有全球性，任何国家都难以仅凭一己之力实现对网络空间的有效治理。中国支持联合国在网络空间国际治理中发挥主渠道作用，坚持真正的多边主义，反对一切形式的单边主义，反对搞针对特定国家的阵营化和排他的小圈子。中国倡导坚持多边参与、多方参与，发挥政府、国际组织、互联网企业、技术社群、民间机构、公民个人等各主体作用。国际社会应坚持共商共建共享，加强沟通交流，深化务实合作，完善网络空间对话协调机制，研究制定全球互联网治理规则，使全球互联网治理体系更加公正合理，更加平衡地反映大多数国家意愿和利益。

（九）共建网上美好精神家园

网络文明是现代社会文明进步的重要标志。加强网络文明建设是坚持以人民为中心、满足亿万网民对美好生活向往的迫切需要。中国倡导尊重网络文化的多样性，提倡各国挖掘自身优秀文化资源，加强优质文化产品的数字化生产和网络化传播，推动各国、各地区、各民族开展网络文化交流和文明互鉴，增进不同文明之间的包容共生。倡导各国政府团结协作，行业组织和企业加强自律，公民个人提升素养，共同反对和抵制网络虚假信息，加强网络空间生态治理，维护良好网络秩序,用人类文明优秀成果滋养网络空间。

（十）坚持互联网的发展成果惠及全人类

互联网发展需要大家共同参与,发展成果应由大家共同分享。中国倡议,国际社会携起手来,推进信息基础设施建设,弥合数字鸿沟,加强对弱势群体的支持和帮助,促进公众数字素养和技能提升,充分发挥互联网和数字技术在抗击疫情、改善民生、消除贫困等方面的作用,推动新技术新应用向上向善,加强数字产品创新供给,推动实现开放、包容、普惠、平衡、可持续的发展,让更多国家和人民搭乘信息时代的快车,共享互联网发展成果,为落实《联合国2030年可持续发展议程》作出积极贡献。

结　束　语

互联网是人类共同的家园。无论数字技术如何创新发展，无论国际环境如何风云变幻，每个人都在网络空间休戚与共、命运相连。建设和维护一个和平、安全、开放、合作、有序的网络空间，关系到人类文明进程和发展命运，是各国的共同期盼和愿望。

我们所处的是一个充满挑战的时代，也是一个充满希望的时代。中国愿同世界各国一道，共同构建更加公平合理、开放包容、安全稳定、富有生机活力的网络空间，携手构建网络空间命运共同体，开创人类更加美好的未来。

第二部分　英文版

China's Space Program: A 2021 Perspective

The State Council Information Office of
the People's Republic of China

January 2022

Preamble

"To explore the vast cosmos, develop the space industry and build China into a space power is our eternal dream," stated President Xi Jinping. The space industry is a critical element of the overall national strategy, and China upholds the principle of exploration and utilization of outer space for peaceful purposes.

Since 2016, China's space industry has made rapid and innovative progress, manifested by a steady improvement in space infrastructure, the completion and operation of the BeiDou Navigation Satellite System, the completion of the high-resolution earth observation system, steady improvement of the service ability of satellite communications and broadcasting, the conclusion of the last step of the three-step lunar exploration program ("orbit, land, and return"), the first stages in building the space station, and a smooth interplanetary voyage and landing beyond the earth-moon system by Tianwen-1, followed by the exploration of Mars. These achievements have attracted worldwide attention.

In the next five years, China will integrate space science, technology and applications while pursuing the new development philosophy, building a new development model and meeting the requirements for high-quality development. It will start a new journey towards a space power. The space industry will contribute more to China's growth as a whole, to global consensus and common effort with regard to outer space exploration and utilization, and to human progress.

We are publishing this white paper to offer a brief introduction to China's major achievements in this field since 2016 and its main tasks in the next five years, in order to help the international community better understand China's space industry.

I. A New Journey Towards a Strong Space Presence

1. Mission

The mission of China's space program is: to explore outer space to expand humanity's understanding of the earth and the cosmos; to facilitate global consensus on our shared responsibility in utilizing outer space for peaceful purposes and safeguarding its security for the benefit of all humanity; to meet the demands of economic, scientific and technological development, national security and social progress; and to raise the scientific and cultural levels of the Chinese people, protect China's national rights and interests, and build up its overall strength.

2. Vision

China aims to strengthen its space presence in an all-round manner: to enhance its capacity to better understand, freely access, efficiently use, and effectively manage space; to defend national security, lead self-reliance and self-improvement efforts in science and technology, and promote high-quality economic and social development; to advocate sound and efficient governance of outer space, and pioneer human progress; and to make a positive contribution to China's socialist modernization and to peace and progress for all humanity.

3. Principles

China's space industry is subject to and serves the overall national strategy. China adheres to the principles of innovation-driven, coordinated, efficient, and peaceful progress based on cooperation and sharing to ensure a high-quality space industry.

– Innovation-driven development

China puts innovation at the core of its space industry. It boosts state strategic scientific and technological strength in the space industry, implements major space programs, strengthens original innovation, optimizes the environment for innovation, achieves industrial production as early as possible, and grows China's independent capacity to build a safe space industry.

– Coordination and efficiency

China adopts a holistic approach in building its space industry. It mobilizes and guides different sectors to take part in and contribute to this key industry, and coordinates all relevant activities under an overall plan. It ensures that technology plays a greater role in promoting and guiding space science and applications, and it facilitates the growth of new forms and models of business for the industry. These measures aim to raise the quality and overall performance of China's space industry.

– For peaceful purposes

China has always advocated the use of outer space for peaceful purposes, and opposes any attempt to turn outer space into a weapon or battlefield or launch an arms race in outer space. China develops and utilizes space resources in a prudent manner, takes effective measures to protect the space environment, ensures that space remains peaceful and clean, and guarantees that its space activities benefit humanity.

– Cooperation and sharing

China always combines independence and self-reliance with opening to the outside world. It actively engages in high-level international exchanges and cooperation, and expands global public services for space technology and products. It takes an active part in solving major challenges facing humanity, helps to realize the goals of the United Nations 2030 Agenda for Sustainable Development, and facilitates global consensus and common effort with regard to outer space exploration and utilization.

II. Development of Space Technology and Systems

China's space industry serves its major strategic needs, and targets cutting-edge technology that leads the world. Spearheaded by the major space projects, the country has accelerated research into core technologies, stepped up their application, and redoubled its efforts to develop space technology and systems. As a result, China's capacity to enter and return from space, and its ability to engage in space exploration, utilization and governance have grown markedly along a sustainable path.

1. Space Transport System

From 2016 to December 2021, 207 launch missions were completed, including 183 by the Long March carrier rocket series. The total launch attempts exceeded 400.

The Long March carrier rockets are being upgraded towards non-toxic and pollution-free launch, and they are becoming smarter boosted by modular technology. The Long March-5 and Long March-5B carrier rockets have been employed for regular launches; Long March-8 and Long March-7A have made their maiden flights, with increased payload capacity.

China now provides a variety of launch vehicle services. The Long March-11 carrier rocket has achieved commercial launch from the sea; the Smart Dragon-1, Kuaizhou-1A, Hyperbola-1, CERES-1 and other commercial vehicles have been successfully launched; successful demonstration flight tests on reusable launch vehicles have been carried out.

In the next five years, China will continue to improve the capacity and performance of its space transport system, and move faster to upgrade launch vehicles. It will further expand the launch vehicle family, send into space new-generation manned carrier rockets and high-thrust solid-fuel carrier rockets, and speed up the R&D of heavy-lift launch vehicles. It will continue to strengthen research into key technologies for reusable space transport systems, and conduct test flights accordingly. In response to the growing need for regular launches, China will develop new rocket engines, combined cycle propulsion, and upper stage technologies to improve its capacity to enter and return from space, and make space entry and exit more efficient.

2. Space Infrastructure
(1) Satellite remote-sensing system
The space-based section of the China High-resolution Earth Observation System has been largely completed, enabling high-spatial-resolution, high-temporal-resolution and high-spectrum-resolution earth observation. China now provides improved land observation services, having launched the Ziyuan-3 03 earth resources satellite, the Huanjing Jianzai-2A/2B satellites for environmental disaster management, a high-resolution multi-mode imaging satellite, a hyper-spectral observation satellite, and a number of commercial remote-sensing satellites.

In ocean observation, China is now able to view multiple indexes of contiguous waters around the globe on all scales, with high-resolution images from the Haiyang-1C/1D satellites and the Haiyang-2B/2C/2D satellites.

China's ability to observe the global atmosphere has achieved a significant increase. Its new-generation Fengyun-4A/4B meteorological satellites in the geostationary orbit are able to perform all-weather, precise and uninterrupted atmospheric monitoring and disaster monitoring to boost response capability. The successful launches of Fengyun-3D/3E satellites enable coordinated morning, afternoon and twilight monitoring, and the Fengyun-2H satellite provides monitoring services for countries and regions participating in the Belt and Road Initiative.

With further improvements to the ground system of its remote-sensing satellites, China is now able to provide remote-sensing satellite data receiving and quick processing services across the world.

(2) Satellite communications and broadcasting system

China has made steady progress in developing fixed communications and broadcasting satellite network, which now covers more areas with greater capacity. The Zhongxing-6C and Zhongxing-9B satellites ensure the uninterrupted, stable operation of broadcasting and television services. The Zhongxing-16 and APSTAR-6D satellites, each with a 50Gbps capacity, signify that satellite communications in China have reached the stage of high-capacity service.

The mobile communications and broadcasting satellite network has expanded with the launch of the Tiantong-1 02/03 satellites, operating in tandem with the Tiantong-1 01 satellite, to provide voice, short message and data services for hand-held terminal users in China, its neighboring areas, and certain parts of the Asia-Pacific.

The relay satellite system is being upgraded with the launch of the Tianlian-1 05 and Tianlian-2 01 satellites, giving a powerful boost to capacity.

The satellite communications and broadcasting ground system has been improved, to form a space-ground integrated network that provides satellite communications and broadcasting, internet, Internet of Things, and information services around the globe.

(3) Satellite navigation system

The completion and operation of the 30-satellite BeiDou Navigation Satellite System (BDS-3) represents the successful conclusion of the system's three-step strategy and its capacity to serve the world. BeiDou's world-leading services include positioning, navigation, timing, regional and global short-message communication, global search and rescue, ground-based and satellite-based augmentation, and precise point positioning.

In the next five years, China will continue to improve its space infrastructure, and integrate remote-sensing, communications, navigation, and positioning satellite technologies. It will:

- Upgrade its spatial information services featuring extensive connection, precise timing and positioning, and all dimension sensoring;
- Develop satellites for geostationary microwave monitoring, new-type ocean color observation, carbon monitoring of the territorial ecosystem, and atmospheric environmental monitoring;
- Develop dual-antenna X-band interferometric synthetic aperture radar (InSAR), land water resources and other satellite technology, for efficient, comprehensive earth observation and data acquisition across the globe;
- Build a satellite communications network with high and low orbit coordination, test new communications satellites for commercial application, and build a second-generation data relay satellite system;
- Study and research navigation-communications integration, low-orbit augmentation and other key technologies for the next-generation BeiDou Navigation Satellite System, and develop a more extensive, more integrated and smarter national positioning, navigation and timing (PNT) system;
- Continue to improve the ground systems for remote-sensing, communications and navigation satellites.

3. Manned Spaceflight

The Tianzhou-1 cargo spacecraft has docked with the earth-orbiting Tiangong-2 space laboratory. With breakthroughs in key technologies for cargo transport and in-orbit propellant replenishment, China has successfully completed the second phase of its manned spaceflight project.

The launch of the Tianhe core module marks a solid step in building China's space station. The Tianzhou-2 and Tianzhou-3 cargo spacecraft and the Shenzhou-12 and Shenzhou-13 manned spacecraft, together with the Tianhe core module to which they have docked, form an assembly in steady operation. Six astronauts have worked in China's space station, performing extravehicular activities, in-orbit maintenance, and scientific experiments.

In the next five years, China will continue to implement its manned spaceflight project. It plans to:

- Launch the Wentian and Mengtian experimental modules, the Xuntian space telescope, the Shenzhou manned spacecraft, and the Tianzhou cargo spacecraft;
- Complete China's space station and continue operations, build a space laboratory on board, and have astronauts on long-term assignments performing large-scale scientific experiments and maintenance;
- Continue studies and research on the plan for a human lunar landing, develop new-generation manned spacecraft, and research key technologies to lay a foundation for exploring and developing cislunar space.

4. Deep Space Exploration
(1) Lunar exploration
Achieving relay communications through the Queqiao satellite, the Chang'e-4 lunar probe performed humanity's first soft landing on the far side of the moon, and conducted roving exploration. The Chang'e-5 lunar probe brought back 1,731 g of samples from the moon, marking China's first successful extraterrestrial sampling and return, and the completion of its three-step lunar exploration program of orbiting, landing and return.

(2) Planetary exploration
The Tianwen-1 Mars probe orbited and landed on Mars; the Zhurong Mars rover explored the planet and left China's first mark there. China has achieved a leap from cislunar to interplanetary exploration.

In the next five years, China will continue with lunar and planetary exploration. It will:

- Launch the Chang'e-6 lunar probe to collect and bring back samples from the polar regions of the moon;

- Launch the Chang'e-7 lunar probe to perform a precise landing in the moon's polar regions and a hopping detection in lunar shadowed area;
- Complete R&D on the key technology of Chang'e-8, and work with other countries, international organizations and partners to build an international research station on the moon;
- Launch asteroid probes to sample near-earth asteroids and probe main-belt comets;
- Complete key technological research on Mars sampling and return, exploration of the Jupiter system, and so forth;
- Study plans for boundary exploration of the solar system.

5. Space Launch Sites and Telemetry, Tracking and Command (TT&C)

(1) Space launch sites

Adaptive improvements have been completed at the Jiuquan, Taiyuan and Xichang launch sites, with new launch pads installed at Jiuquan for the commercial launch of liquid fuel rockets, and the Wenchang Launch Site entering service. China has formed a launch site network covering both coastal and inland areas, high and low altitudes, and various trajectories to satisfy the launch needs of manned spaceships, space station modules, deep space probes and all kinds of satellites. In addition, its first sea launch site has begun operation.

(2) Space TT&C

China's leap from cislunar to interplanetary TT&C communications, with growing space-based TT&C capacity, represents a significant progress. Its space TT&C network has improved to form an integrated space-ground TT&C network providing security, reliability, quick response, flexible access, efficient operation and diverse services. TT&C missions of the Shenzhou and Tianzhou spacecraft series, Tianhe core module, Chang'e lunar probe series, and Tianwen-1 Mars probe have been completed successfully. TT&C station networks for commercial satellites are growing quickly.

In the next five years, China will strengthen unified technical standard-setting for its space products, and on this basis will:

- Further adapt the existing launch site system to better serve most launch missions, and make launch sites smarter, more reliable and more cost-effective to support high-intensity and diversified launch missions;
- Build commercial launch pads and launch sites to meet different commercial launch needs;
- Improve the space TT&C network in terms of organization, technology and methodology, grow the capacity to utilize and integrate space- and ground-based TT&C resources, and build a space TT&C network providing ubiquitous coverage and connections;
- Coordinate the operation and management of the national space system for greater efficiency;
- Strengthen the deep-space TT&C communications network to support missions probing the moon and Mars.

6. Experiments on New Technologies

China has launched a number of new technological test satellites, and tested new technologies such as the common platforms of new-generation communications satellites, very high throughput satellites' telecommunication payload, Ka-band communications, satellite-ground high-speed laser communications, and new electric propulsion.

In the next five years, China will focus on new technology engineering and application, conduct in-orbit tests of new space materials, devices and techniques, and test new technologies in these areas:

- Smart self-management of spacecraft;
- Space mission extension vehicle;
- Innovative space propulsion;
- In-orbit service and maintenance of spacecraft;
- Space debris cleaning.

7. Space Environment Governance

With a growing database, China's space debris monitoring system is becoming more capable of collision warning and space event perception and response, effectively ensuring the safety of in-orbit spacecraft.

In compliance with the *Space Debris Mitigation Guidelines* and the *Guidelines for the Long-term Sustainability of Outer Space Activities*, China has applied upper stage passivation to all its carrier rockets, and completed end of life active deorbit of the Tiangong-2 and other spacecraft, making a positive contribution to mitigating space debris.

Progress has been made in the search and tracking of near-earth objects and in data analysis. A basic space climate service system is now in place, capable of providing services in space climate monitoring, early warning, and forecasting, and is providing broader applications.

In the next five years, China will continue to expand its space environment governance system. It will:

- Strengthen space traffic control;
- Improve its space debris monitoring system, cataloguing database, and early warning services;
- Conduct in-orbit maintenance of spacecraft, collision avoidance and control, and space debris mitigation, to ensure the safe, stable and orderly operation of the space system;
- Strengthen the protection of its space activities, assets and other interests by boosting capacity in disaster backup and information protection, and increasing invulnerability and survivability;
- Study plans for building a near-earth object defense system, and increase the capacity of near-earth object monitoring, cataloguing, early warning, and response;
- Build an integrated space-ground space climate monitoring system, and continue to improve relevant services to effectively respond to catastrophic space climate events.

III. Developing and Expanding Space Application Industry

To serve the economy and society, China has promoted public and commercial application of its satellites and space technology, growing the industry towards greater efficiency.

1. Boosting Public Services with Satellites

The service capacity of satellite applications has markedly improved. The significant role of satellites is seen in the protection of resources and the eco-environment, disaster prevention and mitigation, management of emergencies, weather forecasting and climate change response, and also felt in social management and public services, urbanization, coordinated regional development, and poverty eradication. The space industry helps to improve people's lives.

The satellite remote-sensing system has been used by almost all departments at national and provincial levels to conduct emergency monitoring of over 100 major and catastrophic natural disasters around the country. It provides services to tens of thousands of domestic users and over 100 countries, having distributed over 100 million scenes of data.

The communications and broadcasting satellite network has made direct services available to over 140 million households in China's rural and remote areas, provided returned data for over 500 mobile phone base stations, and ensured efficient emergency communications during the responses to the forest fire in Liangshan, Sichuan Province, to the heavy rainstorm in Zhengzhou, Henan Province and to other major disaster relief work.

The BeiDou Navigation Satellite System has guaranteed the safety of over seven million operating vehicles, provided positioning and short message communication services to over 40,000 seagoing fishing vessels, and offered precise positioning services for the freighting of supplies and tracking of individual movement for Covid-19 control, and for hospital construction.

In the next five years, under the overarching goal of building a safe, healthy, beautiful and digital China, we will intensify the integration of satellite application with the development of industries and regions, and space information with new-generation information technology such as big data and Internet of Things. We will also extend the integrated application of remote-sensing satellite data on land, ocean and meteorology, advance the construction of infrastructure for integrated application of the BeiDou Navigation Satellite System, satellite communications, and the ground communications network, and improve our capacity to tailor and refine professional services. All these efforts will help to achieve the goals of peaking carbon dioxide emissions and carbon neutrality, to revitalize rural areas, and to realize new-type urbanization, coordinated development between regions and eco-environmental progress.

2. Space Application Industry

The commercial use of satellite technology is thriving, which expands the applications market for governments, enterprises and individuals. A group of competitive commercial space enterprises are emerging and realizing industrialized large-scale operation. A variety of products and services such as high-accuracy maps using remote-sensing data, full dimensional images, data processing, and application software are improving the service to users in transport, e-commerce, trading of agricultural products, assessment of disaster losses and insurance claims, and the registration of real estate.

The ability to commercialize satellite communications and broadcasting services has further improved. Four 4K Ultra HD television channels in China were launched and TV viewers now have access to over 100 HD channels. Internet access is also available on board ocean vessels and passenger aircraft. Tiantong-1, a satellite mobile communication system, is in commercial operation.

The satellite navigation industry has witnessed rapid growth as evidenced by sales of over 100 million chips compatible with the BeiDou system. Its industrial applications have been widely introduced into mass consumption, the sharing economy, and daily life. Achievements in space technology have helped traditional industries transform and upgrade, supported emerging industries such as new energy, new materials and environmental protection, enabled new business models such as smart cities, smart agriculture and unmanned driving to grow, making a great contribution to building China's strengths in science and technology, manufacturing, cyberspace and transport.

In the next five years, China's space industry will seize the opportunities presented by the expanding digital industry and the digital transformation of traditional industries, to promote the application and transfer of space technology. Through innovative business models and the deep integration of space application with digital economy, more efforts will be made to expand and extend the scope for applying satellite remote-sensing and satellite communications technologies, and realizing the industrialized operation of the BeiDou Navigation Satellite System. This will provide more advanced, economical, high-quality products and convenient services for all industries and sectors and for mass consumption. New business models for upscaling the space economy such as travel, biomedicine, debris removal and experiment services will be developed to expand the industry.

IV. Research on Space Science

China's research on space science focuses on scientific questions such as the origin and evolution of the universe, and the relationship between the solar system and humanity. It has launched programs to explore space and conduct experiments, advanced research on basic theories, and incubated major research findings.

1. Research on Space Science

(1) Space astronomy

The Dark Matter Particle Explorer (DAMPE) Satellite obtained the precise measurements of the energy spectrums of cosmic ray electrons, protons and the GCR helium. The Huiyan (Insight) Hard X-ray Modulation Telescope was successfully launched; it has since discovered the strongest magnetic field in the universe and obtained a panoramic view of the black hole binary explosion process. The Xihe observation satellite was successfully launched, which obtained multiple solar spectroscopic images at different wavelengths in the Hα waveband.

(2) Lunar and planetary science

Led by its lunar exploration program, China has achieved significant advances in the comprehensive surveying of the moon's geology and subsurface structure, in dating the lunar magmatic activity, and in analyzing its mineralogical features and chemical elements. In planetary exploration, China has built a deeper understanding of the geological evolution of Mars by conducting analysis of its surface structure and soil and the composition of its rocks.

(3) Space earth sciences

Zhangheng-1, also known as the China Seismo-Electromagnetic

Satellite, helped to obtain data on and build models of the global geomagnetic field and the in situ data of ionosphere parameters. A high-precision global carbon flux map, developed by using the data from the Chinese Global Carbon Dioxide Monitoring Scientific Experimental Satellite, is shared globally free of any charge.

(4) Space physics

With the help of Mozi, the world's first quantum communication satellite, China has carried out experiments on satellite-based quantum teleportation and entanglement distribution over thousand kilometers, on gravitational induced decoherence of quantum entanglement, and on entanglement-based secure quantum cryptography over thousand kilometers with no trusted relay. It has also launched the Taiji-1 and Tianqin-1 satellites to support the space gravitational wave detection program.

In the next five years, China will continue with the research and development of programs such as the satellite for space gravitational wave detection, the Einstein Probe, the advanced space-based solar observatory, the panoramic imaging satellite for solar wind and magnetosphere interaction, and the high precision magnetic field measurement satellite, focusing on the subjects of the extreme universe, ripples in time and space, the panoramic view of the sun and the earth, and the search for habitable planets. China will continue to explore frontier areas and research into space astronomy, heliospheric physics, lunar and planetary science, space earth sciences, and space physics, to generate more original scientific findings.

2. Science Experiments in Space

With the help of the Shenzhou spacecraft series, the Tiangong-2 space laboratory, and the Shijian-10 satellite, China has achieved mammalian embryonic development in space and in-orbit verification of the world's first space cold atom clock, expanded the understanding of the mechanisms behind particle segregation in microgravity, pulverized coal combustion, and material preparation, and achieved research findings in space science of international standing.

In the coming five years, China will make use of space experiment platforms such as the Tiangong space station, the Chang'e lunar probe series, and the Tianwen-1 Mars probe to conduct experiments and research on biology, life, medicine, and materials, to expand humanity's understanding of basic science.

V. Modernizing Space Governance

The Chinese government has been proactive in developing the space industry, through policy measures and well-thought-out plans for space activities. Better alignment between a well-functioning market and an enabling government gives full play to the roles of both, endeavoring to create a favorable environment for the growth of a high-quality space industry.

1. Enhancing Innovation

In order to create a new configuration in which the upper, middle and lower industrial chains are coordinated, and large, small and medium-sized enterprises advance in an integrated way, China is building a strategic force of space science and technology, encouraging original innovation by research institutes and bringing together enterprises, universities, research institutes and end-users in creating and applying new technologies. A technological innovation alliance is emerging in key areas of space science.

A number of major space and science projects are in place to promote the leapfrog development of space science and technology, which spearheads overall technical advances.

China is making forward-looking plans for strategic, fundamental and technological breakthroughs in space science – it is integrating the application of new-generation information technology in the space sector, and accelerating the engineering application of advanced and especially revolutionary technologies.

The secondary development of space technologies will be further reinforced to put research findings into industrial production and boost the economy.

2. Strengthening Basic Industrial Capabilities

The space industry will continue to improve its integrated and open industrial system comprising system integrators, specialized contractors, market suppliers, and public service providers, and covering all links from research to production.

To strengthen the industrial and supply chains of its space industry and transform and upgrade the basic capabilities of the industry, China will optimize the industrial structure and upgrade R&D, manufacturing, launch operations, and application services, further integrate industrialization with information technology, and build intelligent production lines, workshops and institutes.

3. Expanding Application

China will improve the policies for its satellite application industry, including coordinating public interest and market demand, integrating facilities and resources, unifying data and product standards, and streamline the channel for sharing and utilization. It is committed to improving satellite application services with unified standards and customized choices.

China will move faster to grow its satellite application market, where various market entities are encouraged to develop value-added products. By creating new application models, China is fostering a "space plus" industrial ecosystem and promoting emerging strategic industries related to space.

4. Encouraging Commercialization

China has formulated guidelines on commercializing its space industry. It will expand the scope of government procurement of space products and services, grant relevant enterprises access and sharing rights to major scientific research facilities and equipment, and support these enterprises in joining the R&D of major engineering projects. It will establish a negative list for market access to space activities, to ensure fair competition and the orderly entry and exit of participating enterprises.

China will optimize the distribution of the space industry in the national industrial chain, and encourage and guide participating enterprises to engage in satellite application and the transfer and transformation of space technologies.

5. Promoting Law-Based Governance

To promote law-based governance of the space industry, China will speed up the formulation of a national space law and establish a legal system with this law at the core. This will include studying and formulating regulations on satellite navigation, strengthening the management of satellite navigation activities, revising measures for the registration of space objects, and regulating the sharing and use of space data and the licensing of civil space launches. It will also include studying and formulating regulations on the management of satellite frequency and orbit resources, and strengthening the declaration, coordination and registration of these resources to safeguard the country's legitimate rights and interests in this regard. China has strengthened research on international space law, and actively participated in formulating International Telecommunication Union standards and international rules regarding outer space, maintaining the international order in outer space based on international space law, and contributing to a fair and reasonable global governance system for outer space.

6. Strengthening Team-Building

China will step up its efforts to become a world center for talent and innovation in space science, and create favorable conditions for the development of professionals and the expansion of their ranks. It will improve the personnel training mechanism – fostering a pool of strategic scientists, leading and young scientists, and teams with strong innovation capacity, and cultivating a large number of outstanding engineers, top technicians championing fine craftsmanship, and visionary entrepreneurs with a sense of social responsibility. China will improve its personnel management mechanisms to regulate and guide the rational flow of professionals. It will also upgrade incentives with greater rewards and stronger support, and strengthen specialty disciplines in universities to cultivate a reserve force of aerospace personnel.

7. Promoting Space Education and Culture

China will continue to hold events to celebrate its Space Day, promote education on space knowledge and culture during World Space Week and National Science and Technology Week, and through Tiangong Classroom and other platforms, and promote the culture and spirit embodied in the development of the atomic and hydrogen bombs, missiles, man-made satellites, manned spaceflight, lunar probes and the BeiDou Navigation Satellite System in the new era. The goal is to inspire the nation, especially the young people, to develop an interest in science, to create and explore the unknown, and to increase scientific knowledge among the general public.

China will protect its major space heritage and build more space museums and experience parks to popularize space science and provide education. It will encourage the creation of space-related literary and art works to promote space culture.

VI. International Cooperation

Peaceful exploration, development and utilization of outer space are rights equally enjoyed by all countries. China calls on all countries to work together to build a global community of shared future and carry out in-depth exchanges and cooperation in outer space on the basis of equality, mutual benefit, peaceful utilization, and inclusive development.

1. Basic Policies

China's basic policies on international exchanges and cooperation are as follows:

- Safeguarding the central role of the United Nations in managing outer space affairs; abiding by the *Treaty on Principles Governing the Activities of States in the Exploration and Use of Outer Space, Including the Moon and Other Celestial Bodies*; upholding the guiding role of relevant UN principles, declarations and resolutions; actively participating in the formulation of international rules regarding outer space; and promoting greater sustainability of space activities;

- Strengthening international exchanges and cooperation on space science, technology and application; working together with the international community to provide public products and services; and contributing to global efforts to address common challenges;

- Strengthening international space cooperation that is based on common goals and serves the Belt and Road Initiative, and ensuring that the space industry benefits the Initiative's participating countries, especially developing countries;

- Supporting the Asia-Pacific Space Cooperation Organization (APSCO) to play an important role, and giving weight to cooperation under the BRICS and Group 20 mechanisms and within the framework of the Shanghai Cooperation Organization;
- Encouraging and endorsing the efforts of domestic research institutes, enterprises, institutions of higher learning, and social organizations to engage in international space exchanges and cooperation in diverse forms and at various levels in accordance with relevant policies, laws and regulations.

2. Major Achievements

Since 2016, China has signed 46 space cooperation agreements or memoranda of understanding with 19 countries and regions and four international organizations. It has actively promoted global governance of outer space, and carried out international cooperation in space science, technology and application through bilateral and multilateral mechanisms. These measures have yielded fruitful results.

(1) Global governance of outer space

- China participates in consultations on issues such as the long-term sustainability of outer space activities, the development and utilization of space resources, and the prevention of arms race in outer space. Together with other parties, it has proposed discussions on space exploration and innovation, and advanced the Space2030 Agenda of the UN.
- China supports the work of the Beijing office of the United Nations Platform for Space-based Information for Disaster Management and Emergency Response, and has participated in the activities of the International Committee on Global Navigation Satellite Systems in an in-depth manner. It has joined international mechanisms such as the Space Missions Planning Advisory Group and the International Asteroid Warning Network.
- China plays its role as the host country of APSCO, and supports

the organization's Development Vision 2030.

- China has strengthened international exchanges on space debris, long-term sustainability of outer space activities, and other issues through mechanisms such as the Space Debris Work Group of China-Russia Space Cooperation Sub-committee and the Sino-US Expert Workshop on Space Debris and Space Flight Safety.
- China supports the activities of international organizations such as the International Telecommunication Union, Group on Earth Observations, Inter-Agency Space Debris Coordination Committee, Consultative Committee for Space Data Systems, International Space Exploration Coordination Group, and the Interagency Operations Advisory Group.

(2) Manned spaceflight

- China has carried out gamma-ray burst polarization monitoring research with the European Space Agency on the Tiangong-2 space laboratory, conducted human body medical research in a microgravitational environment with France during the Shenzhou-11 manned spaceflight mission, carried out joint CAVES training and maritime rescue drills with the European Astronaut Centre.
- China has completed the selection of the first batch of international space science experiments to be conducted on the Chinese space station, and conducted technological cooperation and exchanges with Germany, Italy and Russia on space science experiments and the development of space station sections.

(3) BeiDou Navigation Satellite System

- China has coordinated the development of China's BeiDou Navigation Satellite System and the United States' Global Positioning System, Russia's GLONASS system, and Europe's Galileo system. It has carried out in-depth cooperation with them in the fields of compatibility, interoperability, monitoring and assessment, and joint application.

- China has pressed ahead with international standardization of the BeiDou system, which has been included in the standard systems of the International Electrotechnical Commission and many other international organizations in fields such as civil aviation, maritime affairs, international search and rescue, and mobile communications.
- China has increased the BeiDou system's global service capacity by establishing BeiDou cooperation forum mechanisms with the League of Arab States and the African Union, completing the first overseas BeiDou center in Tunisia, and conducting satellite navigation cooperation with countries such as Pakistan, Saudi Arabia, Argentina, South Africa, Algeria, and Thailand.

(4) Deep-space exploration
- China launched the international lunar research station project together with Russia, and initiated the Sino-Russian Joint Data Center for Lunar and Deep-space Exploration. It is working with Russia to coordinate Chang'e-7's lunar polar exploration mission with Russia's LUNA-Resource-1 orbiter mission.
- In the Chang'e-4 lunar exploration mission China cooperated with Russia and the European Space Agency on engineering technology, and with Sweden, Germany, the Netherlands and Saudi Arabia on payloads. It has launched international onboard payload cooperation in the Chang'e-6 lunar exploration mission.
- In the Tianwen-1 mission, China's first Mars exploration project, China cooperated with the European Space Agency on engineering technology, and with Austria and France on payloads. It has established a Mars probe orbit data exchange mechanism with the United States, and launched international onboard payload cooperation in its asteroid exploration mission.
- In the fields of lunar and deep-space exploration, China cooperated on TT&C with the European Space Agency, Argentina, Namibia, and Pakistan.

(5) Space technology

- Together with relevant partners China has developed and successfully launched the China-France Oceanography Satellite, China-Brazil Earth Resources Satellite 04A, and the Ethiopian Remote-Sensing Satellite. It has launched the Student Small Satellites (SSS) for APSCO. It is jointly developing the MisrSat-2 remote-sensing satellite.

- China completed the in-orbit delivery of the Pakistan Remote-Sensing Satellite (PRSS-1), Venezuelan Remote-Sensing Satellite (VRSS-2), Sudan Remote-Sensing Satellite (SRSS-1), and the Algerian Communications Satellite (Alcomsat-1).

- China has provided satellite carrying or launching services for countries including Saudi Arabia, Pakistan, Argentina, Brazil, Canada, and Luxembourg.

- China has conducted space product and technology cooperation with countries including Russia, Ukraine, Belarus, Argentina, Pakistan, and Nigeria.

- China has helped developing countries boost their space science and research. It has built satellite research and development infrastructure with countries including Egypt, Pakistan and Nigeria. It has pressed ahead with the construction of the Belt and Road Initiative Space Information Corridor, and opened China's space facilities to developing countries.

(6) Space applications

- China has established an emergency support mechanism for disaster prevention and mitigation for international users of the Fengyun meteorological satellites, and data from China's meteorological satellites have been widely used in 121 countries and regions.

- China has signed cooperation agreements for the BRICS Remote-Sensing Satellite Constellation, cooperated with the European Space Agency on earth observation satellite data exchange, and built the China-ASEAN Satellite Information Offshore Service

Platform and the Remote-Sensing Satellite Data-Sharing Service Platform. It has worked with Laos, Thailand, Cambodia, and Myanmar to build the Lancang-Mekong Space Information Exchange Center.

- China has built satellite data receiving stations with countries including Bolivia, Indonesia, Namibia, Thailand and South Africa.
- China actively participates in the mechanism of the International Charter on Space and Major Disasters, providing satellite remote-sensing data totaling 800 scenes and adding eight new on-duty satellites (constellations) to the satellite system, thereby improving the international community's capacity for disaster prevention and mitigation.
- China actively provides satellite emergency monitoring services. It has initiated emergency monitoring in response to 17 major disasters in 15 countries. For instance, in response to the severe drought in Afghanistan and the dam collapse in Laos in 2018, and to the cyclone that struck Mozambique in 2019, it provided monitoring services for the authorities of affected countries.
- China released its *GEO Strategic Plan 2016-2025: Implementing GEOSS*. It served as the rotating chair of the Group on Earth Observations in 2020 and promoted the construction of a global earth observation system.
- China participates in the international Space Climate Observatory platform, promoting China's best practices in space technology to address climate change, and facilitating international cooperation on space climate observation.

(7) Space science
- Using science satellites including Wukong, Mozi, Shijian-10, and Insight, China has conducted joint scientific research and experiments with countries including Switzerland, Italy, Austria, the United Kingdom, and Japan.
- China co-developed and successfully launched the China-Italy

Electromagnetic Monitoring Experiment Satellite. It has continued the joint development of the Sino-European Panoramic Imaging Satellite for Solar Wind and Magnetosphere Interaction, Sino-French Astronomic Satellite, and China-Italy Electromagnetic Monitoring Experiment Satellite 02. It has joined countries including Italy and Germany in developing and calibrating the payloads of satellites such as the advanced space-based solar observatory, Einstein Probe, and enhanced X-ray timing and polarimetry observatory.

- Using the China-Brazil Joint Laboratory for Space Weather, it co-built the space environment monitoring and research platform for South America.

(8) Personnel and academic exchanges

- China has taken part in the activities organized by the International Astronautical Federation, International Committee on Space Research, International Academy of Astronautics, and International Institute of Space Law. It has hosted the 2017 Global Space Exploration Conference, the 13th Meeting of the International Committee on Global Navigation Satellite Systems, the United Nations/China Forum on Space Solutions: Realizing the Sustainable Development Goals, the Wenchang International Aviation and Aerospace Forum, the Zhuhai Forum, the International Summit on BDS Applications, and the Fengyun Satellite User Conference.

- China has helped developing countries train professionals. Through the Regional Centre for Space Science and Technology Education in Asia and the Pacific (China) (Affiliated to the United Nations), it has trained almost 1,000 space-industry professionals for more than 60 countries, and established the "Belt and Road" Aerospace Innovation Alliance and the Association of Sino-Russian Technical Universities. It has also promoted personnel exchanges in remote-sensing and navigation technology through the International Training Program and other channels.

- China has promoted scientific and technological exchanges in the fields of space science, remote sensing and navigation through the China-Europe Space Science Bilateral Meeting, the China-EU-ESA Dialogue on Space Technology Cooperation, and the Dragon Programme – a joint undertaking between ESA and the Ministry of Science and Technology of China.

3. Key Areas for Future Cooperation

In the next five years China will be more open and active in broadening bilateral and multilateral cooperation mechanisms, and will engage in extensive international exchanges and cooperation in the following key areas:

(1) Global governance of outer space

- Under the framework of the United Nations, China will actively participate in formulating international rules regarding outer space, and will work together with other countries to address the challenges in ensuring long-term sustainability of outer space activities.
- China will actively participate in discussions on international issues and the development of relevant mechanisms, such as those in the fields of space environment governance, near-earth objects monitoring and response, planet protection, space traffic management, and the development and utilization of space resources.
- China will cooperate in space environment governance, improve the efficiency of space crisis management and comprehensive governance, conduct dialogue with Russia, the United States and other countries as well as relevant international organizations on outer space governance, and actively support the construction of APSCO's space science observatory.

(2) Manned spaceflight

- China will employ its space station to conduct space-based astronomical observations, earth science and research, and space science experiments under conditions of microgravity.

- China will promote more extensive international cooperation in astronaut selection and training, joint flights and other fields.

(3) BeiDou Navigation Satellite System

- China will continue to participate in the activities of the UN's International Committee on Global Navigation Satellite Systems and promote the establishment of a fair and reasonable satellite navigation order.
- China will actively improve compatibility and interoperability of global satellite navigation systems such as the BeiDou Navigation Satellite System and other such systems as well as satellite-based augmentation systems.
- China will prioritize cooperation and exchanges, and share with others mature solutions, on the application of the BeiDou Navigation Satellite System, thereby boosting the socio-economic development of partner countries.

(4) Deep-space exploration

- China will advance cooperation on the international lunar research station project. It welcomes international partners to participate in the research and construction of the station at any stage and level of the mission.
- It will expand cooperation in the fields of asteroid and interplanetary exploration.

(5) Space technology

- China will support cooperation on satellite engineering and technology. It will complete the joint research and development of MisrSat-2, and launch the SVOM (Space-based multiband astronomical Variable Objects Monitor), and the China-Italy Electromagnetic Monitoring Experiment Satellite 02. It will press ahead with follow-up cooperation in the China-Brazil Earth Resources Satellites program.
- China will engage in cooperation on space TT&C support. It will continue to cooperate with the European Space Agency in the field

of TT&C support, and further advance the building of ground station networks.

- China will support international cooperation on commercial spaceflight, including:

  (a) launching services;

  (b) technical cooperation on whole satellites, on sub-systems, spare parts, and electronic components of satellites and launch vehicles, on ground facilities and equipment, and on other related items.

  It will give priority to developing communications satellites for Pakistan and to cooperating on the construction of the Pakistan Space Center and Egypt's Space City.

(6) Space applications

- China will promote global application of data from Chinese meteorological satellites, support the provision of data from the China-France Oceanography Satellite to the World Meteorological Organization, and promote global sharing and scientific application of the data obtained by Zhangheng-1, China's seismo-electromagnetic satellite.

- China will press ahead with the construction of the Belt and Road Initiative Space Information Corridor, and strengthen cooperation on the application of remote-sensing, navigation, and communications satellites.

- China will press ahead with the construction of the data-sharing service platform of APSCO.

- China will advance the construction and application of the BRICS remote-sensing satellite constellation.

- China will participate in the construction and use of the Space Climate Observatory.

(7) Space science

- By means of the deep-space exploration project, and using extra-terrestrial samples and exploration data, China will conduct joint research in fields such as the space environment and planetary origin and evolution. Through the United Nations scientific data obtained by the Chang'e 4 satellite will be made available to the international community.

- China will boost joint R&D on space science satellites and research subjects such as dark matter particles, solar burst activities and their influence, and spatial gravitational wave.

(8) Personnel and academic exchanges

- China will conduct personnel exchanges and training in the space industry.
- China will hold high-level international academic exchange conferences and forums.

Conclusion

In today's world, a growing number of countries are seeing the importance of space and are investing more on their space programs. Space industry around the world has entered a new stage of rapid development and profound transformation that will have a major and far-reaching impact on human society.

At this new historical start towards a modern socialist country, China will accelerate work on its space industry. Guided by the concept of a global community of shared future, it will work actively with other countries to carry out international space exchanges and cooperation, safeguard outer space security, and strive for long-term sustainability in activities related to outer space. By doing so, China will contribute more to protecting the earth, improving people's wellbeing, and serving human progress.

China's Parasports
Progress and the Protection of Rights

The State Council Information Office of
the People's Republic of China

March 2022

Preamble

Sports are important for all individuals, including those with a disability. Developing parasports is an effective way to help persons with disabilities to improve physical fitness, pursue physical and mental rehabilitation, participate in social activities, and achieve all-round development. It also provides a special opportunity for the public to better understand the potential and value of the disabled, and promote social harmony and progress. In addition, developing parasports is of great importance in ensuring that persons with disabilities can enjoy equal rights, integrate readily into society, and share the fruits of economic and social progress. Participation in sports is an important right of persons with disabilities as well as an integral component of human rights protection.

The Central Committee of the Communist Party of China (CPC) with Xi Jinping at the core attaches great importance to the cause of the disabled, and provides them with extensive care. Since the 18th CPC National Congress in 2012, guided by Xi Jinping Thought on Socialism with Chinese Characteristics for a New Era, China has included this cause in the Five-sphere Integrated Plan and the Four-pronged Comprehensive Strategy, and taken concrete and effective measures to develop parasports. With the steady advance of parasports in China, many athletes with disabilities have worked hard and won honors for the country in the international arena, inspiring the public through their sporting prowess. Historic progress has been made in developing sports for persons with disabilities.

With the Beijing 2022 Paralympic Winter Games just around the corner, athletes with disabilities are once again drawing global attention. The Games will certainly provide an opportunity for the development of parasports in China; they will enable the international parasports movement to advance "together for a shared future".

I. Parasports Have Progressed Through National Development

Since the founding of the People's Republic of China (PRC) in 1949, in the cause of socialist revolution and reconstruction, reform and opening up, socialist modernization, and socialism with Chinese characteristics for a new era, along with making progress in the cause of the disabled, parasports have steadily developed and prospered, embarking on a path that carries distinct Chinese features and respects the trends of the times.

1. Steady progress was made in parasports after the founding of the PRC. With the founding of the PRC, the people became masters of the country. Persons with disabilities were granted equal political status, enjoying the same lawful rights and obligations as other citizens. The 1954 *Constitution of the People's Republic of China* stipulated that they "have the right to material assistance". Welfare factories, welfare institutions, special education schools, specialized social organizations and a positive social environment have guaranteed the basic rights and interests of disabled people and improved their lives.

In the early years of the PRC, the CPC and the Chinese government attached great importance to sports for the people. Parasports made gradual progress in schools, factories and sanatoriums. Large numbers of disabled people actively participated in sports activities such as radio calisthenics, workplace exercises, table tennis, basketball, and tug of war, laying the foundations for more disabled people to participate in sports.

In 1957, the first national games for blind youth took place in Shanghai. Sports organizations for people with hearing impairments were established all over the country, and they organized regional sports events. In

1959, the first national men's basketball competition for those with hearing impairments was held. National sports competitions encouraged more disabled people to participate in sports, improved their physical fitness, and increased their enthusiasm for social integration.

2. Parasports progressed rapidly following the launch of reform and opening up. Following the introduction of reform and opening up in 1978, China achieved a historic transformation – raising the living standards of its people from bare subsistence to a basic level of moderate prosperity. This marked a tremendous step forward for the Chinese nation – from standing upright to becoming better-off.

The CPC and the Chinese government launched a host of major initiatives to champion the progress of parasports and improve the lives of disabled people. The state promulgated the *Law of the People's Republic of China on the Protection of Persons with Disabilities*, and ratified the *Convention on the Rights of Persons with Disabilities*. As reform and opening up progressed, promoting the interests of disabled people evolved from social welfare, provided mainly in the form of relief, into a comprehensive social undertaking. Greater efforts were made to increase opportunities for disabled people to participate in social activities, and to respect and protect their rights in all respects, laying the foundations for the development of parasports.

The *Law of the People's Republic of China on Physical Culture and Sports* stipulates that society as a whole should concern itself with and support the participation of the disabled in physical activities, and that governments at all levels shall take measures to provide conditions for disabled people to participate in physical activities. The law also prescribes that disabled people should have preferential access to public sports installations and facilities, and that schools shall create conditions for organizing sports activities suited to the particular conditions of students who are in poor health or disabled.

Parasports were included in the national development strategies and in development plans for the disabled. Relevant work mechanisms and public services were improved, enabling parasports to enter a stage of rapid development.

In 1983, a national sports invitational for persons with disabilities was held in Tianjin. In 1984, the First National Games for Persons with Disabilities took place in Hefei, Anhui Province. In the same year, Team China made its debut at the 7th Paralympic Summer Games in New York, and won its first ever Paralympic gold medal. In 1994, Beijing hosted the 6th Far East and South Pacific Games for the Disabled (FESPIC Games), the first international multi-sport event for disabled people held in China. In 2001, Beijing won the bid to host the 2008 Olympic and Paralympic Summer Games. In 2004, Team China led both the gold medal count and the overall medal count for the first time at the Athens Paralympic Summer Games. In 2007, Shanghai hosted the Special Olympics World Summer Games. In 2008, the Paralympic Summer Games were held in Beijing. In 2010, Guangzhou hosted the Asian Para Games.

Over this period, China set up a number of sports organizations for disabled people, including the China Sports Association for the Disabled (later renamed the National Paralympic Committee of China), the China Sports Association for the Deaf, and the China Association for the Mentally Challenged (later renamed Special Olympics China). China also joined a number of international sports organizations for the disabled, including the International Paralympic Committee. Meanwhile, various local sports organizations for disabled people were set up across the country.

3. Historic progress has been made in parasports in the new era. Since the 18th CPC National Congress in 2012, socialism with Chinese characteristics has entered a new era. China has built a moderately prosperous society in all respects as scheduled, and the Chinese nation has achieved a tremendous transformation – from standing upright to becoming prosperous and growing in strength.

Xi Jinping, general secretary of the CPC Central Committee and president of China, has a particular concern for people with disabilities.

He emphasizes that disabled people are equal members of society, and an important force for the development of human civilization and for upholding and developing Chinese socialism. He notes that the disabled are just as capable of leading rewarding lives as able-bodied people. He also instructed that no individuals with disabilities should be left behind when moderate prosperity in all respects was to be realized in China in 2020. Xi has committed that China will develop further programs for the disabled, promote their all-round development and shared prosperity, and strive to ensure access to rehabilitation services for every disabled person. He pledged that China would deliver an excellent and extraordinary Winter Olympics and Paralympics at Beijing 2022. He has also emphasized that the country must be considerate in providing convenient, efficient, targeted and meticulous services for athletes, and in particular, in meeting the special needs of athletes with disabilities by building accessible facilities. These important observations have pointed the direction for the cause of disabled people in China.

Under the leadership of the CPC Central Committee with Xi Jinping at its core, China incorporates programs for disabled people into its overall plans for economic and social development and its human rights action plans. As a result, the rights and interests of people with disabilities have been better protected, and the goals of equality, participation and sharing have drawn closer. Disabled people have a stronger sense of fulfillment, happiness and security, and parasports have bright prospects for development.

Parasports have been included in China's national strategies of Fitness-for-All, Healthy China initiative, and Building China into a Country Strong in Sports. The *Law of the People's Republic of China on Ensuring Public Cultural Services* and the *Regulations on Building an Accessible Environment* provide that top priority shall be given to improving accessibility of public service facilities including sports facilities. China has built a National Ice Sports Arena for People with Impairments. More and more disabled people are engaging in rehabilitation and fitness activities, participating in parasports in their communities and homes, and taking part in outdoor sports activities. The Disability Support Project under the National Fitness Program has been implemented, and sports instructors for people with disabilities have been trained. People with severe disabilities have access to rehabilitation and fitness services in their homes.

Every effort has been made to prepare for the Beijing 2022 Paralympic Winter Games, and Chinese athletes will participate in all events. In the 2018 Pyeongchang Paralympic Winter Games, Chinese athletes won gold in Wheelchair Curling, China's first medal in Winter Paralympics. In the Tokyo 2020 Paralympic Summer Games, Chinese athletes achieved extraordinary results, ranking top in the gold medal and medal tallies for the fifth time in a row. Chinese athletes have scaled new heights in the Deaflympics and the Special Olympics World Games.

Parasports have made enormous progress in China, demonstrating China's institutional strength in promoting programs for the disabled, and displaying its notable achievements in respecting and protecting the rights and interests of people with disabilities. Throughout the country, understanding, respect, care and help for the disabled are growing in strength. More and more disabled people are realizing their dreams and achieving remarkable improvements in their lives through sports. The courage, tenacity and resilience that disabled people show in pushing boundaries and forging ahead have inspired the whole nation and promoted social and cultural progress.

II. Physical Activities for Persons with Disabilities Have Flourished

China regards rehabilitation and fitness activities for persons with disabilities as one of the main components in implementing its national strategies of Fitness-for-All, Healthy China initiative, and Building China into a Country Strong in Sports. By carrying out parasports activities across the whole country, enriching the content of such activities, improving sports services, and intensifying scientific research and education, China has encouraged the disabled to become more active participants in rehabilitation and fitness activities.

1. Physical activities for persons with disabilities are flourishing. At community level, a variety of rehabilitation and fitness activities for persons with disabilities have been organized, adapted to local conditions in urban and rural China. To promote the participation of persons with disabilities in grassroots fitness activities and competitive sports, China has extended rehabilitation activities and fitness sports services to communities through government procurement. The participation rate in grassroots cultural and sports activities for persons with disabilities in China has spiraled, from 6.8 percent in 2015 to 23.9 percent in 2021.

Schools at all levels and of all types have organized specially designed regular physical activities for their disabled students, and have promoted line dancing, cheerleading, dryland curling, and other group-based sports. College students and those in primary and secondary schools have been encouraged to participate in projects such as the Special Olympics University Program and in Special Olympics Unified Sports. Medical workers have been mobilized to engage in activities such as sports rehabilitation, para-athletics classification, and the Special Olympics Healthy Athletes program, and physical educators have been encouraged to participate in professional services such as physical fitness and sports training for the disabled, and to provide voluntary services for parasports.

China's National Games for Persons with Disabilities have incorporated rehabilitation and fitness events. The National Football Games for Persons with Disabilities have been held with multiple categories for persons with visual or hearing impairments or intellectual disabilities. Teams participating in the National Line Dancing Open Tournament for Persons with Disabilities now come from around 20 provinces and equivalent administrative units. A growing number of special education schools have made line dancing a physical activity for their main recess.

2. Parasports events are carried out nationwide. Persons with disabilities regularly participate in national parasports events, such as the National Special Olympics Day, Fitness Week for Persons with Disabilities, and Winter Sports Season for Persons with Disabilities. Since 2007, China has been organizing activities to popularize National Special Olympics Day, which falls on July 20 every year. Participation in the Special Olympics has tapped into the potential of persons with intellectual disabilities, improved their self-esteem, and brought them into the community. Since 2011, around the National Fitness Day each year, China has been organizing nationwide parasports activities to mark the Fitness Week for Persons with Disabilities, during which events such as wheelchair Tai Chi, Tai Chi ball, and blind football games have been held.

Through participating in rehabilitation and fitness events and activities, persons with disabilities have become more familiar with parasports, begun to take part in sports activities, and learned to use rehabilitation and fitness equipment. They have had the opportunity to demonstrate and exchange rehabilitation and fitness skills. Greater fitness and a more positive mindset have inspired their passion for life, and they have become more confident about integrating into society. Events such as the Wheelchair Marathon for the Disabled, the Chess Challenge among Blind Players, and the National Tai Chi Ball Championships for Persons with Hearing Impairments have developed into national parasports events.

3. Winter sports for persons with disabilities are on the rise. Every year since 2016 China has hosted a Winter Sports Season for Persons with Disabilities, providing them with a platform to participate in winter sports, and fulfilling the Beijing 2022 bid commitment of engaging 300 million people in winter sports. The scale of participation has expanded from 14 provincial-level units in the first Winter Sports Season to 31 provinces and equivalent administrative units. Various winter parasports activities suited to local conditions have been held, allowing participants to experience Paralympic Winter Games events, and take part in mass-participation winter sports, winter rehabilitation and fitness training camps, and ice and snow festivals. A variety of winter sports for mass participation have been created and promoted, such as mini skiing, dryland skiing, dryland curling, ice Cuju (a traditional Chinese game of competing for a ball on the ice rink), skating, sledding, sleighing, ice bikes, snow football, ice dragon boating, snow tug-of-war, and ice fishing. These novel and fun sports have proved very popular among persons with disabilities. In addition, availability of winter sports and fitness services for persons with disabilities at community level, and technical support, have been improved with the promulgation of materials such as *A Guidebook on Winter Sports and Fitness Programs for Persons with Disabilities*.

4. Rehabilitation and fitness services for persons with disabilities keep improving. China has introduced a series of measures to engage persons with disabilities in rehabilitation and physical activities, and to cultivate rehabilitation and fitness service teams. These include: launching a Self-improvement Fitness Project and a Sports Rehabilitation Care Plan, developing and promoting programs, methodology and equipment for rehabilitation and fitness of the disabled, enriching sports services and products for persons with disabilities, and promoting community-level fitness services for them and home-based rehabilitation services for persons with severe disabilities.

The *National Basic Public Service Standards for Mass Sports (2021 Edition)* and other national policies and regulations stipulate that the fitness environment for persons with disabilities is to be improved, and require that they have access to public facilities free of charge or at reduced prices. As of 2020, a total of 10,675 disabled-friendly sports venues had been built nationwide, a total of 125,000 instructors had been trained, and 434,000 households with severely disabled people had been provided with home-based rehabilitation and fitness services. Meanwhile, China has actively guided the construction of winter sports facilities for persons with disabilities with the focus on supporting less developed areas, townships and rural areas.

5. Progress has been made in parasports education and research. China has incorporated parasports in special education, teacher training, and physical education programs, and has accelerated the development of parasports research institutions. China Administration of Sports for Persons with Disabilities, the Sports Development Committee of the China Disability Research Society, together with parasports research institutions in many colleges and universities, form the main force in parasports education and research. A system for cultivating parasports talent has taken shape. Some universities and colleges have opened selective courses on parasports. A number of parasports professionals have been cultivated. Considerable progress has been made in parasports research. As of 2021, more than 20 parasports projects were being supported by the National Social Science Fund of China.

III. Performances in Parasports Are Improving Steadily

Disabled people are becoming increasingly active in sports. More and more athletes with disabilities have competed in sporting events both at home and abroad. They are seeking to meet challenges, pursuing self-improvement, demonstrating an indomitable spirit, and fighting for a wonderful and successful life.

1. Chinese parasports athletes have given outstanding performances at major international sporting events. Since 1987, Chinese athletes with intellectual disabilities have participated in nine Special Olympics World Summer Games and seven Special Olympics World Winter Games. In 1989, Chinese deaf athletes made their international debut at the 16th World Games for the Deaf in Christchurch of New Zealand. In 2007, the Chinese delegation earned a bronze medal at the 16th Winter Deaflympics in Salt Lake City of the United States – the first medal won by Chinese athletes at the event. Subsequently, Chinese athletes achieved outstanding performances at several Summer and Winter Deaflympics. They also took an active part in Asian sporting events for the disabled and won many honors. In 1984, 24 athletes from the Chinese Paralympic delegation competed in Athletics, Swimming and Table Tennis at the Seventh Summer Paralympics in New York, and brought home 24 medals, including two golds, generating an upsurge of enthusiasm for sports among disabled people in China. At the following Summer Paralympics, Team China's performance showed a marked improvement. In 2004, at the 12th Summer Paralympics in Athens, the Chinese delegation won 141 medals, including 63 golds, ranking first in both medals and golds won. In 2021, at the 16th Summer Paralympics in Tokyo, Team China claimed 207 medals, including 96 golds, topping both the gold medal tally and the overall medal standings for the fifth consecutive time. During the 13th Five-year Plan period (2016-2020), China sent disabled athletes delegations to participate in 160 international sporting events, bringing home a total of 1,114 gold medals.

2. Influence of national parasports events keeps expanding. Since China organized its first National Games for Persons with Disabilities (NGPD) in 1984, 11 such events have been held, with the number of sports increasing from three (Athletics, Swimming and Table Tennis) to 34. Since the third games in 1992, the NGPD has been listed as a large-scale sporting event ratified by the State Council and held once every four years. This confirms the institutionalization and standardization of parasports in China. In 2019, Tianjin hosted the 10th NGPD (together with the Seventh National Special Olympic Games) and the National Games of China. This made the city the first to host both the NGPD and the National Games of China. In 2021, Shaanxi hosted the 11th NGPD (together with the Eighth National Special Olympic Games) and the National Games of China. It was the first time that the NGPD had been held in the same city and during the same year as the National Games of China. This allowed synchronized planning and implementation and both games were equally successful. In addition to the NGPD, China also organizes national individual events for categories such as blind athletes, deaf athletes, and athletes with limb deficiencies, for the purpose of engaging more people with various types of disabilities in sports activities. Through these national sporting events for disabled people on a regular basis, the country has trained a number of athletes with disabilities and improved their sports skills.

3. Chinese athletes show growing strength in winter Paralympic sports. China's successful bid for 2022 Paralympic Winter Games has generated great opportunities for the development of its Winter Paralympic sports. The country attaches great importance to the preparation for

Winter Paralympics. It has designed and implemented a series of action plans, pressed ahead with sporting events planning, and coordinated the creation of training facilities, equipment support, and research services. It has organized training camps to select outstanding athletes, strengthened the training of technical personnel, hired capable coaches from home and abroad, established national training teams, and promoted international cooperation. All the six Winter Paralympic sports – Alpine Skiing, Biathlon, Cross-Country Skiing, Snowboard, Ice Hockey, and Wheelchair Curling – have been included in the NGPD, which pushed forward winter sports activities in 29 provinces and equivalent administrative units.

From 2015 to 2021, the number of Winter Paralympic sports in China increased from 2 to 6, so that all Winter Paralympic sports are now covered. The number of athletes increased from fewer than 50 to nearly 1,000, and that of technical officials from 0 to more than 100. Since 2018, annual national competitions for sporting events in Winter Paralympics have been held, and these sporting events were included in the 2019 and 2021 NGPD. Chinese parasports athletes have participated in the Winter Paralympic Games since 2016, and won 47 gold, 54 silver, and 52 bronze medals. In the Beijing 2022 Paralympic Winter Games, a total of 96 athletes from China will take part in all 6 sports and 73 events. Compared with the Sochi 2014 Paralympic Winter Games, the number of athletes will increase by more than 80, the number of sports by 4, and the number of events by 67.

4. Mechanisms for athlete training and support are improving. In order to ensure fair competition, parasports athletes are classified medically and functionally according to their categories and the sports that are suitable for them. A four-tiered parasports athlete spare-time training system has been established and improved, in which the county level is responsible for identification and selection, the city level training and development, the provincial level for intensive training and games participation, and the national level for the training of key talent. Youth selection competitions and training camps have been organized for the training of reserve talent.

Greater efforts have been made to build a contingent of parasports coaches, referees, classifiers and other professionals. More parasports training bases have been built, and 45 national training bases have been nominated for parasports, providing support and services for research, training and competition. Governments at all levels have taken measures to address problems of education, employment and social security for parasports athletes, and to carry out pilot work for enrolling top athletes into higher learning institutions without examination. *Measures for the Administration of Parasports Events and Activities* have been issued to promote orderly and standard development of parasports games. Parasports ethics have been strengthened. Doping and other violations are forbidden so as to ensure fairness and justice in parasports.

IV. Contributing to International Parasports

An open China actively takes on its international responsibilities. It has succeeded in hosting the Beijing 2008 Summer Paralympics, the Shanghai 2007 Special Olympics World Summer Games, the Sixth Far East and South Pacific Games for the Disabled, and the Guangzhou 2010 Asian Para Games, and made full preparations for the Beijing 2022 Paralympic Winter Games and Hangzhou 2022 Asian Para Games. This has given a strong boost to the cause of the disabled in China and made an outstanding contribution to international parasports. China is fully engaged in international sports affairs for the disabled and continues to strengthen exchanges and cooperation with other countries and with international organizations for disabled people, building friendship among peoples of all countries, including those with disabilities.

1. Asian multi-sport events for the disabled have been staged successfully. In 1994, Beijing held the Sixth Far East and South Pacific Games for the Disabled, in which a total of 1,927 athletes from 42 countries and regions took part, making it the biggest event in the history of these games at that time. This was the first time that China had held an international multi-sport event for the disabled. It showcased China's achievements in reform and opening up and modernization, gave the rest of society a deeper understanding of its work for the disabled, boosted the development of China's programs for persons with disabilities, and raised the profile of the Asian and Pacific Decade of Disabled Persons.

In 2010, the First Asian Para Games were held in Guangzhou, attended by athletes from 41 countries and regions. This was the first sports event held after the reorganization of Asian parasports organizations. It was also the first time that the Asian Para Games were held in the same city and the same year as the Asian Games, promoting a more barrier-free environment in Guangzhou. The Asian Para Games helped to display the sporting prowess of the disabled, created a sound atmosphere for assisting persons with disabilities to integrate better into society, enabled more disabled people to share in the fruits of development, and improved the level of parasports in Asia.

In 2022, the Fourth Asian Para Games will be held in Hangzhou. Around 3,800 parasports athletes from over 40 countries and regions will compete in 604 events across 22 sports. These games will vigorously promote friendship and cooperation in Asia.

2. The Shanghai 2007 Special Olympics World Summer Games were a big success. In 2007, the 12th Special Olympics World Summer Games were held in Shanghai, attracting over 10,000 athletes and coaches from 164 countries and regions to compete in 25 sports. This was the first time that a developing country had held the Special Olympics World Summer Games and the first time the games had been held in Asia. It boosted the confidence of persons with intellectual disabilities in their efforts to integrate into society, and promoted the Special Olympics in China.

To mark the Shanghai Special Olympics World Summer Games, July 20, the opening day of the event, was designated as the National Special Olympics Day. A volunteer association named "Sunshine Home" was founded in Shanghai to help persons with intellectual disabilities to receive rehabilitative training, educational training, day care, and vocational rehabilitation. Based on this experience, the "Sunshine Home" program was rolled out nationwide to support care centers and households in providing services and help for persons with intellectual or mental disabilities and for the severely disabled.

3. The Beijing 2008 Paralympic Games were delivered to the highest possible standard. In 2008, Beijing hosted the 13th Paralympic Games, attracting 4,032 athletes from 147 countries and regions to compete in 472 events across 20 sports. The number of participating athletes, countries and regions and the number of competition events all hit a record high in the history of the Paralympic Games. The 2008 Paralympic Games made Beijing the first city in the world to bid for and host the Olympic Games and Paralympic Games at the same time; Beijing fulfilled its promise to stage "two games of equal splendor", and delivered a unique Paralympics to the highest possible standards. Its motto of "transcendence, integration and sharing" reflected China's contribution to the values of the international Paralympic Movement. These games have left a rich legacy in sports facilities, urban transport, accessible facilities, and volunteer services, representing a significant advance in China's work for persons with disabilities.

Beijing built a batch of standardized service centers named "Sweet Home" to help the disabled and their families to enjoy access to vocational rehabilitation, educational training, day care, and recreational and sports activities, creating conditions for them to integrate into society on an equal basis.

The public's understanding of provision for the disabled and their sports has increased. The concepts of "equality, participation and sharing" are taking root, while understanding, respecting, helping, and caring for the disabled are becoming the norm in society. China has delivered on its solemn promise to the international community. It has carried on the Olympic spirit of solidarity, friendship and peace, promoted mutual understanding and friendship among peoples of all countries, made the slogan of "One World, One Dream" resonate throughout the world, and won high acclaim from the international community.

4. China is going all out to prepare for the Beijing 2022 Paralympic Winter Games. In 2015, together with Zhangjiakou, Beijing won the bid to host the 2022 Olympic and Paralympic Winter Games. This made the city the first ever to host both the Summer and Winter Paralympics, and created major development opportunities for winter parasports. China committed to organizing a "green, inclusive, open and clean" sports event, and one that is "streamlined, safe and splendid". To this end the country has made every effort to proactively communicate and cooperate with the International Paralympic Committee and other international sports organizations in implementing all the protocols for Covid-19 control and prevention. Detailed preparations have been made for the organization of the Games and the related services, for the application of science and technology and for cultural activities during the Games.

In 2019, Beijing launched a special program to foster a barrier-free environment, focusing on 17 major tasks to rectify problems in key areas such as urban roads, public transport, public services venues, and information exchange. A total of 336,000 facilities and sites have been modified, realizing basic accessibility in the core area of the capital city, making its barrier-free environment more standardized, accomodating and systemic. Zhangjiakou has also actively nurtured a barrier-free environment, leading to a significant improvement in accessibility.

China has established and improved a winter sport system with ice and snow sports as the pillar, to encourage more disabled people to engage in winter sports. The Beijing Paralympic Winter Games will be held from March 4 to 13, 2022. As of February 20, 2022, 647 athletes from 48 countries and regions registered and would be competing in the Games. China is fully prepared to welcome athletes from all around the world to the Games.

5. China actively participates in international parasports. Greater international engagement is allowing China to play an increasingly important role in international parasports. The country has a greater say in relevant affairs, and its influence is growing. Since 1984, China has joined many international sports organizations for persons with disabilities, including the International Paralympic Committee (IPC), International Organizations of Sports for the Disabled (IOSDs), International Blind Sports Federation (IBSA), Cerebral Palsy International Sports and Recreation Association (CPISRA), International Committee of Sports for the Deaf (ICSD), International Wheelchair and Amputee Sports Federation (IWAS), Special Olympics International (SOI), and Far East and South Pacific

Games Federation for the Disabled (FESPIC).

It has established friendly relations with sports organizations for the disabled in numerous countries and regions. The National Paralympic Committee of China (NPCC), China Sports Association for the Deaf, and Special Olympics China have become important members of international organizations of sports for the disabled. China has proactively participated in important conferences on international sports for the disabled, such as the IPC General Assembly, that will chart the future course for development. Chinese parasports officials, referees, and experts have been elected as members of the executive board and special committees of the FESPIC, ICSD, and IBSA. In order to advance sports skills for the disabled, China has recommended and appointed professionals to serve as technical officials and international referees of relevant international sports organizations for the disabled.

6. Extensive international exchanges on parasports have been carried out. China first sent a delegation to the Third FESPIC Games in 1982 – the first time for Chinese athletes with disabilities to compete at an international sporting event. China has actively carried out international exchanges and cooperation on parasports, which are an important component of people-to-people exchanges in bilateral relations and multilateral cooperation mechanisms, including the Belt and Road Initiative and the Forum on China-Africa Cooperation.

In 2017, China hosted the Belt and Road High-level Event on Disability Cooperation and issued an initiative for promoting cooperation and exchanges on disability among Belt and Road countries and other documents, and established a network to cooperate on sharing sports facilities and resources. This includes 45 national-level training centers for summer and winter parasports that are open to athletes and coaches from Belt and Road countries. In 2019, a forum on parasports under the Belt and Road framework was held to promote mutual learning among various sports organizations for persons with disabilities, providing a model for exchanges and cooperation in the field of parasports. That same year, the NPCC signed strategic cooperation agreements with the Paralympic committees of Finland, Russia, Greece and other countries. Meanwhile, a growing number of exchanges on parasports have taken place between China and other countries at city and other local levels.

V. Achievements in Parasports Reflect Improvements in China's Human Rights

The remarkable achievements of parasports in China reflect both the sportsmanship and sporting prowess of the disabled, and the progress China is making in human rights and national development. China adheres to a people-centered approach that treats people's wellbeing as the primary human right, promotes the all-round development of human rights, and effectively protects the rights and interests of vulnerable groups, including persons with disabilities. Participation in sports is an important element of the right to subsistence and development for those with disabilities. The development of parasports accords with China's general development; it effectively responds to the needs of persons with disabilities and promotes their physical and mental health. Parasports are a vivid reflection of the development and progress of human rights in China. They promote the common values of humanity, advance exchanges, understanding and friendship among peoples around the world, and contribute China's wisdom to building a fair, just, reasonable and inclusive global governance order on human rights, and to maintaining world peace and development.

1. China adheres to a people-centered approach and promotes the physical and mental health of persons with disabilities. China upholds a people-centered approach in protecting human rights, and protects rights and interests of persons with disabilities through development. The country has included programs for persons with disabilities in its development strategies and achieved the goal of "building a moderately prosperous society in all respects, leaving no one behind, including persons with disabilities". Sports are an effective means of boosting people's health and meeting their desire for a better life. For those with disabilities, participating in sports can help build up fitness and mitigate and remove functional impairment. It can increase the individual's capacity to self-support, to pursue interests and hobbies, to increase social interaction, to improve life quality, and to achieve their life's potential.

China attaches great importance to protecting the right to health of persons with disabilities and emphasizes that "every disabled person should have access to rehabilitation services". Sports for the disabled have been incorporated into rehabilitation services. Governments at all levels have explored new ways of serving persons with disabilities at the grassroots, and carried out extensive rehabilitation and fitness activities by way of sports. In schools, students with disabilities have been guaranteed equal participation in sports in a bid to ensure their physical and mental health and promote their sound growth. The disabled have a stronger guarantee of the right to health through physical activities.

2. China upholds equality and integration for persons with disabilities in the context of the national conditions. China always applies the principle of universality of human rights in the context of the national conditions, and firmly believes that the rights to subsistence and development are the primary and basic human rights. Improving people's wellbeing, making sure that they are the masters of the country, and promoting their all-round development are key goals, and China works hard to uphold social equality and justice.

Chinese laws and regulations stipulate that persons with disabilities are entitled to equal participation in cultural and sport activities. In consequence, the disabled enjoy stronger protection of rights and are rendered special assistance. China has built and improved public sport facilities, provided related services, and ensured equal public sport services for persons with disabilities. It has also adopted other vigorous measures to create an accessible environment in sports – renovating sports venues and facilities to make them more accessible for the disabled, upgrading and opening stadiums and gymnasiums to all disabled people, providing necessary support in the convenient use of these facilities, and eliminating external barriers hindering their full participation in sports.

Sports events such as the Beijing Paralympic Games have led to greater participation of the disabled in social activities, not only in sports but also in economic, social, cultural and environmental affairs, and in urban and regional development. Major parasports venues across China continue to serve the disabled after the events are over, becoming a model for barrier-free urban development.

In order to raise the participation of the disabled in community art and sport activities, local authorities have also improved community parasports facilities, nurtured and supported their sport and art organizations, purchased diverse social services, and hosted sport activities involving both the disabled and those in good health. Relevant organizations and agencies have developed and popularized small-scale rehabilitation and fitness equipment suited to local conditions and customized for persons with various types of disability. They have also created and provided popular programs and methods.

The disabled can fully participate in sports in order to explore the limits of their potential and break through boundaries. Through unity and hard work, they can enjoy equality and participation and a successful life. Parasports promote traditional Chinese cultural values such as harmony, inclusion, cherishing life, and helping the weak, and inspire many more persons with disabilities to develop a passion for parasports and begin to participate. Demonstrating self-esteem, confidence, independence, and strength, they carry forward the spirit of China's sports. Showcasing their vitality and character through sports, they better secure their rights to equality and participation in society.

3. China attaches equal importance to all human rights to achieve all-round development for persons with disabilities. Parasports are a mirror reflecting the living standards and human rights of persons with disabilities. China guarantees their economic, political, social and cultural rights, laying a solid foundation for them to participate in sports, be active in other fields, and achieve all-round development. While building whole-process people's democracy, China has solicited suggestions from the disabled, their representatives, and their organizations, to make the national sports system more equal and inclusive.

Numerous services for persons with disabilities have been strengthened and improved: social security, welfare services, education, the right to employment, public legal services, protection of their personal and property rights, and efforts to eliminate discrimination. Outstanding athletes in the field of parasports are regularly commended, as are individuals and organizations contributing to the development of parasports.

Publicity to promote parasports has been intensified, spreading new concepts and trends through various channels and means, and creating a favorable social environment. The general public has gained a deeper understanding of the Paralympic values of "courage, determination, inspiration and equality". They endorse the ideas of equality, integration, and elimination of barriers, take a greater interest in undertakings concerning persons with disabilities, and offer their support.

There is wide social participation in events such as Fitness Week for Persons with Disabilities, Cultural Week for Persons with Disabilities, National Special Olympic Day, and Winter Sports Season for Persons with Disabilities. Activities such as sponsorship, volunteer services and cheering squads support and encourage persons with disabilities to take part in sports and share the benefits brought by social progress.

Parasports have helped to create a milieu encouraging society as a whole to better respect and guarantee the inherent dignity and equal rights of persons with disabilities. In so doing they have made an effective contribution to social progress.

4. China encourages international cooperation and exchanges in parasports. China upholds mutual learning and exchanges between civilizations, and regards parasports as a major part of international exchanges among the disabled. As a major sport power, China plays a growing role in international parasports affairs, vigorously promoting the development of parasports in the region and the world at large.

The boom in parasports in China is the result of the country's active implementation of the *Convention on the Rights of Persons with Disabilities*, and the UN 2030 Agenda for Sustainable Development. China respects diversity in other countries' cultural, sport and social systems, and promotes equality and justice in international sport activities and rules. It has made unconditional donations to the Development Fund for the International Paralympic Committee, and it has built a sports infrastructure and resource-sharing mechanism, and opened its national parasports training centers to disabled athletes and coaches from other countries.

China encourages persons with disabilities to engage in widespread international sport activities, so as to expand people-to-people exchanges, enhance mutual understanding and connectivity, bring people of various countries closer, achieve fairer, more rational and inclusive global human rights governance, and promote world peace and development.

China upholds humanism and internationalism, emphasizes that all those with disabilities are equal members of the human family, and promotes international parasports cooperation and exchanges. This contributes to mutual learning through exchanges between civilizations, and to the building of a global community of shared future.

Conclusion

The care that is provided for the disabled is a marker of social progress. Developing parasports plays a vital role in encouraging persons with disabilities to build self-esteem, confidence, independence, and strength, and pursue self-improvement. It carries forward the spirit of continuous self-renewal and creates an atmosphere that encourages the whole of society to understand, respect, care for and support disabled people and their cause. It encourages people to work together to promote the all-round development and common prosperity of the disabled.

Since the founding of the PRC, and especially following the 18th CPC National Congress, China has made remarkable progress in parasports. At the same time, it should be noted that progress remains imbalanced and inadequate. There is a huge gap between different regions and between rural and urban areas, and the capacity to provide services remains insufficient. The rate of participation in rehabilitation, fitness and sport activities needs to be increased, and winter parasports should be further popularized. There is much more work yet to be done in further developing parasports.

Under the strong leadership of the CPC Central Committee with Xi Jinping at the core, the Party and the Chinese government will continue to uphold the people-centered development philosophy in building China into a modern socialist country in all respects. They will spare no effort to provide assistance to vulnerable groups, ensure that the disabled enjoy equal rights, and improve their wellbeing and their self-development skills. Concrete measures will be taken to respect and protect disabled people's rights and interests, including the right to participate in sports, in order to promote the cause of persons with disabilities and meet their expectations for a better life.

Youth of China in the New Era

The State Council Information Office of
the People's Republic of China

April 2022

Preamble

Youth is the most active and vital force in society. The hopes of a country and the future of a nation lie in the hands of its young generation. Young Chinese have always played a vanguard role in the quest for national rejuvenation.

After 1840, China was gradually reduced to a semi-colonial, semi-feudal society and suffered enormous hardships. The country endured intense humiliation, the people were subjected to great pain, and China's civilization was plunged into darkness. China's youth gradually came to recognize the mounting national crisis.

The enlightenment of its youth lit a beacon of hope for the rejuvenation of the Chinese nation. Around the May Fourth Movement in 1919, a large number of aspiring and progressive young intellectuals assumed the lead in accepting new ideas, new culture, and new knowledge. After careful consideration they chose to follow Marxism-Leninism, which led to a widespread awakening of the people and the nation for the first time since the Opium War. In July 1921, 13 delegates, of an average age of only 28, participated in the first National Congress of the Communist Party of China (CPC) and announced the founding of the Party, an epoch-making event that sounded the clarion call for the awakening and rise of the nation. This marked the beginning of a new era of national rejuvenation for China. Under the CPC's leadership, the Communist Youth League of China (CYLC) was established in 1922, opening a new chapter of the Chinese youth movement.

Looking back on a century of relentless change, China's youth have never wavered in their determination to love the Party, the country and the people, nor in their commitment to the original aspiration of following the instructions and guidance of the Party. During the New Democratic Revolution (1919-1949), they rose to the occasion without fear of death and fought bravely for national independence and the people's liberation. During the socialist revolution and reconstruction (1949-1978), they endured hardships and dedicated themselves to building the newly-founded country. In the new period of reform, opening up and socialist modernization, those with a talent for innovation who were open to challenges stood out and forged ahead, led reform, and ensured that China progressed with the times.

The 18th CPC National Congress held in 2012 marks the beginning of a new era in the development of socialism with Chinese characteristics. The CPC Central Committee with Comrade Xi Jinping at its core attaches great importance to young people, and cares deeply about them, and fully trusts them. It is committed to the principle that the Party exercises leadership over youth, gives top priority to youth development, and ensures the CYLC plays its role to the full as an aide to the Party and a reserve force. This will enable the younger generations to develop fully and achieve historic progress. In this great new era, China's youth have shown amazing vibrancy and great passion.

Young Chinese people in the new era are confident, aspirant and responsible. They wholeheartedly support the leadership of the Party. With a global vision, they stand at the forefront of the times bursting with commitment: pursuing lofty ideals with a firm belief in Marxism, communism and socialism with Chinese characteristics; full of patriotism, sharing weal and woe with the country and the people; displaying the sterling quality of living up to responsibilities; being the first in the country to worry about the affairs of the state and the last to enjoy themselves; striving to be pioneers in, pacesetters for and contributors to the country's development.

History shows clearly that without the CPC, the Chinese youth movement would have achieved little. For China's youth, commitment to the CPC is the most valuable experience, and the revolutionary traditions passed down are the most precious wealth accumulated over the past century.

In his speech addressing a ceremony celebrating the CPC centenary on July 1, 2021, Xi Jinping, general secretary of the CPC Central Committee, emphasized that "In the new era, our young people should make it their mission to contribute to national rejuvenation and aspire to become more proud, confident, and assured in their identity as Chinese people, so that they can live up to the promise of their youth and the expectations of our times, our Party and our people."

We have stood at a new historical starting point and embarked on a new journey in achieving the rejuvenation of the Chinese nation. Looking ahead to the new era, China's youth are embracing precious opportunities to realize their ambitions and display their talents, as they shoulder the important responsibility of building a great modern socialist country and realizing the Chinese Dream of national rejuvenation.

The Chinese Dream is a dream about history, the present and the future. It is cherished by all of the people, but even more so by the young. China's youth in the new era will keep on striving with boundless energy, to turn the Chinese Dream of national rejuvenation into reality.

In order to fully showcase the vigorous image and the invaluable contribution of China's youth in the new era, China is releasing this white paper on the occasion of the 100th anniversary of the founding of the CYLC.

I. The New Era: Great Times with Ample Opportunities

Great times make fine young people and flourishing ages nurture true talent. The Chinese nation has achieved a tremendous transformation from obtaining independence and becoming prosperous to growing in strength, and the current new era bestows prosperity and hope. China's rejuvenation has become an unstoppable process.

Living in the best times in Chinese history, the current young generation enjoys an enabling environment for development, a broad space to grow, and wonderful opportunities to make a good career.

(1) Better Conditions for Development

China's economic and technological influence and composite national strength keep growing, which offers a sound foundation for China's youth to develop with increasing confidence.

Better material conditions. Affluence provides a good foundation for the young generation to develop and grow.

China has achieved two miracles – rapid economic growth and lasting social stability. In 2021, its economy ranked second in the world in size, with GDP exceeding 110 trillion yuan. As more than 25 million young people have escaped poverty, this generation can look forward to a better future of greater prosperity.

In pursuing a life of high quality, young people are changing their consumption habits from consuming mass products and services to customized ones. They are changing from buying to meet their basic needs to buying to enjoy life, from having clothing to wear to dressing fashionably, from having food to eat to eating well for good health, and from taking affordable transportation to choosing fast and comfortable vehicles. Their standard of living has seen qualitative changes and their prospects for development are supported by a solid material foundation.

Greater space for rich intellectual and cultural life. A rich and colorful intellectual and cultural life is a precondition for young people to prosper and grow.

With a growing number of libraries, museums, cultural centers, art galleries and other public cultural facilities being built,[1] young people now enjoy notably improved public cultural services. Instead of feeling amazed at any new place they visit, they are getting used to visiting all kinds of places, thus refining their cultural tastes. Through the buoyant growth of traditional cultural industries such as publishing, television, movies, and artistic performance, and emerging cultural sectors such as the digital creative industry, online audio and visual, digital publishing, digital entertainment and online performance and broadcasting, young people now find diverse public cultural products available to them. Instead of reading and watching whatever they could get hold of, they can read and watch whatever they would like, thus broadening their vision. As a huge variety of tourist products are created for them to choose, such as cultural tours, countryside tours, CPC heritage tours and international travel packages, their desire to travel around the world is now satisfied. Instead of affordable sightseeing trips near their homes, they can travel anywhere they wish, thus enriching their knowledge and experience. These expanding intellectual and cultural spaces offer greater possibilities for young Chinese to achieve more, set lofty goals, and refine their tastes.

Growing with the internet. The internet has profoundly shaped the current generation, and the current generation has also influenced the internet.

---

[1] By the end of 2020, the number of registered museums had reached 5,788 across the country, with one new museum being opened every two days on average during the period 2016-2020.

At the end of 2020, the number of netizens aged 6 to 18 reached 180 million in China, with the internet available to 94.9 percent of minors, and the gap in internet accessibility between cities and rural areas narrowed to 0.3 percentage point from 5.4 percentage points in 2018. The internet has become the "sixth sense" of contemporary young people and part of their lives, and offers them a space to grow.

Along with rapid popularization of the internet, more and more young people are using the internet to access information, exchange ideas, make friends, and shop, and their ways of learning, living and working are changing profoundly. Young people make up the majority of the users of short online videos, live-streaming viewers, and ride-hailing customers. As they become the main producers of information, consumers of servic-es, and promoters of technologies related to cyberspace, they are exerting

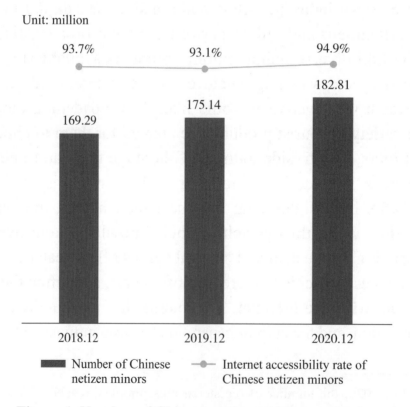

Figure 1. Number of Chinese netizen minors and internet accessibility rate from 2018 to 2020

a tremendous influence on internet trends. In a complex online environment, young people are spreading positive energy and shaping new social trends in an effort to ensure a clean cyberspace.

(2) More Opportunities to Fulfill Potential

Only when the country prospers can its young people prosper. With rapid economic and social development, young people in China in the new era have access to better opportunities for development and a growing stage on which to fulfill their potential.

Equal access to education. Young people in China enjoy more equal and higher-quality educational opportunities as the country continues giving high priority to education. In 2021, the completion rate of compulsory education in China reached 95.4 percent, the gross enrollment rate in senior secondary education reached 91.4 percent, and the gross enrollment rate in higher education reached 57.8 percent, with 44.3 million students on campus, ranking first in the world. More and more young people have stepped onto this important path to success and excellence.

The country has established and been improving the system of financial aid to students, which offers full coverage from preschool to postgraduate education. By 2020, subsidies had totaled over 240 billion yuan and assisted nearly 150 million students, achieving full coverage from preschool education, compulsory education, and senior secondary education to undergraduate and postgraduate education, across public and privately-run schools, and for all students from families with financial difficulties. The right of particular groups to receive compulsory education and their interests have been well protected, including children living in cities with their parents who are migrant workers, and students from rural and poor areas. In 2020, 85.8 percent of children living in cities with migrant worker parents studied in public schools or filled the slots purchased by the government in privately-run schools. From 2012 to 2021, more than 820,000 students from rural and poor areas were enrolled in key universities through special enrollment plans. More young people have thus

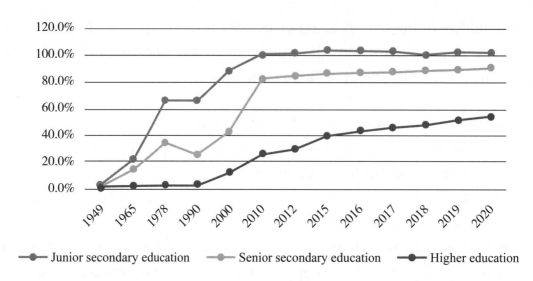

Figure 2. Gross enrollment rate in junior secondary education, senior secondary education, and higher education in China from 1949 to 2020

been granted equal opportunities to receive better education, which prevents poverty from passing down from one generation to the next.

Diverse career options. The career choices of young people in China are increasingly diverse and market-oriented, and made, more often than not, on their own. Young people now look beyond a stable lifelong job in the traditional sense, and non-public economic entities and new social organizations are gradually becoming their main channels for employment. The options of "either workers or farmers" are a thing of the past, and the tertiary industry has become an important gathering place for the young workforce. In 2020, the tertiary industry employed 47.7 percent of those in employment across the country, up 13.1 percentage points from a decade ago. In particular, new and rapidly-rising industries and new business forms have given birth to a large number of new career options, such as esports players, live-streaming hosts, and web writers, and engaged a large number of young people in flexible employment, such as parcel and food couriers. There have emerged what they call "*Slash*" people with multiple titles, jobs, and ways of working and living. All these have testified to the greater range of opportunities and choices available to young people as times change.

Unimpeded mobility and more development opportunities. As the socialist market economy develops, the vitality of market players increases, and various factors of production flow more easily, young people enjoy more development opportunities and greater mobility. With the extension of the strategy for coordinated regional development, young people in China, who used to flock to economically developed southern and eastern regions of the country, have gradually diversified the target cities where they seek development opportunities and where they can fit in and thrive. Many young people from rural areas settle down and realize dreams in cities through hard work. In 2020, the number of migrant workers reached nearly 170 million and most of them were young people. Young permanent urban residents accounted for 71.1 percent of the total young population in the country, 15.3 percentage points higher than ten years ago and 7.2 percentage points higher than that of the permanent urban residents in the country's total population. More young people are making their homes in the city and leaping forward in development through urbanization.

(3) More All-round Protection and Support

The development of young people calls for strong protection and support of the state. As fairness and justice in society have steadily improved and people's rights and interests have been effectively safeguarded, young people in China in the new era can grow and prosper in a better legal environment and enjoy stronger policy support, more reliable social security, and greater care from a range of organizations.

Better legal protection. With progress in the rule of law in all respects, the system of the socialist rule of law with Chinese characteristics is steadily improving, providing strong protection for young people to develop. As the fundamental law of the country, China's Constitution clearly stipulates that "the state shall foster the all-round moral, intellectual and physical development of young adults, youths and children", which has laid a basic foundation for a legal framework to protect youth development. The youth development involves a wide range of areas and requires highly systematic, concerted efforts from all sectors. The Civil Code stipulates various civil rights and interests of young people. Laws including the *Education Law, Compulsory Education Law, Vocational Education Law, Higher Education Law, Law on the Promotion of Privately-run Schools*, and *Family Education Promotion Law*, among others, have prescribed a sound legal environment to ensure young people their right to education. Laws including the *Employment Promotion Law, Labor Law, Labor Contract Law, Social Insurance Law, Law on Scientific and Technological Progress, Law on Population and Family Planning, Law on Physical Culture and Sports*, and *Law on the Protection of Rights and Interests of Women* have effectively safeguarded the rights and interests of young people in various fields. Laws including the *Criminal Law, Law on the Protection of Minors, Law on the Prevention of Juvenile Delinquency,* and *Anti-Domestic Violence Law* have helped build a legal shield protecting the legitimate rights and interests of young people.

More considerate policy support. China has made policies and improved its policy system to cater to the diverse needs of young people in the country. Considerations for young people have been clearly embodied in the 13th and 14th Five-year Plans for National Economic and Social Development, and the needs of young people have been given particular attention when putting in place major national strategies, such as the strategy for invigorating China through science and education, the strategy on developing a quality workforce, the innovation-driven development strategy, the rural revitalization strategy, and the Healthy China initiative. Increasing attention and support have been given to young people in top-level design. In April 2017, the CPC Central Committee and the State Council issued the Middle- and Long-term Youth Development Plan (2016-2025), the first national-level plan directed towards young people in the history of the People's Republic of China, providing fundamental policy guidance for young people in China to grow and develop in the new era. The Party and the government have paid close attention to issues of immediate concern to young people in areas including job-hunting after graduation, innovation and entrepreneurship, social integration, dating and marriage, support for the elderly, and children's education. A series of policies and measures have been introduced, and the building of youth-development-friendly cities is in full swing, with the concept of prioritizing young people growing in popularity. Now, a basic mechanism

Panel 1　Middle- and Long-term Youth Development Plan (2016-2025)	
中长期青年发展规划 （2016—2025年） 人 民 出 版 社	**Overall Objectives** By 2020, a preliminary policy system and work mechanism for youth development with Chinese characteristics will be in place. The theoretical and political literacy of the vast number of youth, and their all-round development will be further improved. They will have the opportunity to play a full role as a new driving force and pioneer in securing a decisive victory in building a moderately prosperous society in all respects. By 2025, the policy system and work mechanism for youth development with Chinese characteristics will be more developed. The young people will have greater theoretical and political literacy, significantly upgrade their all-round development, and they will grow into a generation with high aspirations, moral integrity, professional competence, a good sense and a broad mind, and an enterprising spirit who can shoulder the important responsibility of realizing the Chinese Dream of national rejuvenation.

Areas of Youth Development	Key Projects
Theoretical Literacy and Moral Standards Education Health Dating and Marriage Employment and Entrepreneurship Culture Social Integration and Engagement Safeguarding Legitimate Rights and Interests Preventing Juvenile Delinquency Social Security	Young Marxists Training Project Youth Core Socialist Values Study Project Youth Physical Health Improvement Project Youth Internship Plan Youth Choicest Cultural Works Project Youth Internet Civilization Development Project Young Chinese Volunteer Campaign Youth Ethnic Unity and Progress Promotion Project

for youth work from the central level to the local level has been generally put in place, and a preliminary policy system for youth development with Chinese characteristics has taken shape. Young people have been benefiting from the policies fully and they feel that they have been taken care of and their important needs are being addressed.

Improved social security services. As China has built the largest social security system in the world and further developed inclusive social security services, young people in China are shielded by social security when they enter the workforce, and free from various worries when pursuing their dreams. They can therefore live a more comfortable life, feel more at ease at work, and have greater confidence about the future. The government has introduced a series of policies to support flexible employment through multiple channels, gradually improved the social security services for those engaged in such employment, and supported young people in taking up flexible jobs. Housing supply for young people has been increased, and more big cities have increased the supply of government-subsidized rental housing for new urban residents and young people, mitigating housing problems for young people. The country is working towards an integrated national scheme for basic old-age insurance, and will continue to expand the coverage of such insurance policies as unemployment insurance and work-related injury insurance to young working population. Young people are better protected by the social security system.

Strong institutional safeguards and support. Organizations help young people grow and develop. As a CPC-led people's organization composed of progressive young people, the CYLC has always prioritized safeguarding the rights and interests of young people, and their development opportunities. It has earnestly advocated the idea of prioritizing youth development, made full use of its organizational strengths and vigorously mobilized social resources to carry out policy advocacy on the pressing difficulties and problems that are of the greatest concern to young people. It has been doing its best to address specific problems by every means possible to create a good environment for young people to grow and develop. As one of the basic people's organizations under the leadership of the CPC, the All-China Youth Federation has always represented and safeguarded the legitimate rights and interests of young people of all ethnic groups and all sectors of society, guided them in their active and healthy participation in public activities, and worked hard to help them healthily grow and prosper. As a federative body of student unions and graduate student unions at universities and colleges and student unions at secondary schools under the leadership of the CPC, the All-China Students' Federation has voiced and safeguarded the specific interests of young students in accordance with the law and the Constitution of the Federation, and organized healthy, positive, and colorful extracurricular and community service activities to help them grow and develop.

Panel 2 Project Hope

Project Hope, launched by the Central Committee of the Communist Youth League of China and implemented by the China Youth Development Foundation, is a social public welfare undertaking whose mission is to improve basic education facilities in poor areas and help children in poor areas who have dropped out of school to return. As of the end of 2021, Project Hope nationwide had received 19.42 billion yuan in donations, provided financial aid to 6.63 million students from families with financial difficulties, and helped build 20,878 Hope primary schools.

Upholding the tradition of financially aiding students and helping them grow and develop, Project Hope has launched programs in five major areas – financial aid, health protection, skills training, funding asistance, and integrity – and implemented public welfare programs such as building Hope Kitchens in schools in poor rural areas and organizing field trips to sites of significance in early CPC history, effectively promoting education in poor areas and assisting young people from poor families to grow.

In 2019, the 30th anniversary of Project Hope, General Secretary Xi Jinping spoke highly of its important role in alleviating poverty, promoting education, helping young people grow and develop, and leading the trend for positive social activities. Xi emphasized the need to manage Project Hope effectively in order to provide young people with new support and hope, so that they may experience the loving care of the Party and of the big socialist family.

II. All-Round Development in the New Era

Hard work builds ability, and adversity builds resilience. In the new era, China's youth actively study the theory and practice of science and other knowledge and skills, improving their physical and moral qualities and their all-round ability. They are growing into a new generation that is capable of shouldering the responsibility of national rejuvenation.

(1) Firmer in Ideals and Convictions

Ideals provide direction in life, and convictions determine the success of a cause. In the new era, young Chinese should hold lofty ideals and be firm in their convictions, which are fundamental to their success, and they should strive to become aspiring young people, living up to the expectations of the Party, the country and the people.

Confidence in the Chinese path. Through comparison with the past and the rest of the world, and through social observation and hands-on practice, young Chinese keenly understand the importance of the Party's leadership and leader's guidance, the merits of the socialist system, and the strength of the people. A youth survey conducted in 2020 demonstrated that the majority of China's youth wholeheartedly support socialism with Chinese characteristics, and are full of confidence about the rejuvenation of the Chinese nation.

Under the guidance of Xi Jinping Thought on Socialism with Chinese Characteristics for a New Era, they have learned about China's speed, the China miracle, and the governance of China through vivid examples and objective data showcasing the country's achievements, and through their own personal experience. They become prouder to be a member of the Chinese nation, and are more determined to join forces

Panel 3　Young Marxists Training Project (YMTP)

Launched in 2007, the YMTP aims to train young political workers for the Party with firm beliefs, outstanding capability, sound character, and solid working practices. In 2013, it was incorporated into the Marxist Theory Research and Development Project of the CPC Central Committee. In 2017, it was listed as one of the 10 key projects of the Middle- and Long-term Youth Development Plan (2016-2025). In 2020, the Central Committee of the Communist Youth League of China released the *Opinions on Further Implementing the Young Marxists Training Project*, in cooperation with the Ministry of Education, the Ministry of Civil Affairs, the Ministry of Agriculture and Rural Affairs, and the State-owned Assets Supervision and Administration Commission of the State Council.

Currently, a YMTP network has been set up at the county, city and provincial levels, which covers institutions of higher learning, state-owned enterprises, rural areas, and social organizations, as well as people engaging in work related to Young Pioneers. The major part of the project involves the study of theory, revolutionary education, and training in practical circumstances. The project aims to nurture a large base of Marxists armed with the latest achievements in adapting Marxism to the Chinese context, and to prepare the younger generations for carrying forward the socialist cause.

Training for colleges and universities: highlighting political and theoretical training for college students.

Training for state-owned enterprises: enhancing political training for youth in these enterprises.

Training for rural areas: zooming in on the rural revitalization strategy to cultivate youth who are well versed in agriculture, love the rural areas, and value rural workers, and to make them a major force in rural governance.

Training for social organizations: highlighting instruction in politics and values for youth in these organizations.

Training for people engaging in work related to Young Pioneers: improving the political ability of Young Pioneers counsellors.

As of the end of 2021, the project had trained nearly 3 million people.

and achieve the Chinese Dream – the rejuvenation of the Chinese nation.

Commitment to core socialist values. The value orientation of youth will decide the values of the whole of society. Young Chinese learn morals and values from heroes and role models of our times. They proactively uphold and promote core socialist values – prosperity, democracy, civility, harmony, freedom, equality, justice, the rule of law, patriotism, dedication, good faith and amity. A large number of outstanding youth have become role models for others to emulate, including more than 1,500 youth who have been awarded the China Youth May 4th Medal, and Excellent Communist Youth League Members at various levels. More than 20,000 young people have been honored as Positive and Kind Youth for exuding positive youthful energy. Although sometimes confused by exchanges, mingling and clashes of ideas, young Chinese always love the Party and the country sincerely, and continue to pursue their lofty values and ideals.

Stronger cultural confidence. Culture is the soul of a nation, and strong cultural confidence is a vital foundation for realizing national rejuvenation. China's youth draw nutrients from the best of China's traditional culture, revolutionary culture, and advanced socialist culture, and gain strength from the time-honored Chinese civilization.

A youth survey in 2020 showed that more than 80 percent of the respondents believed that the reason for the enthusiasm for Sinology among youth and adolescents is that "Chinese citizens have begun to pay attention to the innate value of traditional culture". Young people have switched from coveting foreign brands to preferring national ones, from wearing Western attire to wearing traditional costumes, and from favoring Western dance styles to traditional Chinese ones. Young Chinese identify more and more with the splendors of Chinese civilization. They are deeply proud of the Chinese nation, and are more active in promoting traditional Chinese culture and boosting cultural confidence across society.

(2) Better Physical and Mental Health

The key to China's development lies in the younger generations. A strong body and mind are important for the healthy development of young people. Chinese youth in the new era are of the highest caliber. This is first reflected in their sound physical and mental health, which sustain them in trials and tribulations.

Improved physical health. In schools, as the class hours for physical education continue to increase, students study academic courses in class, and engage in physical activities on the playground. More than 37 million rural students receiving compulsory education have benefited from the student nutrition improvement program, and their physical health has markedly improved. In 2018, 92 percent of students aged between 14 and 19 passed the physical fitness test, and the proportion of those rated good or excellent increased substantially.

In communities, young people participate actively in mass sports. Running, swimming and ball games are popular. Sport and fitness venues are crowded. The Beijing Olympic Winter Games have boosted young people's enthusiasm for winter sports in China. Youth aged 18 to 30 are the main force in winter sports, with the participation rate reaching 37.3 percent, the highest among all age groups.

In competitive sports arenas, especially in international events such as the Olympic Games and the Asian Games, Chinese youth have taken golds and silvers inspired by the Chinese Women's Volleyball Team known for its unyielding spirit, living up to the new Olympic motto "Faster, Higher, Stronger – Together". They have manifested the vigorous spirit of the Chinese nation. Chinese youth enjoy, value, and participate in sports, becoming an active force in building a country strong in sports.

Confidence and optimism. Young Chinese begin by doing small things around them, then work hard to turn their firm ideals and convictions, sound values, and strong cultural confidence into a healthy social mindset. Although they are under significant pressure in terms of employment, education, housing, dating and marriage, and often have to take

> **Panel 4   Nutrition Improvement Program for Rural Students in Compulsory Education**
>
> In 2011, China launched a program to improve the nutrition of rural students in compulsory education. The central government paid three yuan per day (which was increased to five yuan per day from the fall semester of 2021) as a nutrition subsidy to every rural student in compulsory education. As of the end of 2020, 1,732 counties in 28 provinces had implemented the nutrition improvement program, covering 131,600 rural schools, benefiting almost 38 million students. In the past 10 years, both the nutrition and the health of students in underdeveloped rural areas have improved remarkably, as has their physical fitness. The rate of students passing the physical fitness test has gone up from 70.3 percent in 2012 to 86.7 percent now. The rates of malnutrition and underweight have plummeted, and average height and weight have increased measurably. These have laid a good foundation for the continuous improvement of young people's health.

care of elderly family members, yet with care and support from the Party, government and society, they rise up to the challenge.

A 2021 questionnaire on the emotions of China's young people showed that 88 percent of the respondents believed that they were capable of managing their emotions. China's mainstream youth are confident about their future, and dream of and pursue a beautiful life. Confidence, optimism and self-motivation are their salient characteristics.

(3) Stronger Intellectual Foundations

Knowledge can shape one's future and education may change one's life. As China makes headway with its education programs, the younger generations have borne witness to and benefited from the historic progress. They have received a better education on a fairer footing; their enthusiasm for learning keeps growing and their scientific and cultural achievements have flourished.

A much better education. Thanks to the strategy for invigorating

China through science and education and the strategy on developing a quality workforce, hundreds of millions of young Chinese have been provided with opportunities to tap their potential and hone their talents through education. This has enabled them to create a better life and realize their value.

Take 2020 for example. The new additions to the workforce that year had an average education of 13.8 years, 1.1 years more than a decade earlier. More than 50 percent of employees with college or higher education were young people while young employees accounted for only 30 percent of the total workforce. Receiving higher and better education is still one of the best ways for young Chinese to shape their future, realize their dreams, and attain their ideals.

Learning is becoming popular. More and more young people take delight in learning and make it part of their everyday life, fostering a positive atmosphere of self-improvement through continuous learning.

A large number of young graduates pursue advanced studies after leaving school. In 2020, the number of adults receiving continuing on-campus education exceeded 7.7 million and more than 8.4 million people

---

Panel 5   "Challenge Cup" National Contest of Extracurricular Academic Sci-Tech Projects by College Students

This is a national contest initiated by renowned universities and the press and jointly sponsored by the Central Committee of the CYLC, China Association for Science and Technology, Ministry of Education, All-China Students' Federation and the government of the host location.

Since the first event in 1989, these contests have been organized on the theme of "respect for science, pursuing truth, working hard, rising to the challenge, and innovating". The events have promoted the growth of young innovative talent, helped improve well-rounded higher education, and advanced economic and social development. They exert extensive influence among college students and wider society.

received online college education. Enthusiasm for on-the-job training is also very high. Surveys show that more than half of young workers have taken vocational training, choosing to add to their knowledge base after work. Thanks to the fast-growing network media, they have more study choices available: through MOOC (massive open online courses) for instance.

(4) Active Participation in Social Activities

Society offers an important space for young people to learn and practice skills. The younger generations of the new era have actively adapted to and integrated with society with more confidence and kept pace with social progress, displaying an acute sense of participation in society and the skills required, and acting as advocates and creators of positive energy.

Participation in political activities in an orderly manner. The younger generations are actively involved in politics and in China's application of whole-process people's democracy. Inspired by the lofty ideals of communism, they work hard and forge ahead, and an increasing number of them have applied to join the CPC and CYLC organizations.

By June 2021, the CPC had nearly 24 million members under the age of 35, accounting for 25 percent of its total membership. More than 80 percent of the CPC members admitted each year since the Party's 18th National Congress in 2012 were under 35. The number of CYLC members (age range: 14-28) almost reached 74 million at the end of 2021.

A large number of young people have served as deputies to the people's congresses or as members of the Chinese People's Political Consultative Conference (CPPCC) committees at all levels. Through these organizations they have performed their duties and participated in the deliberation and administration of state affairs. In 2019, young people accounted for 10.9 percent of the deputies to the county-level people's congresses and 13.7 percent of the county-level CPPCC committees. Young people are active participants in democratic elections, decision-making, management and oversight, making suggestions on major issues relating to economic and social development, and exercising their democratic rights and engaging in consultation to reach agreement on issues concerning youth.

Active participation in social programs. In recent years, a growing number of young people have taken part in charity and public-welfare activities, providing services in the communities, protecting the eco-environment, conducting cultural programs, and offering elderly care and assistance to people with disabilities. While playing an important role in influential social organizations, they have also set up self-management and self-service bodies.

At present, there are more than 7,600 county-level organizations of volunteers or artistic and sports organizations for young people, which are operating under the guidance of the CYLC. With these as the driver, more than 150,000 youth organizations have been set up, covering all counties. Through such organizations, young people have played a constructive role in providing many public services on behalf of the government, enforcing industrial discipline, meeting diverse public needs for services, leading socially conscious lifestyles, and promoting communication between the public and the government. All of this displays their strong sense of participation and social responsibility.

III. Shouldering Heavy Tasks and Responsibilities

The new era of socialism with Chinese characteristics is a grand stage on which young people can enjoy bright prospects and accomplish great things. In the new era, China's youth are striving to support high-quality economic growth, participate in the development of socialist democratic politics, create a flourishing socialist culture, promote socialist moral and ethical progress, and build a beautiful China. They are working hard and forging ahead boldly on this new quest to realize the second centenary goal of building a modern socialist country.

(1) Dedicated in Grassroots Work Posts

In the new era, respecting the PRC's great tradition of "perpetual struggle", treating their grassroots work posts as a stage to realize the value of their life, and applying their diligence, young Chinese are working for social progress and striving for happiness, national rejuvenation, and a bright future for the country.

Young people work in various fields – conventional fields such as industry, agriculture, commerce and the military, as well as in science, education, culture, health, and sports, and now in internet-based new business models, areas and occupations. Through their hard work in their grassroots work posts, they have turned the ordinary into the extraordinary, and make the impossible achievable.

In factory workshops, young workers hone their skills and strive for excellence. They tighten every screw and weld every joint to perfection. They vie to be "young people who excel at their jobs" and they help "made-in-China" gain a competitive edge in the global market. In rural areas, young farmers cultivate the fields meticulously, increase grain yield and field fertility with technology, and work hard to ensure food security. On construction sites, young migrant workers painstakingly work all hours of the day and night to build skyscrapers, making the city more beautiful. At training venues, young athletes train hard and persevere in spite of all difficulties. With sporting prowess and indomitable spirit, they strive for Olympic games medals and see China's national flag being raised at the awards ceremony. In city streets, couriers and takeaway delivery riders brave wind and rain to pass on happiness and warmth. Their sweat and toil demonstrate that Chinese youth have not forgotten the hard times, even though they now live in better days and no longer need to worry about food and clothing. They work hard and shine in their grassroots posts.

(2) Leading the Charge in Difficult Situations and Emergencies

In the new era China's youth have shown no fear of difficulties and hardships in times of crisis, displaying their grit at critical moments. They rise to the occasion whenever the country and the people need them; they shoulder their responsibilities, make selfless contributions, and press ahead with the intrepidity typical of their generation.

Young people stand at the forefront in major projects emblematic of China's composite national strength and national pride, in catastrophic natural disasters, and in other emergencies.

Youth teams have played a prominent role in the strategic projects that transport natural gas and electricity from western to eastern regions, divert water from the south to the north, and channel computing resources from the east to the west, as well as the construction of many milestone facilities, including the Hong Kong-Zhuhai-Macao Bridge, Beijing Daxing International Airport, and Hualong One nuclear generator.

During the Covid-19 pandemic, young people have been risking their lives to combat this deadly disease. More than 5.5 million of them in 320,000 task groups have worked on the front lines of this combat, providing

Panel 6　Youth Task Group

The first youth task group in China, consisting of 18 CYLC members, was established in Beijing in 1954. Under the leadership of the CPC and with the organizing and support of the CYLC, many more emerged in the following decades. They have played an active role in economic activities, innovation and research breakthroughs, disaster relief, etc., all of which are important elements to China's economic and social reform, and national development and stability. The youth task group is an innovation of Chinese socialism and an important channel for the CYLC to accomplish the central task of economic development and serve the overall interests of the country.

Youth task groups are mostly organized by CYLC organizations in enterprises, public institutions, counties, cities and districts, townships and sub-districts, villages and urban communities, and institutions of higher learning. They are composed of young people, with CYLC members as the political core.

In enterprises, these groups focus on tasks involving production and operation, engineering projects, innovation, business performance, and workplace safety. They promote science-based management and advocate excellence at work. In public institutions, they take on tasks in the fields of government services, commercial services, and social services. They promote professional ethics and present a positive image of their professions. In cities, they primarily work on issues of grassroots-level governance, including the development of model cities, emergency response, aid for the needy, and dispute resolution. In the countryside, they tackle problems in the production and marketing of farm products, popularization of cultivation and livestock breeding technologies, infrastructure construction, and improvements to the living environment, all in relation to the implementation of the rural revitalization strategy. In institutions of higher learning, they leverage the academic strength of college students to complete their school assignments and provide assistance to local communities. Groups in other fields also rally young people in relevant sectors for targeted programs.

As the presence of youth task groups expands and their performance improves, the exemplary and leading role of CYLC members has become more pronounced in the completion of pressing, challenging, dangerous, onerous and unprecedented tasks. Young people are working for China's economic and social progress with a stronger sense of purpose and greater determination.

medical care, transporting supplies, and building facilities. They have made a tremendous contribution to the all-out people's war on the virus. Of the 28,600 nurses from the medical teams sent to Hubei, 90 percent were born between 1980 and 1999. During the construction of the Huoshenshan and Leishenshan hospitals in Wuhan, young workers, who accounted for 60 percent of the workforce, established 13 task groups to spearhead the project. With an iron will and boundless courage, they created an engineering miracle. This was a shining example of how young Chinese can hold their own in the face of difficulties, face down threats, and rise to the challenge at critical moments.

(3) Tempering Themselves Through Community Service

The local community is the best place to temper young people in the new era, where they can learn through practice. By aligning their personal ambitions with the grand goals of the state and the Party, young people turn their pursuit of the Chinese Dream into pragmatic work, and hone their skills and increase their abilities through trial and experimentation.

Helping villagers solve problems in rural areas, providing services to residents in cities, and patrolling and guarding the frontiers ... More and more young people are now working in communities and in the places where they are most needed, fighting hardship to drive China's modernization and realize their dreams.

Of the 1,981 individuals and 1,501 groups commended by the central authorities in 2021 who had stood out in China's poverty alleviation campaign, many were young people. More than 1,800 people have died in the battle against poverty, and many of them were young people.

As the country implements the rural revitalization strategy, young people have led the efforts to establish specialized cooperatives, apply modern agricultural technologies, and develop new industries and new forms of business in rural areas. They have taken the lead in abandoning outdated social mores, nurturing civil social norms of conduct, and improving rural living environments, and helped villagers increase their incomes. All of these have contributed to giving rural areas a bright new image.

By 2021, 470,000 college graduates had worked in rural areas on posts related to teaching, agriculture, medical service and poverty alleviation, and during their vacations, millions of college students had conducted surveys or taken part in cultural activities and other activities to spread understanding of science and technology and information on health in the countryside. Through these efforts, young people have offered their support to China's poverty alleviation and rural revitalization.

(4) Taking the Lead in Innovation and Entrepreneurship

In the new era, China's youth have shown rich imagination and creativity, open-mindedness, and a pioneering spirit. They have the spirit to engage in the field of international competition as it grows ever fiercer, and have become a strong force driving innovation and entrepreneurship.

Backed by policy incentives of the Party and the state, young people take the lead in innovation, starting businesses, and striving for excellence, serving the country and the people with their ingenuity and expertise in economic, social, technological and cultural fields. Under the innovation-driven development strategy and open competition mechanisms, a large number of world-class young scientists have come to the fore in major sci-tech programs, including China's space station *Tiangong*, deep-sea manned submersible *Jiaolong*, the five-hundred-meter aperture spherical telescope (FAST) *Tianyan*, the dark matter probe satellite *Wukong*, the quantum science satellite *Mozi*, the Mars probe *Tianwen-1*, and the lunar mission *Chang'e*. The average age of the core members of the research groups on the Beidou Navigation Satellite System is 36; the corresponding figures are 35 for *Mozi* and 30 for *Tianyan*. Every year more than 3 million science and technology and engineering students graduate from Chinese universities, which continuously replenish the country's ranks of engineers. Well-educated and highly-skilled, they give China an "engineering bonus", adding impetus to the country's development and improving its standing in international competition.

China has introduced a raft of policies supporting business startups, and young people are responding warmly. They are active in entrepreneurship programs like the China College Students' Entrepreneurship Competition, China International "Internet+" College Students Innovation and Entrepreneurship Competition, carving out careers with their knowledge and ingenuity. Among the founders of market entities registered since 2014, more than 5 million are college students and new graduates. In creative industries such as IT services, culture, sports, entertainment and sci-tech, young people account for half or more of the workforce, and are at the helm of many unicorn and gazelle companies. Aligning individual inclination with national development, young people are putting their talents to use in innovation and starting businesses, and serving society in the process.

Unit: 10,000 people

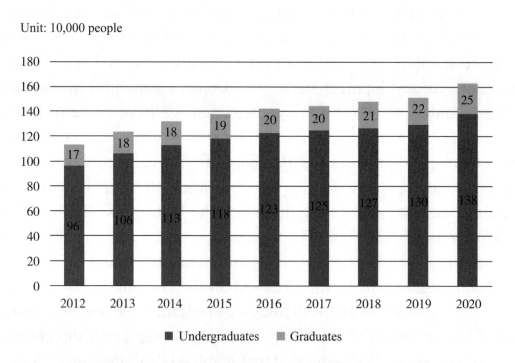

Figure 3. Number of engineering majors graduated from undergraduate
and graduate programs in China from 2012 to 2020

Panel 7 Report on Chinese Youth Entrepreneurship and Employment 2021

In December 2021, the China Foundation for Youth Entrepreneurship and Employment and its research partners released the *Report on Chinese Youth Entrepreneurship and Employment 2021.*

The report showed that entrepreneurship was thriving across China. The number of startups was huge, venture capital investment was robust, and the quality of startups and the business environment in which they operated were both improving. People aged 19-23 constituted the main driving force behind startups.

Based on startup environment, entrepreneurial spirit, and startup results, the report has established 17 indexes for China's youth entrepreneurship. Fifty cities were rated as being friendly to young entrepreneurs.

Between 2015 and 2020, China's youth entrepreneurship indexes rose from 100 to 167.5. Beijing, Shanghai, and Guangzhou scored the top three in 2020; and other first-tier cities, provincial capitals, and prefecture-level cities in developed eastern regions were also high on the list. And 60 percent of the top 50 cities for youth entrepreneurship were in eastern provinces, leading the nation in this regard. When it came to startup results, core cities were the magnet for entrepreneurship activities, with those in the Yangtze River Delta having the greatest geographic advantages. There was a large presence of high-performing innovative tech companies in Jiangsu, Shanghai, Beijing and Guangdong.

The report created a detailed portrait of young entrepreneurs by delving into their common characteristics, startup funding, motivation, current situation and difficulties. On this basis it provided suggestions on how to further stimulate youth entrepreneurship.

(5) Spearheading Cultural and Ethical Progress

In the new era China's youth advance with the times, adapt to the need to modernize China's system and capacity for governance, and set the pace in making cultural and ethical progress. They advocate and follow new, positive trends.

In both urban and rural areas, in the workplace or on campus, young people embrace good moral values and ethical conduct. They champion pursuit of excellence and the greater good, and set healthy trends.

A growing number of young people are engaged in community governance and services in both urban and rural areas. By participating in programs like Youth Action in Communities launched by the CYLC Central Committee, they gain practical experience, and improve their ability to serve society. In all sectors of the economy, young people work in a spirit of dedication, collaboration, excellence and contribution, and have created many model worker teams. They represent the work ethic and professionalism of the new era. Young athletes, demonstrating good sportsmanship, score excellent results at games.

Since the China Young Volunteers initiative was launched in 1993, volunteering has become an important avenue for young Chinese to participate in social governance, fulfill social responsibilities, and temper themselves in the course of serving the people and society.

Panel 8　Model Youth Groups

Since 1994, the CYLC Central Committee has been calling on young people to establish model worker groups, and has organized 20 rounds of selection. More than 20,000 groups have won the title at the national level, in addition to more than 100,000 recognized at the provincial level or in their respective sectors. Model youth groups have become a highlight of China's effort to advance cultural and ethical progress and professionalism.

In the new era the initiative of model youth groups carries on the spirit of dedication, collaboration, excellence and contribution. It targets young frontline workers in all sectors, primarily those providing administrative, commercial and social services. Through activities to encourage science-based management, people-centered management, self-management, innovation, higher efficiency and better performance, the initiative promotes professional ethics, supports work achievements, builds strong teams, and cultivates young professionals. It is a broad-based, practice-focused initiative with a strong brand identity, under which young people contribute their wisdom and strength to cultural, ethical, economic and social progress.

Panel 9　China Young Volunteers

In 1993, the CYLC Central Committee launched the China Young Volunteers initiative. With support from all sectors of the society, it has since spread across the country, instilling the spirit of contribution, friendship, mutual aid and progress in the people. The volunteer network is growing stronger, volunteer services are expanding, the number of volunteers is increasing, and their working mechanisms are improving. The initiative is playing an increasingly positive role in serving society, educating youth, and promoting moral values.

As of 2021, the Chinese Young Volunteers Association has set up organizations in all provinces and equivalent administrative units on the mainland, in Xinjiang Production and Construction Corps, in 95 percent of prefectures (prefecture-level cities), in 69 percent of counties (districts), and in more than 2,000 universities.

The "Go West" Program featuring volunteer services by postgraduates and college graduates in central and western China has gained widespread recognition. More than 700 young volunteers have taken on missions abroad, sowing the seed of friendship globally. Nearly six million young volunteers have paired up with rural children whose parents are migrant workers and children with disabilities to provide long-term assistance. More than 4.9 million young volunteers participated in relief efforts during the Wenchuan Earthquake in 2008 and the Yushu Earthquake in 2010. And millions more have provided outstanding service at major sport galas and international events, including the Beijing 2008 Summer Olympic and Paralympic Games, Beijing 2022 Winter Olympic and Paralympic Games, the Shanghai World Expo, and the G20 Hangzhou Summit.

As of the end of 2021, more than 90 million people aged between 14 and 35 had registered at the volunteering platform Chinavolunteer.mac. gov.cn. They are active in community affairs, large sport events, environmental protection, development-driven poverty alleviation, healthcare, emergency response and cultural preservation. By spreading the spirit of volunteerism – contribution, friendship, mutual aid and progress – they promote unity, equality, amity, mutual aid, and common progress across the society.

Over the past 18 years, China's "Go West" Program has dispatched 410,000 postgraduates and college graduates to 2,100 counties in central and western regions to support poverty reduction endeavors there through teaching and healthcare service. Young people have always been the mainstay of volunteers providing services in large-scale events. They have made a deep impression on the world.

IV. Having a Global Vision and a Strong Sense of Responsibility

The younger generation is the future of a country and the hope of the world. China's youth in the new era care about their family and country, and share that concern for the rest of humanity. They uphold the beliefs advocated by Chinese culture that all peoples are one family and the world is a commonwealth. They actively draw inspiration from the experience and achievements of other countries and civilizations. They work along with their peers from around the world to build a global community of shared future, and advocate peace, development, equity, justice, democracy and freedom, which are the common values of humanity, for the purpose of creating a better future for all.

(1) Embracing the World with Greater Openness and Confidence

As China opens its doors wider to the outside world, the country's young people today are building a greater understanding of international exchanges and cooperation. They are embracing the world, pursuing broader and deeper integration with others, and showing greater rationality, inclusiveness, self-confidence and self-reliance, by studying, working, traveling, and participating in visiting programs abroad.

Studying abroad is the most important way for Chinese youngsters to learn about the world. In 1978, China sent just over 800 students abroad. In 2019, more than 700,000 Chinese students went abroad to undertake education courses. Over the past four decades, the total number of Chinese people studying abroad has exceeded 6.5 million. The number of Chinese overseas returnees grew from 248 in 1978 to more than 580,000 in 2019. The total number of overseas returnees has exceeded 4.2 million in the past more than four decades. In addition, a large number of Chinese young people go abroad for travel, visiting programs, business tours, and labor cooperation, which enable them to better understand the world. In 2019 alone, Chinese citizens made 170 million

**Table 1 Number of Chinese students going abroad to study,
and returned overseas Chinese students from 1978 to 2019**

Year	Number of Chinese Students Going Abroad to Study	Number of Returned Overseas Chinese Students
1978	860	248
1980	2,124	1,223
1985	7,144	3,880
1990	19,352	2,099
1995	21,934	5,090
2000	38,989	9,121
2005	118,515	34,987
2010	284,700	134,800
2015	523,700	409,100
2016	544,500	432,500
2017	608,400	480,900
2018	662,100	519,400
2019	703,500	580,300

overseas trips. The channels for Chinese youth to know about the world continue to expand, and their global vision is steadily broadening.

The "circle of friends" with whom China can communicate and cooperate continues to grow. China's youth seize every opportunity to tell China's stories and participate in global governance of youth affairs in various international arenas, and promote win-win cooperation through active exchanges and interactions under bilateral and multilateral frameworks. As young Chinese people take a more active part in bilateral exchange mechanisms, they become closer to their peers in other countries and build deeper bilateral ties. Under the framework of the Chinese Youth Global Partnership, China has established exchange and cooperation relationships with more than 100 international organizations, government youth agencies, political parties, and non-governmental youth organizations. Chinese youth are engaged in frequent international exchanges in fields like education, science, culture, arts, sports, and the media under the cultural and people-to-people exchange mechanisms between China and other countries and regions such as Russia, the United States, Europe, India and Japan. China's youth and their partners in neighboring countries and developing countries carry out cultural and people-to-people exchanges that bring fruitful results; they also achieve mutual benefit through incubating startups, promoting economic and trade cooperation, advancing technological exchange, and other efforts. China's young people have become more active in joining international organizations, attending international conferences, and participating in global governance. As a result, they have succeeded in enhancing the international image of China's youth.

Hundreds of young people from China work hard for the UN and other international organizations and contribute to world peace and development. China's young people are growing in confidence as they spread China's voice and express China's ideas at the UN Youth Forum, the UNESCO Youth Forum, and other multilateral mechanisms and in international youth organizations such as the Asian Youth Council. This allows them to serve as young ambassadors of Sino-foreign friendship.

(2) Meeting the Responsibility to Build a Global Community of Shared Future

Young Chinese of the new era are fully aware that the future of each and every nation and country is interlocked. We should stand together and help each other in the face of adversity, and endeavor to build this planet of ours into a single family of shared future.

Building consensus among youth through heart-to-heart communication and dialogue. Young Chinese actively advocate and practice the idea of building a global community of shared future. They are committed to telling the stories of global youth, spreading the voice of global youth, and building consensus among global youth on issues such as poverty alleviation, climate change, and anti-Covid cooperation. In 2020, at an online seminar on Covid-19 organized by the World Health Organization and other UN agencies, a young representative of China shared her moving story as a volunteer, recounted some experiences, and explained China's science-based response to the epidemic. Young Chinese also contribute their wisdom and ideas for safeguarding global youth rights to subsistence, development, protection and participation in the process of formulating documents on youth cooperation under international mechanisms such as the Shanghai Cooperation Organization, BRICS, and G20. During the Beijing 2022 Olympic and Paralympic Winter Games, the youth volunteers of China and young athletes from many countries overcame language barriers and cultural differences as they expressed goodwill with smiles, build friendships through personal contact, and pooled their strengths through heart-to-heart communication. Those young people worked together to build bridges towards a shared future, and spread the vision of building a global community of shared future around the world in their own way.

Hand in hand on the journey towards a brighter future. China's youth firmly bear in mind the concept of building a global community of

Panel 10   International Youth Sustainable Development Index Report 2021

In December 2021, a joint research group formed by China Youth and Children Research Center, China International Youth Exchange Center, the Center for Youth Moral Education at Tsinghua University, and the Research Center for Contemporary China at Peking University released the *International Youth Sustainable Development Index Report 2021*. Through multi-dimensional and multi-level assessment, the report presents an overall picture of the present status, characteristics, trends and problems of youth development in various countries, with the goal of promoting international exchanges and mutual learning on youth development.

The report assesses youth development in 85 countries. In terms of overall results, the top three countries in the ranking are Singapore, Norway, and Belgium. In terms of geographical distribution, the top 10 countries include four Asian countries, five European countries, and one country from Oceania. In terms of development level, the top 10 countries include eight developed countries and two developing countries.

According to the report, China ranks among the top 30% (23rd) of the 85 countries in terms of youth development index, higher than its positions in per capita GDP and Human Development Index (HDI) rankings. In the domains of "Civic Participation" and "Health & Wellbeing", China ranks among the top 15% (9th and 12th, respectively), higher than its overall ranking and topping many developed countries. This evidences China's remarkable achievements in youth development.

shared future, and actively implement it in practice. They devote themselves to the construction of the Belt and Road while following the principles of "extensive consultation, joint contribution and shared benefits". Hundreds of thousands of young employees in Chinese companies operating overseas work hard in foreign lands far from home, contributing to local economic and social development. They also take an active part in volunteer services, charitable donations, and cultural exchanges, building friendships and cooperation with young people in the host countries. At present, many volunteer Chinese teachers, most of whom are young people, are working in more than 100 countries to help youth in other countries to study Chinese culture. The China Youth Volunteer Overseas Service Program has sent more than 700 young volunteers to over 20 countries in Asia, Africa, and Latin America to provide services in areas like medical care, agricultural technology, civil engineering, industrial technology, economic management, and social development. Demonstrating a great love for humanity and upholding a spirit of humanism, young Chinese soldiers actively participate in UN peacekeeping missions; they have made their contributions to defending world peace. By 2020, China had dispatched more than 40,000 peacekeepers, and 16 of them, under the age of 30 on average, had sacrificed their lives. The actions of Chinese youth have demonstrated that as long as people around the world unite with one heart and one mind and move forward hand in hand, we will build a global community with a brighter future.

(3) Global Action Initiative of China's Youth

Humanity has entered a new era of interconnection, with countries sharing common interests and their futures closely linked. Across the globe greater deficits of governance, trust, peace and development are emerging, and we are seeing escalating chaos, discord and injustice. Profound changes of a scale unseen in a century, together with the Covid-19 pandemic, are presenting grave challenges to the global economy and people's prospects of a better life. Humanity has found itself at a crossroads: peace or war, light or darkness, progress or regression – there are significant choices that we need to make. The era calls on global youth to unite with one heart, strengthen mutual understanding, learn from each other, view the world from the angle of mutual appreciation, mutual learning, and mutual benefit, so as to jointly build a global community of shared future. China's youth therefore call on young people around the world:

– To uphold the values of beauty, uprightness, and goodness. Young people should set themselves lofty ideals and conduct themselves with moral integrity. They should follow the right path, value kindness, goodness, and beauty, have an ardent love for life, and contribute to society. They should make every possible effort to promote truth and spread positive energy.

— To maintain a spirit of youth and vigor. Young people should be self-confident, self-reliant, and high in spirits. They should seek to improve and extend themselves, fulfill their dreams, and show their worth, and strive to present themselves in the best possible light. They should advocate healthy lifestyles, pursue physical and mental health, foster a sound outlook, and maintain vigor.

— To shoulder the responsibility for national development. Young people, as masters of their respective countries, should study hard to improve their skills and abilities, leverage their wisdom, and be bold in innovation. Ready to struggle and willing to work hard, they should be at the forefront of the times and shoulder the historic mission to realize the development and progress of their countries.

— To contribute wisdom and strength to world peace and development. With the world and the future in mind, young people should uphold the common values of humanity, set the trends of history and lead the tides of the times, and stand on the side of fairness, justice, and human progress. They should safeguard world peace, promote common development, defend democracy and freedom, and make a greater contribution to building a prosperous, beautiful world.

China's youth look forward to a world of peace, stability, development and prosperity. They expect every country and region to provide favorable conditions for youth development, and hope all young people across the globe will shoulder their responsibilities and contribute their wisdom and strength to building an open, inclusive, clean, and beautiful world that enjoys lasting peace, universal security, and common prosperity.

Conclusion

A country will be full of hope and can look forward to a bright prospect when its young generation has ideals, abilities, and a strong sense of responsibility. The future of China and the future of the wider world both belong to the young.

In the future, the young Chinese generation will, "with their youthfulness, create a vibrant family, country, nation, human community, Earth and the universe." They will make their youthful dreams come true.

In the future, with successive efforts from one generation of young people to the next, China will scale new heights in every dimension, achieving economic, political, cultural, ethical, social, and eco-environmental progress. The Chinese people will enjoy a happier and healthier life and the Chinese nation will become a proud and active member of the community of nations. The great Chinese Dream will eventually become a reality.

The future of the world is related to the destiny of every young person, and it also depends on the efforts that every young person makes. If young people from all countries unite for the common goal, uphold justice, work in harmony, help each other, conduct consultation as equals, and commit to openness and innovation, we will be able to steer clear of strife and war, build a "global village" that pursues peaceful development and harmony, jointly create a future of prosperity, health, safety, mutual respect, mutual learning, and shared benefits, and ultimately realize the common dream of all of humanity.

China's youth stand ready to work with their counterparts from all over the world and contribute their wisdom and strength to building a global community of shared future and a better world.

The Taiwan Question and China's Reunification in the New Era

The People's Republic of China

The Taiwan Affairs Office of the State Council
and
The State Council Information Office

August 2022

Preamble

Resolving the Taiwan question and realizing China's complete reunification is a shared aspiration of all the sons and daughters of the Chinese nation. It is indispensable for the realization of China's rejuvenation. It is also a historic mission of the Communist Party of China (CPC). The CPC, the Chinese government, and the Chinese people have striven for decades to achieve this goal.

The 18th National Congress of the CPC in 2012 heralded a new era in building socialism with Chinese characteristics. Under the strong leadership of the CPC Central Committee with Xi Jinping at the core, the CPC and the Chinese government have adopted new and innovative measures in relation to Taiwan. They have continued to chart the course of cross-Straits relations, safeguard peace and stability across the Taiwan Straits, and promote progress towards national reunification. However, in recent years the Taiwan authorities, led by the Democratic Progressive Party (DPP), have redoubled their efforts to divide the country, and some external forces have tried to exploit Taiwan to contain China, prevent the Chinese nation from achieving complete reunification, and halt the process of national rejuvenation.

The CPC has united the Chinese people and led them in fulfilling the First Centenary Goal of building a moderately prosperous society in all respects as scheduled, and in embarking on a new journey towards the Second Centenary Goal of building China into a modern socialist country.

The Chinese nation has achieved a historic transformation from standing upright to becoming prosperous and growing in strength, and national rejuvenation is driven by an unstoppable force. This marks a new starting point for reunification.

The Chinese government has published two previous white papers on Taiwan. One was *The Taiwan Question and Reunification of China* in August 1993, and the other was *The One-China Principle and the Taiwan Issue* in February 2000. These two white papers provided a comprehensive and systematic elaboration of the basic principles and policies regarding the resolution of the Taiwan question. This new white paper is being released to reiterate the fact that Taiwan is part of China, to demonstrate the resolve of the CPC and the Chinese people and their commitment to national reunification, and to emphasize the position and policies of the CPC and the Chinese government in the new era.

I. Taiwan Is Part of China – This Is an Indisputable Fact

Taiwan has belonged to China since ancient times. This statement has a sound basis in history and jurisprudence. New archeological discoveries and research findings regularly attest to the profound historical and cultural ties between the two sides of the Taiwan Straits. A large number of historical records and annals document the development of Taiwan by the Chinese people in earlier periods.

The earliest references to this effect are to be found, among others, in *Seaboard Geographic Gazetteer* compiled in the year 230 by Shen Ying of the State of Wu during the Three Kingdoms Period. The royal court of the Sui Dynasty had on three occasions sent troops to Taiwan, called Liuqiu at that time. Starting from the Song and Yuan dynasties, the imperial central governments of China all set up administrative bodies to exercise jurisdiction over Penghu and Taiwan.

In 1624, Dutch colonialists invaded and occupied the southern part of Taiwan. In 1662, General Zheng Chenggong, hailed as a national hero, led an expedition and expelled them from the island. Subsequently, the Qing court gradually set up more administrative bodies in Taiwan. In 1684, a Taiwan prefecture administration was set up under the jurisdiction of Fujian Province. In 1885, Taiwan's status was upgraded and it became the 20th province of China.

In July 1894, Japan launched a war of aggression against China. In April 1895, the defeated Qing government was forced to cede Taiwan and the Penghu Islands to Japan. During the Chinese People's War of Resistance Against Japanese Aggression (1931-1945), China's Communists called for the recovery of Taiwan. Talking with American journalist Nym Wales on May 15, 1937, Mao Zedong said that China's goal was to achieve a final victory in the war – a victory that would recover the occupied Chinese territories in Northeast China and to the south of the Shanhai Pass, and secure the liberation of Taiwan.

On December 9, 1941, the Chinese government issued a declaration of war against Japan, and proclaimed that all treaties, conventions, agreements, and contracts regarding relations between China and Japan had been abrogated, and that China would recover Taiwan and the Penghu Islands.

The Cairo Declaration issued by China, the United States and the United Kingdom on December 1, 1943 stated that it was the purpose of the three allies that all the territories Japan had stolen from China, such as Northeast China, Taiwan and the Penghu Islands, should be restored to China.

The Potsdam Proclamation was signed by China, the United States and the United Kingdom on July 26, 1945, and subsequently recognized by the Soviet Union. It reiterated: "The terms of the Cairo Declaration shall be carried out." In September of the same year, Japan signed the instrument of surrender, in which it promised that it would faithfully fulfill the obligations laid down in the Potsdam Proclamation. On October 25 the Chinese government announced that it was resuming the exercise of sovereignty over Taiwan, and the ceremony to accept Japan's surrender in Taiwan Province of the China war theater of the Allied powers was held in Taibei (Taipei). China had thereby recovered Taiwan *de jure* and *de facto* through a host of documents with international legal effect.

On October 1, 1949, the People's Republic of China (PRC) was founded, becoming the successor to the Republic of China (1912-1949), and the Central People's Government became the only legitimate government of the whole of China. The new government replaced the previous Kuomintang regime in a situation where China, as a subject under international law, did not change and China's sovereignty and inherent territory did not change. As a natural result, the government of the PRC should enjoy and exercise China's full sovereignty, which includes its sovereignty over Taiwan.

As a result of the civil war in China in the late 1940s and the interference of external forces, the two sides of the Taiwan Straits have fallen into a state of protracted political confrontation. But the sovereignty and territory of China have never been divided and will never be divided, and Taiwan's status as part of China's territory has never changed and will never be allowed to change.

In October 1971, during its 26th session the United Nations General Assembly adopted Resolution 2758, which undertook "to restore all its rights to the People's Republic of China and to recognize the representatives of its Government as the only legitimate representatives of China to the United Nations, and to expel forthwith the representatives of Chiang Kai-shek from the place which they unlawfully occupy at the United Nations and in all the organizations related to it". This resolution settled once and for all the political, legal and procedural issues of China's representation in the UN, and it covered the whole country, including Taiwan. It also spelled out that China has one single seat in the UN, so there is no such thing as "two Chinas" or "one China, one Taiwan".

The specialized agencies of the UN later adopted further resolutions restoring to the PRC its lawful seat and expelling the representatives of the Taiwan authorities. One of these is Resolution 25.1 adopted at the 25th World Health Assembly in May 1972. It was clearly stated in the official legal opinions of the Office of Legal Affairs of the UN Secretariat that "the United Nations considers 'Taiwan' as a province of China with no separate status", and the "'authorities' in 'Taipei' are not considered to ... enjoy any form of government status". At the UN the island is referred to as "Taiwan, Province of China"[1].

Resolution 2758 is a political document encapsulating the one-China

---

[1] *United Nations Juridical Yearbook 2010*, p. 516.

principle whose legal authority leaves no room for doubt and has been acknowledged worldwide. Taiwan does not have any ground, reason, or right to join the UN, or any other international organization whose membership is confined to sovereign states.

In recent years some elements in a small number of countries, the US foremost among them, have colluded with forces in Taiwan, to falsely claim that the resolution did not conclusively resolve the issue of Taiwan's representation. Puffing up the illegal and invalid Treaty of San Francisco[2] and disregarding the Cairo Declaration, the Potsdam Proclamation and other international legal documents, they profess that the status of Taiwan has yet to be determined, and declare their support for "Taiwan's meaningful participation in the UN system". What they are actually attempting to do is to alter Taiwan's status as part of China and create "two Chinas" or "one China, one Taiwan" as part of a political ploy – using Taiwan to contain China. These actions in violation of Resolution 2758 and international law are a serious breach of political commitments made by these countries. They damage China's sovereignty and dignity, and treat the basic principles of international law with contempt. The Chinese government has condemned and expressed its resolute opposition to them.

---

[2] Between September 4 and 8, 1951, the United States gathered a number of countries in San Francisco for what they described as the San Francisco Peace Conference. Neither the PRC nor the Soviet Union received an invitation. The treaty signed at this meeting, commonly known as the Treaty of San Francisco, included an article under which Japan renounced all rights, title and claim to Taiwan and the Penghu Islands. This treaty contravened the provisions of the Declaration by United Nations signed by 26 countries – including the United States, the United Kingdom, the Soviet Union and China – in 1942, the fundamental principles of the UN Charter, and the basic norms of international law. The PRC was excluded from its preparation, drafting and signing, and its rulings on the territory and sovereign rights of China – including the sovereignty over Taiwan – are therefore illegal and invalid. The Chinese government has always refused to recognize the Treaty of San Francisco, and has never from the outset deviated from this stance. Other countries, including the Soviet Union, Poland, Czechoslovakia, the Democratic People's Republic of Korea, Mongolia, and Vietnam, have also refused to recognize the document's authority.

The one-China principle represents the universal consensus of the international community; it is consistent with the basic norms of international relations. To date, 181 countries including the United States have established diplomatic relations with the PRC on the basis of the one-China principle. The China-US Joint Communique on the Establishment of Diplomatic Relations, published in December 1978, states: "The Government of the United States of America acknowledges the Chinese position that there is but one China and Taiwan is part of China." It also states: "The United States of America recognizes the Government of the People's Republic of China as the sole legal Government of China. Within this context, the people of the United States will maintain cultural, commercial, and other unofficial relations with the people of Taiwan."

The Constitution of the People's Republic of China, adopted at the Fifth Session of the Fifth National People's Congress (NPC) in December 1982, stipulates: "Taiwan is part of the sacred territory of the People's Republic of China. It is the inviolable duty of all Chinese people, including our compatriots in Taiwan, to accomplish the great task of reunifying the motherland."

The Anti-Secession Law, adopted at the Third Session of the 10th NPC in March 2005, stipulates: "There is only one China in the world. Both the mainland and Taiwan belong to one China. China's sovereignty and territorial integrity brook no division. Safeguarding China's sovereignty and territorial integrity is the common obligation of all Chinese people, the Taiwan compatriots included. Taiwan is part of China. The state shall never allow the 'Taiwan independence' secessionist forces to make Taiwan secede from China under any name or by any means."

The National Security Law, adopted at the 15th meeting of the Standing Committee of the 12th NPC in July 2015, stipulates: "The sovereignty and territorial integrity of China brook no violation or separation. Safeguarding national sovereignty, unity and territorial integrity is the common duty of all Chinese citizens, including Hong Kong, Macao and Taiwan compatriots."

We are one China, and Taiwan is part of China. This is an indisputable fact supported by history and the law. Taiwan has never been a state; its status as part of China is unalterable. Any attempt to distort these facts and dispute or deny the one-China principle will end in failure.

II. Resolute Efforts of the CPC to Realize China's Complete Reunification

The CPC has always been dedicated to working for the wellbeing of the Chinese people and the rejuvenation of the Chinese nation. Soon after its founding in 1921, the CPC set itself the goal of freeing Taiwan from colonial rule, reuniting it with the rest of the country and liberating the whole nation, including compatriots in Taiwan. It has made a tremendous effort to achieve this goal.

The CPC is committed to the historic mission of resolving the Taiwan question and realizing China's complete reunification. Under its resolute leadership, people on both sides of the Taiwan Straits have worked together to de-escalate tension across the Straits. They have set out on a path of peaceful development and made many breakthroughs in improving cross-Straits relations.

After the founding of the PRC in 1949, China's Communists, under the leadership of Mao Zedong, proposed the essential guideline, underlying principle, and basic policy for peaceful settlement of the Taiwan question. The CPC prepared and worked for the liberation of Taiwan, thwarted the Taiwan authorities' plans to attack the mainland, and foiled attempts to create "two Chinas" and "one China, one Taiwan". Through their efforts, the lawful seat and rights of the PRC in the United Nations were restored and the one-China principle was subscribed to by the majority of countries, laying important groundwork for peaceful reunification. The CPC central leadership established high-level contact with the Taiwan authorities through proper channels in pursuit of a peaceful solution to the Taiwan question.

Following the Third Plenary Session of the 11th CPC Central Committee in

1978, with the establishment of diplomatic relations between the PRC and the United States, China's Communists, led by Deng Xiaoping, defined the fundamental guideline for peaceful reunification in the vital interests of the country and the people and on the basis of the consensus for peaceful settlement of the Taiwan question. The CPC introduced the creative and well-conceived concept of One Country, Two Systems, and applied it first in resolving the questions of Hong Kong and Macao. It took action to ease military confrontation across the Taiwan Straits, restore contact, and open up people-to-people exchanges and cooperation, opening a new chapter in cross-Straits relations.

After the Fourth Plenary Session of the 13th CPC Central Committee in 1989, China's Communists, led by Jiang Zemin, made eight proposals for the development of cross-Straits relations and the peaceful reunification of China[3]. The CPC facilitated agreement across the Straits on the 1992 Consensus, which embodies the one-China principle. It initiated cross-Straits consultations and negotiations, resulting in the first talks between heads of the non-governmental organizations authorized by the two sides of the Straits, and expanded cross-Straits exchanges and cooperation in various fields. The CPC took firm action against separatist activities led by Lee Teng-hui, and struck hard at the separatist forces seeking "Taiwan independence". It ensured the smooth return of Hong Kong and Macao to China, and applied the policy of One Country, Two Systems, which had a constructive impact on the settlement of the Taiwan question.

---

[3] In his speech titled "Continue to Promote the Reunification of the Motherland" on January 30, 1995, Jiang Zemin, then general secretary of the CPC Central Committee and president of China, made eight proposals for the development of cross-Straits relations and peaceful national reunification. He emphasized, "Adhering to the one-China principle is the basis and prerequisite for peaceful reunification", and "in not promising to renounce the use of force, we are in no way targeting our Taiwan compatriots, but rather foreign forces conspiring to interfere in China's peaceful reunification and bring about Taiwan independence". (See *Selected Works of Jiang Zemin*, Vol. I, Eng. ed., Foreign Languages Press, Beijing, 2009, pp. 407-412.)

After the 16th CPC National Congress in 2002, China's Communists, led by Hu Jintao, highlighted the importance of peaceful development of cross-Straits relations. The CPC pushed for the enactment of the Anti-Secession Law to curb separatist activities in Taiwan, hosted the first talks between the leaders of the CPC and the Kuomintang in six decades since 1945, and defeated attempts by Chen Shui-bian to fabricate a legal basis for "independence". The CPC effected profound changes in moving the peaceful development of cross-Straits relations forward by promoting institutionalized consultations and negotiations that produced fruitful results, establishing overall direct two-way links in mail, business and transport, and facilitating the signing and implementation of the Economic Cooperation Framework Agreement.

After the 18th CPC National Congress in 2012, China's Communists, under the leadership of Xi Jinping, took a holistic approach to cross-Straits relations in keeping with changing circumstances, added substance to the theory on national reunification and the principles and policies concerning Taiwan, and worked to keep cross-Straits relations on the right track. The CPC developed its overall policy for resolving the Taiwan question in the new era, and set out the overarching guideline and a program of action.

At its 19th National Congress in October 2017, the CPC affirmed the basic policy of upholding One Country, Two Systems and promoting national reunification, and emphasized its resolve never to allow any person, any organization, or any political party, at any time or in any form, to separate any part of Chinese territory from China.

In January 2019, Xi Jinping, general secretary of the CPC Central Committee and president of China, addressed a meeting marking the 40th anniversary of the release of the Message to Compatriots in Taiwan. In his speech, Xi Jinping proposed major policies to advance the peaceful development of cross-Straits relations and the peaceful reunification of China in the new era. These are: first, working together to promote China's rejuvenation and its peaceful reunification; second, seeking a Two Systems solution to the Taiwan question and making innovative efforts towards peaceful reunification; third, abiding by the one-China principle and safeguarding the prospects for peaceful reunification; fourth, further integrating development across the Straits and consolidating the foundations for peaceful reunification; fifth, forging closer bonds of heart and mind between people on both sides of the Straits and strengthening joint commitment to peaceful reunification.

The CPC and the Chinese government have thereby adopted a series of major measures for charting the course of cross-Straits relations and realizing China's peaceful reunification:

– The CPC and the Chinese government have facilitated the first meeting and direct dialogue between leaders of the two sides since 1949, raising exchanges and interactions to new heights, opening up a new chapter, and creating new space for cross-Straits relations. This is a new milestone. The departments in charge of cross-Straits affairs on both sides have established regular contact and communication mechanisms on a common political foundation, and the heads of the two departments have exchanged visits and set up hotlines.

– Upholding the one-China principle and the 1992 Consensus, the CPC and the Chinese government have facilitated exchanges between political parties across the Straits, and conducted dialogues, consultations, and in-depth exchanges of views on cross-Straits relations and the future of the Chinese nation with relevant political parties, organizations, and individuals in Taiwan. These efforts have resulted in consensus on multiple issues, and promoted a number of joint initiatives exploring the Two Systems solution to the Taiwan question with all sectors of Taiwan society.

– Guided by the conviction that people on both sides of the Taiwan Straits are of the same family, the CPC and the Chinese government have promoted peaceful development of cross-Straits relations and integrated development of the two sides for the benefit of both the mainland and Taiwan. We have also refined the institutional arrangements, policies and measures to promote cross-Straits exchanges and cooperation, designed to advance the wellbeing of the people of Taiwan. These include the delivery of water from the coastal province of Fujian to Kinmen Island, electronic travel passes for Taiwan residents to enter or leave the mainland, residence permits for Taiwan residents, progressively ensuring that Taiwan compatriots have equal access to public services so as to facilitate their studying, starting businesses, working and living on the mainland, and an ongoing effort to pave the way for Taiwan to benefit first from the mainland's development opportunities.

– While countering interference and obstruction from separatist forces, the CPC and the Chinese government have called on the people of Taiwan to promote effective and in-depth cooperation and people-to-people exchanges in various fields across the Straits. Having overcome the impact of Covid-19, we have held a number of exchange events such as the Straits Forum, and maintained the momentum of cross-Straits exchanges and cooperation.

– Resolute in defending state sovereignty and territorial integrity and opposing separatist activities and external interference, the CPC and the Chinese government have safeguarded peace and stability in the Taiwan Straits and the fundamental interests of the Chinese nation. We have taken lawful action against and effectively deterred separatist forces. We have handled Taiwan's external exchanges in a sound manner, and consolidated the international community's commitment to the one-China principle.

Under the guidance of the CPC, great progress has been made in cross-Straits relations over the past seven decades, especially since the estrangement between the two sides was ended. Increased exchanges, broader cooperation and closer interactions have brought tangible benefits to people across the Straits, especially of Taiwan. This fully demonstrates that cross-Straits amity and cooperation are mutually beneficial.

The volume of cross-Straits trade was only US$46 million in 1978. It rose to US$328.34 billion in 2021, up by a factor of more than 7,000. The mainland has been Taiwan's largest export market for the last 21 years, generating a large annual surplus for the island. The mainland is also the largest destination for Taiwan's off-island investment. By the end of 2021 Taiwan businesses had invested in almost 124,000 projects on the mainland, to a total value of US$71.34 billion[4].

In 1987 less than 50,000 visits were made between the two sides; by 2019 this number had soared to about 9 million. In the past three years, affected by Covid-19, online communication has become the main form of people-to-people interactions across the Straits, and the numbers of people participating in and covered by online communication are reaching new highs.

The CPC has always been the spine of the Chinese nation, exercising strong leadership in realizing national rejuvenation and reunification. Its consistent efforts over the decades to resolve the Taiwan question and achieve complete national reunification are based on the following:

First, the one-China principle must be upheld, and no individual or force should be allowed to separate Taiwan from China.

Second, it is imperative to strive for the wellbeing of all Chinese people, including those in Taiwan, and to realize the aspirations of all Chinese people for a better life.

Third, we must follow the principles of freeing the mind, seeking truth from facts, maintaining the right political orientation, and breaking new ground, and defend the fundamental interests of the nation and the core interests of the state in formulating principles and policies on work related to Taiwan.

Fourth, it is necessary to have the courage and skill to fight against any force that attempts to undermine China's sovereignty and territorial integrity or stands in the way of its reunification.

Fifth, extensive unity and solidarity must be upheld to mobilize all factors to fight against any force that would divide the country, and pool strengths to advance national reunification.

---

[4] This figure does not include reinvestment by Taiwan investors through a third place.

III. China's Complete Reunification Is a Process That Cannot Be Halted

Against a backdrop of profound and complex changes in the domestic and international situation, our cause of complete national reunification is facing new challenges. The CPC and the Chinese government have the strength and the confidence to deal with complexities and overcome risks and threats, and the ability to take great strides forward on the path to national reunification.

1. Complete Reunification Is Critical to National Rejuvenation

Throughout China's 5,000-year history, national reunification and opposition to division have remained a common ideal and a shared tradition of the whole nation. In the modern era from the mid-19th century, due to the aggression of Western powers and the decadence of feudal rule, China was gradually reduced to a semi-feudal, semi-colonial society, and went through a period of suffering worse than anything it had previously known. The country endured intense humiliation, the people were subjected to great pain, and the Chinese civilization was plunged into darkness. Japan's 50-year occupation of Taiwan epitomized this humiliation and inflicted agony on both sides of the Taiwan Straits. Our two sides face each other just across a strip of water, yet we are still far apart. The fact that we have not yet been reunified is a scar left by history on the Chinese nation. We Chinese on both sides should work together to achieve reunification and heal this wound.

National rejuvenation has been the greatest dream of the Chinese people and the Chinese nation since the modern era began. Only by realizing complete national reunification can the Chinese people on both sides of the Straits cast aside the shadow of civil war and create and enjoy lasting peace. National reunification is the only way to avoid the risk of Taiwan being invaded and occupied again by foreign countries, to foil the attempts of external forces to contain China, and to safeguard the sovereignty, security, and development interests of our country. It is the most effective remedy to secessionist attempts to divide our country, and the best means to consolidate Taiwan's status as part of China and advance national rejuvenation. It will enable us to pool the strengths of the people on both sides, build our common home, safeguard our interests and well-being, and create a brighter future for the Chinese people and the Chinese nation. As Dr Sun Yat-sen, the great pioneer of China's revolution, once said, "Unification is the hope of all Chinese nationals. If China can be unified, all Chinese will enjoy a happy life; if it cannot, all will suffer."

In exploring the path to rejuvenation and prosperity, China has endured vicissitudes and hardships. "Unification brings strength while division leads to chaos." This is a law of history. The realization of complete national reunification is driven by the history and culture of the Chinese nation and determined by the momentum towards and circumstances surrounding our national rejuvenation. Never before have we been so close to, confident in, and capable of achieving the goal of national rejuvenation. The same is true when it comes to our goal of complete national reunification. The Taiwan question arose as a result of weakness and chaos in our nation, and it will be resolved as national rejuvenation becomes a reality. When all the Chinese people stick together and work together, we will surely succeed in realizing national reunification on our way to national rejuvenation.

2. National Development and Progress Set the Direction of Cross-Straits Relations

China's development and progress are a key factor determining the course of cross-Straits relations and the realization of complete national reunification. In particular, the great achievements over four decades of reform, opening up and modernization have had a profound impact on the historical process of resolving the Taiwan question and realizing complete national reunification. No matter which political party or group is in power in Taiwan, it cannot alter the course of progress in cross-Straits relations or the trend towards national reunification.

International Monetary Fund statistics show that in 1980 the GDP of the mainland was about US$303 billion, just over 7 times that of Taiwan, which was about US$42.3 billion; in 2021, the GDP of the mainland was about US$17.46 trillion, more than 22 times that of Taiwan, which was about US$790 billion.[5]

China's development and progress, and in particular the steady increases in its economic power, technological strength, and national defense capabilities, are an effective curb against separatist activities and interference from external forces. They also provide broad space and great opportunities for cross-Straits exchanges and cooperation. As more and more compatriots from Taiwan, especially young people, pursue their studies, start businesses, seek jobs, or go to live on the mainland, cross-Straits exchanges, interaction and integration are intensified in all sectors, the economic ties and personal bonds between the people on both sides run deeper, and our common cultural and national identities grow stronger, leading cross-Straits relations towards reunification.

The CPC has united the Chinese people and led them in embarking on the new journey of building China into a modern socialist country in all respects. Following the path of socialism with Chinese characteristics, the mainland has improved its governance and maintained long-term economic growth; it enjoys a solid material foundation, a wealth of human resources, a huge market, strong resilience in development, and social stability. It therefore has many strengths and favorable conditions

---

[5] From the statistics of the April 2022 edition of the World Economic Outlook databases of the International Monetary Fund.

for further development, and these have become the driving force for re-unification.

Grounding its effort in the new development stage, the mainland is committed to applying the new development philosophy, creating a new development dynamic, and promoting high-quality development. As a result, the overall strength and international influence of the mainland will continue to increase, and its influence over and appeal to Taiwan society will keep growing. We will have a more solid foundation for resolving the Taiwan question and greater ability to do so. This will give a significant boost to national reunification.

3. Any Attempt by Separatist Forces to Prevent Reunification Is Bound to Fail

Taiwan has been an integral part of China's territory since ancient times. Moves to separate Taiwan from China represent the serious crime of secession, and undermine the common interests of compatriots on both sides of the Taiwan Straits and the fundamental interests of the Chinese nation. They will lead nowhere.

The DPP authorities have adopted a separatist stance, and colluded with external forces in successive provocative actions designed to divide the country. They refuse to recognize the one-China principle, and distort and deny the 1992 Consensus. They assert that Taiwan and the mainland should not be subordinate to each other, and proclaim a new "two states" theory. On the island, they constantly press for "de-sinicization" and promote "incremental independence". They incite radical separatists in and outside the DPP to lobby for amendments to their "constitution" and "laws". They deceive the people of Taiwan, incite hostility against the mainland, and obstruct and undermine cross-Straits exchanges, cooperation and integrated development. They have steadily built up their military forces with the intention of pursuing "independence" and preventing reunification. They join with external forces in trying to sow the seeds of "two Chinas" or "one China, one Taiwan". The actions of the DPP authorities have resulted in tension in cross-Straits relations, endangering peace and stability in the Taiwan Straits, and undermining the prospects and restricting the space for peaceful reunification. These are obstacles that must be removed in advancing the process of peaceful reunification.

Taiwan belongs to all the Chinese people, including the 23 million Taiwan compatriots. The Chinese people are firm in their resolve and have a deep commitment to safeguarding China's sovereignty and territorial integrity, and the fundamental interests of the Chinese nation, and this resolve and commitment will frustrate any attempt to divide the country. When Taiwan was invaded by a foreign power more than 100 years ago, China was a poor and weak country. More than 70 years ago, China defeated the invaders and recovered Taiwan. Today, China has grown into the world's second largest economy. With significant growth in its political, economic, cultural, technological, and military strength, there is no likelihood that China will allow Taiwan to be separated again. Attempts to reject reunification and split the country are doomed, because they will founder against the history and culture of the Chinese nation as well as the resolve and commitment of more than 1.4 billion Chinese people.

4. External Forces Obstructing China's Complete Reunification Will Surely Be Defeated

External interference is a prominent obstacle to China's reunification. Still lost in delusions of hegemony and trapped in a Cold War mindset, some forces in the US insist on perceiving and portraying China as a major strategic adversary and a serious long-term threat. They do their utmost to undermine and pressurize China, exploiting Taiwan as a convenient tool. The US authorities have stated that they remain committed to the one-China policy and that they do not support "Taiwan independence". But their actions contradict their words. They are clouding the one-China principle in uncertainty and compromising its integrity. They are contriving "official" exchanges with Taiwan, increasing arms sales, and colluding in military provocation. To help Taiwan expand its "international space", they are inducing other countries to interfere in Taiwan affairs, and concocting Taiwan-related bills that infringe upon the sovereignty of China. They are creating confusion around what is black and white, right and wrong. On the one hand, they incite separatist forces to create tension and turmoil in cross-Straits relations. On the other hand, they accuse the mainland of coercion, pressurizing Taiwan, and unilaterally changing the status quo, in order to embolden these forces and create obstacles to China's peaceful reunification.

The important principles of respecting state sovereignty and territorial integrity as enshrined in the Charter of the United Nations are the cornerstones of modern international law and basic norms of international relations. It is the sacred right of every sovereign state to safeguard national unity and territorial integrity. It goes without saying that the Chinese government is entitled to take all measures necessary to settle the Taiwan question and achieve national reunification, free of external interference.

Behind the smokescreens of "freedom, democracy, and human rights" and "upholding the rules-based international order", some anti-China forces in the US deliberately distort the nature of the Taiwan question – which is purely an internal matter for China – and try to deny the legitimacy and justification of the Chinese government in safeguarding national sovereignty and territorial integrity. This clearly reveals their intention of using Taiwan to contain China and obstruct China's reunification, which should be thoroughly exposed and condemned.

These external forces are using Taiwan as a pawn to undermine China's development and progress, and obstruct the rejuvenation of the Chinese nation. They are doing so at the cost of the interests, wellbeing and future of the people of Taiwan rather than for their benefit. They have encouraged and instigated provocative actions by the separatist forces; these have intensified cross-Straits tension and confrontation, and undermined peace and stability in the Asia-Pacific region. This runs counter to the underlying global trends of peace, development and win-win cooperation, and goes against the wishes of the international community and the aspiration of all peoples.

Shortly after the PRC was founded, even though the country itself had to be rebuilt on the ruins of decades of war, China and its people won a resounding victory in the War to Resist US Aggression and Aid Korea (1950-1953). We defeated a powerful and well-armed enemy through gallantry and tenacity. In doing so, we safeguarded the security of the newly founded People's Republic, reestablished the status of China as a major country in the world, and demonstrated our heroic spirit, our lack of fear, and our will to stand up against the abuse of the powerful.

China is firmly committed to peaceful development. At the same time, it will not flinch under any external interference, nor will it tolerate any infringement upon its sovereignty, security and development interests. Relying on external forces will achieve nothing for Taiwan's separatists, and using Taiwan to contain China is doomed to fail.

Tranquility, development and a decent life are the expectations of our Taiwan compatriots, and the common aspiration of those on both sides of the Taiwan Straits. Under the strong leadership of the CPC, the Chinese people and the Chinese nation have stood upright, won prosperity, and grown in strength. A moderately prosperous society in all respects has been built on the mainland, where a large population once lived in dire poverty. We now have better conditions, more confidence, and greater capabilities. We can complete the historic mission of national reunification, so that both sides of the Straits can enjoy a better life. The wheel of history rolls on towards national reunification, and it will not be stopped by any individual or any force.

IV. National Reunification in the New Era

Taking into consideration the overall goal of national rejuvenation in the context of global change on a scale unseen in a century, the CPC and the Chinese government have continued to follow the CPC's fundamental guidelines on the Taiwan question and implement its principles and policies towards Taiwan, and have made concrete efforts to promote peaceful cross-Straits relations, integrate the development of the two sides, and work towards national reunification.

1. Upholding the Basic Principles of Peaceful Reunification and One Country, Two Systems

National reunification by peaceful means is the first choice of the CPC and the Chinese government in resolving the Taiwan question, as it best serves the interests of the Chinese nation as a whole, including our compatriots in Taiwan, and it works best for the long-term stability and development of China. We have worked hard to overcome hardships and obstacles to peaceful reunification over the past decades, showing that we cherish and safeguard the greater good of the nation, the wellbeing of our compatriots in Taiwan, and peace on both sides.

The One Country, Two Systems principle is an important institutional instrument created by the CPC and the Chinese government to enable peaceful reunification. It represents a great achievement of Chinese socialism. Peaceful reunification and One Country, Two Systems are our basic principles for resolving the Taiwan question and the best approach to realizing national reunification. Embodying the Chinese wisdom – we thrive by embracing each other – they take full account of Taiwan's realities and are conducive to long-term stability in Taiwan after reunification.

We maintain that after peaceful reunification, Taiwan may continue its current social system and enjoy a high degree of autonomy in accordance with the law. The two social systems will develop side by side for a long time to come. One Country is the precondition and foundation of Two Systems; Two Systems is subordinate to and derives from One Country; and the two are integrated under the one-China principle.

We will continue working with our compatriots in Taiwan to explore a Two Systems solution to the Taiwan question and increase our efforts towards peaceful reunification. In designing the specifics for implementing One Country, Two Systems, we will give full consideration to the realities in Taiwan and the views and proposals from all walks of life on both sides, and fully accommodate the interests and sentiments of our compatriots in Taiwan.

Ever since the One Country, Two Systems principle was proposed, certain political forces have been misrepresenting and distorting its objectives. The DPP and the authorities under its leadership have done everything possible to target the principle with baseless criticisms, and this has led to misunderstandings about its aims in some quarters of Taiwan. It is a fact that since Hong Kong and Macao returned to the motherland and were reincorporated into national governance, they have embarked on a broad path of shared development together with the mainland, and each complements the others' strengths. The practice of One Country, Two Systems has been a resounding success.

For a time, Hong Kong faced a period of damaging social unrest caused by anti-China agitators both inside and outside the region. Based on a clear understanding of the situation there, the CPC and the Chinese government upheld the One Country, Two Systems principle, made some appropriate improvements, and took a series of measures that addressed both the symptoms and root causes of the unrest. Order was restored and prosperity returned to Hong Kong. This has laid a solid foundation for the law-based governance of Hong Kong and Macao and the long-term continuation of One Country, Two Systems.

To realize peaceful reunification, we must acknowledge that the mainland and Taiwan have their own distinct social systems and ideologies. The One Country, Two Systems principle is the most inclusive solution to this problem. It is an approach that is grounded in democratic principles, demonstrates good will, seeks peaceful resolution of the Taiwan question, and delivers mutual benefit. The differences in social system are neither an obstacle to reunification nor a justification for secessionism. We firmly believe that our compatriots in Taiwan will develop a better understanding of the principle, and that the Two Systems solution to the Taiwan question will play its full role while compatriots on both sides work together towards peaceful reunification.

Peaceful reunification can only be achieved through consultation and discussion as equals. The long-standing political differences between the two sides are the fundamental obstacles to the steady improvement of cross-Straits relations, but we should not allow this problem to be passed down from one generation to the next. We can phase in flexible forms of consultation and discussion. We are ready to engage with all parties, groups, or individuals in Taiwan in a broad exchange of views aimed at resolving the political differences between the two sides based on the one-China principle and the 1992 Consensus. Representatives will be recommended by all political parties and all sectors of society on both sides, and they will engage in democratic consultations on peaceful development of cross-Straits relations, integrated development of the two sides, and the peaceful reunification of our country.

2. Promoting Peaceful Cross-Straits Relations and Integrated Development

Peaceful cross-Straits relations and integrated development pave the way for reunification and serve to benefit our people on both sides. Thus, both sides should work together towards this goal. We will extend integrated development, increase exchanges and cooperation, strengthen bonds, and expand common interests in the peaceful development of cross-Straits relations. In this way, we will all identify more closely with the Chinese culture and Chinese nation, and heighten the sense of our shared future. This lays solid foundations for peaceful reunification.

We will explore an innovative approach to integrated development and take the lead in setting up a pilot zone for integrated cross-Straits development in Fujian Province, advancing integration through better connectivity and more preferential policies, and based on mutual trust and understanding. Both sides should continue to promote connectivity in any area where it is beneficial, including trade and economic cooperation, infrastructure, energy and resources, and industrial standards. We should promote cooperation in culture, education, and health care, and the sharing of social security and public resources. We should support neighboring areas or areas with similar conditions on the two sides in providing equal, universal, and accessible public services. We should take active steps to institutionalize cross-Straits economic cooperation and create a common market for the two sides to strengthen the Chinese economy.

We will improve the systems and policies to guarantee the wellbeing of Taiwan compatriots and ensure that they are treated as equals on the mainland, and we will protect their legitimate rights and interests here in accordance with the law. We will support our fellow Chinese and enterprises from Taiwan in participating in the Belt and Road Initiative, major regional development strategies, and the strategy for coordinated regional development. We will help them integrate into the new development dynamic, participate in high-quality development, share in more development opportunities, and benefit from national socio-economic development.

We will expand cross-Straits exchanges and cooperation in various fields and overcome any obstacles and obstruction. We will encourage our people on both sides to pass on the best of traditional Chinese culture and ensure that it grows in new and creative ways. We will strengthen communication among the general public and the younger generations on both sides, and encourage more fellow Chinese in Taiwan – young people in particular – to pursue studies, start businesses, seek jobs, or live on the mainland. This will help people on both sides to expand mutual understanding, strengthen mutual trust, consolidate a shared sense of identity, and forge closer bonds of heart and mind.

3. Defeating Separatism and External Interference

Separatism will plunge Taiwan into the abyss and bring nothing but disaster to the island. To protect the interests of the Chinese nation as a whole, including our compatriots in Taiwan, we must resolutely oppose it and work for peaceful reunification. We are ready to create vast space for peaceful reunification; but we will leave no room for separatist activities in any form.

We Chinese will decide our own affairs. The Taiwan question is an internal affair that involves China's core interests and the Chinese people's national sentiments, and no external interference will be tolerated. Any attempt to use the Taiwan question as a pretext to interfere in China's internal affairs or obstruct China's reunification will meet with the resolute opposition of the Chinese people, including our compatriots in Taiwan. No one should underestimate our resolve, will and ability to defend China's sovereignty and territorial integrity.

We will work with the greatest sincerity and exert our utmost efforts to achieve peaceful reunification. But we will not renounce the use of force, and we reserve the option of taking all necessary measures. This is to guard against external interference and all separatist activities. In no way does it target our fellow Chinese in Taiwan. Use of force would be the last resort taken under compelling circumstances. We will only be forced to take drastic measures to respond to the provocation of separatist elements or external forces should they ever cross our red lines.

We will always be ready to respond with the use of force or other necessary means to interference by external forces or radical action by separatist elements. Our ultimate goal is to ensure the prospects of China's peaceful reunification and advance this process.

Some forces in the US are making every effort to incite groups inside Taiwan to stir up trouble and use Taiwan as a pawn against China. This has jeopardized peace and stability across the Taiwan Straits, obstructed the Chinese government's efforts towards peaceful reunification, and undermined the healthy and steady development of China-US relations. Left unchecked, it will continue to escalate tension across the Straits, further disrupt China-US relations, and severely damage the interests of the US itself. The US should abide by the one-China principle, deal with Taiwan-related issues in a prudent and proper manner, stand by its previous commitments, and stop supporting Taiwan separatists.

4. Working with Our Fellow Chinese in Taiwan Towards National Reunification and Rejuvenation

National reunification is an essential step towards national rejuvenation. The future of Taiwan lies in China's reunification, and the wellbeing of the people in Taiwan hinges on the rejuvenation of the Chinese nation, an endeavor that bears on the future and destiny of the people on both sides. A united and prosperous China will be a blessing for all Chinese, while a weak and divided China will be a disaster. Only China's rejuvenation and prosperity can bring lives of plenty and happiness to both sides. But it requires the joint efforts of both sides, as does the complete reunification of the country.

Separatist propaganda and the unresolved political dispute between the two sides have created misconceptions over cross-Straits relations, problems with national identity, and misgivings over national reunification among some fellow Chinese in Taiwan. Blood is thicker than water, and people on both sides of the Straits share the bond of kinship. We have great patience and tolerance and we will create conditions for closer exchanges and communication between the two sides, and to increase our compatriots' knowledge of the mainland and reduce these misconceptions and misgivings, in order to help them resist the manipulation of separatists.

We will join hands with our fellow Chinese in Taiwan to strive for national reunification and rejuvenation. We hope they will stand on the right side of history, be proud of their Chinese identity, and fully consider the position and role of Taiwan in China's rejuvenation. We hope they will pursue the greater good of the nation, resolutely oppose separatism and any form of external interference, and make a positive contribution to the just cause of China's peaceful reunification.

V. Bright Prospects for Peaceful Reunification

Once peaceful reunification is achieved under One Country, Two Systems, it will lay new foundations for China to make further progress and achieve national rejuvenation. At the same time, it will create huge opportunities for social and economic development in Taiwan and bring tangible benefits to the people of Taiwan.

1. Taiwan Will Have a Vast Space for Development

Taiwan boasts a high level of economic growth, industries with distinctive local features, and robust foreign trade. Its economy is highly complementary with that of the mainland. After reunification, the systems and mechanisms for cross-Straits economic cooperation will be further improved. Backed up by the vast mainland market, Taiwan's economy will enjoy broader prospects, become more competitive, develop steadier and smoother industrial and supply chains, and display greater vitality in innovation-driven growth. Many problems that have long afflicted Taiwan's economy and its people can be resolved through integrated cross-Straits development with all possible connectivity between the two sides. Taiwan's fiscal revenues can be better employed to improve living standards, bringing real benefits to the people and resolving their difficulties.

Taiwan's cultural creativity will also enjoy a great boost. Both sides of the Taiwan Straits share the culture and ethos of the Chinese nation. Nourished by the Chinese civilization, Taiwan's regional culture will flourish and prosper.

2. The Rights and Interests of the People in Taiwan Will Be Fully Protected

Provided that China's sovereignty, security and development interests are guaranteed, after reunification Taiwan will enjoy a high degree of autonomy as a special administrative region. Taiwan's social system and its way of life will be fully respected, and the private property, religious beliefs, and lawful rights and interests of the people in Taiwan will be fully protected. All Taiwan compatriots who support reunification of the country and rejuvenation of the nation will be the masters of the region, contributing to and benefitting from China's development. With a powerful motherland in support, the people of Taiwan will enjoy greater security and dignity and stand upright and rock-solid in the international community.

3. Both Sides of the Taiwan Straits Will Share the Triumph of National Rejuvenation

The people of Taiwan are brave, diligent and patriotic, and have made unremitting efforts to improve themselves. They revere their ancestry and love their homeland. Working together and applying their talents, people on both sides of the Taiwan Straits will create a promising future. After reunification, we Chinese will bridge gaps and differences caused by long-term separation, share a stronger sense of national identity, and stand together as one. After reunification, we can leverage complementary strengths in pursuit of mutual benefit and common development. After reunification, we can join hands to make the Chinese nation stronger and more prosperous, and stand taller among all the nations of the world.

The people separated by the Taiwan Straits share the same blood and a common destiny. After reunification, China will have greater international influence and appeal, and a stronger ability to shape international public opinion, and the Chinese people will enjoy greater self-esteem, self-confidence and national pride. In Taiwan and on the mainland the people will share the dignity and triumph of a united China and be proud of being Chinese. We will work together to refine and implement the Two Systems solution to the Taiwan question, to improve the institutional arrangements for implementing the One Country, Two Systems policy, and to ensure lasting peace and stability in Taiwan.

4. Peaceful Reunification of China Is Conducive to Peace and Development in the Asia-Pacific and the Wider World

Peaceful cross-Straits reunification is of benefit not only to the Chinese nation, but to all peoples and the international community as a whole. The reunification of China will not harm the legitimate interests of any other country, including any economic interests they might have in Taiwan. On the contrary, it will bring more development opportunities to all countries; it will create more positive momentum for prosperity and stability in the Asia-Pacific and the rest of the world; it will contribute more to building a global community of shared future, promoting world peace and development, and propelling human progress.

After reunification, foreign countries can continue to develop economic and cultural relations with Taiwan. With the approval of the central government of China, they may set up consulates or other official and quasi-official institutions in Taiwan, international organizations and agencies may establish offices, relevant international conventions can be applied, and relevant international conferences can be held there.

Conclusion

Over its 5,000-year history, China has created a splendid culture that has shone throughout the world from past times to present, and has made an enormous contribution to human society. After a century of suffering and hardship, the nation has overcome humiliation, emerged from backwardness, and embraced boundless development opportunities. Now, it is striding towards the goal of national rejuvenation.

Embarking on a new journey in a new era, the CPC and the Chinese government will continue to rally compatriots on both sides of the Taiwan Straits, and lead the efforts to answer the call of the times, shoulder historic responsibilities, grasp our fate and our future in our own hands, and work hard to achieve national reunification and rejuvenation.

The journey ahead cannot be all smooth sailing. However, as long as we Chinese on both sides of the Taiwan Straits devote our ingenuity and energy to the same goal, let there be no doubt – we will tolerate no foreign interference in Taiwan, we will thwart any attempt to divide our country, and we will combine as a mighty force for national reunification and rejuvenation. The historic goal of reuniting our motherland must be realized and will be realized.

China's BeiDou Navigation Satellite System in the New Era

The State Council Information Office of
the People's Republic of China

November 2022

Preamble

The BeiDou Navigation Satellite System (BDS) is a project built and operated by China as a component of the country's national security and economic and social development strategy. After many years in development, it has become an important new element of China's infrastructure, providing high-accuracy, round-the-clock positioning, navigation and timing services to global users in all weathers.

From the 18th National Congress of the Communist Party of China (CPC) held in 2012, BDS entered a new era of rapid development. On July 31, 2020, President Xi Jinping announced to the world that BDS-3 was officially commissioned – a sign that BDS began to provide global services. From the launch of reform and opening up in 1978 to the beginning of the new era, from BDS-1 to BDS-3, from two-satellite positioning to a configuration covering the entire globe, from serving the Asia-Pacific to serving the whole world, BDS has progressed together with China's development and advanced the process of national rejuvenation.

In the new era, BDS benefits not only the Chinese people but also the people of other countries. A first-class navigation satellite system developed by China and dedicated to the world, it has been applied worldwide, integrated with global infrastructure, and introduced into mass markets, empowering industries and profoundly changing people's lives and the way they work. It provides an essential spatiotemporal reference for economic and social development, contributing Chinese wisdom and strength to making navigation satellite systems better serve the world and benefit humanity.

In the new era, BDS demonstrates China's resolve and confidence in striving for greater strength and self-reliance in science and technology.

It embodies the Chinese people's spirit and commitment to independence and self-reliance in overcoming difficulties through hard work, showcases the strength of China's socialist system in pooling resources on major projects, and epitomizes China's global vision and its sense of responsibility in helping others to achieve common development.

The Chinese government is publishing this white paper to present China's achievements and vision in developing BDS, and to share its ideas and experience.

I. BeiDou in the New Era

As China makes historic progress and undergoes historic transformations in the new era, BDS has also entered a new period of high-quality development, making further breakthroughs and reaching higher levels in its mechanisms and in the speed and scale of its deployment. It is a miracle created by China in the vault of the sky.

1. A Path of Independent Development

China has relied on independent innovation and taken a phased approach in developing BDS. Starting from scratch, the system has undergone steady improvements and upgrades, providing both active and passive positioning and expanding from regional to global coverage.

The three-step BDS strategy. China began to develop its own navigation satellite system in 1994. BDS-1 entered service and began providing positioning services in China at the end of 2000. At this point, China became the third country in the world with a navigation satellite system. BDS-2 was completed in 2012, providing passive positioning services to the Asia-Pacific region. In 2020, BDS-3 was formally commissioned to provide satellite navigation services worldwide. This marked the successful conclusion of the three-step BDS strategy.

Accelerated progress towards a global era. In December 2012, BDS-2 entered into service, marking a new stage of development. In March 2015, China launched the first BDS-3 experimental satellite. In November 2017, the first two Medium Earth Orbit (MEO) satellites joined the BDS-3 system. The global deployment of the BDS configuration began to gather pace. In December 2018, China completed the primary deployment of 19 satellites. In June 2020, it completed the entire constellation deployment of 24 MEO satellites, three Geostationary Earth Orbit (GEO) satellites, and three Inclined Geosynchronous Orbit (IGSO) satellites. The next month, BDS-3 began to provide global services, upgrading BDS to a worldwide system.

2. Better Services for the Whole World

In the new era, BDS will provide better services around the globe for the benefit of all humanity. To this end, China will intensify integration of different technologies, improve its capacity for diversified and specialized services, promote industries engaged in BDS applications, and reinforce international cooperation and exchanges on all fronts. Through this process, we can promote economic and social development, meet the people's desire for a better life, and share the results and benefits of BDS throughout the world.

Open services and greater compatibility. BDS provides open, free satellite navigation services, and its ability to serve the public across the world is being constantly improved. Through active international cooperation and exchanges, China calls for and works towards greater compatibility and broader sharing among different navigation satellite systems.

Innovation and upgrading. Under the innovation-driven development strategy, China is building up its capacity for independent development based on innovation. BDS is consistently being upgraded by adopting new and emerging technologies such as the latest communication technologies and low earth orbiter navigation augmentation. Efforts are also under way to incorporate non-satellite navigation technologies into its scope.

Quality services. BDS ensures stable and uninterrupted operation, shows strength in specialized services, and delivers high-quality satellite navigation services to users worldwide. In order to foster a more enabling environment for BDS-related industries, China has improved relevant standards, policies and regulations, intellectual property rights protection, and dissemination and promotion.

Sharing for the common good. China will expand BDS applications and promote higher quality in related industries, so that the system will be incorporated into every aspect of society and facilitate work and daily life. China shares the progress of its navigation satellite system with the rest of the world, with the goal of benefits for all.

3. BeiDou Spirit in the New Era

The BDS development team have worked hard through successive generations to surmount all difficulties in their research. In the new era, they have fostered a BeiDou spirit of independent innovation, openness and inclusiveness, unity of purpose, and pursuit of excellence. It is a telling example of China's national spirit centered on patriotism and defined by reform and innovation in the new era. It also makes a fine addition to the CPC's long line of inspiring principles.

Independent innovation as the core competitive advantage. China has maintained independence in the research, design, construction and operation of BDS, keeping core technologies in key fields firmly in our own hands. This is the approach we have taken in confronting challenges and overcoming difficulties in the development of BDS.

A global vision of openness and inclusiveness. The world is becoming increasingly open and integrated. By making BDS available worldwide, China honors its commitment to helping people of all countries share the opportunities and fruits of development. This clearly demonstrates China's farsighted vision and its will to share the best it has to offer.

Unity of purpose for success. BDS is the fruit of the cooperation and dedication of its developers, the support of the whole nation, and the collaboration among all parties concerned. It embodies China's great tradition of working together and the Chinese people's deep love for their country.

The constant pursuit of excellence. China is striving to make BDS one of the best navigation satellite systems in the world by achieving excellence in technology, construction, management and services. It is designed to become one of China's most recognizable brands in the new era.

4. Outlook for the Future

In the years to come, China will further upgrade BDS technologies, functions and services. The goal is to create a comprehensive spatiotemporal system that is more extensive, more integrated, and more intelligent, and that provides flexible, smart, precise and secure navigation, positioning and timing services. In doing so, China will help improve people's wellbeing and promote human progress.

In building a more powerful BDS, China will create its own smart and distinctive system for operation, maintenance and management, and gain a competitive edge in services such as short message communication, ground-based and satellite-based augmentation, and international search and rescue. By steadily improving the quality and increasing the scope of its services, BDS will build the capacity to provide global decimeter-level positioning and navigation with high integrity, thereby delivering better services to users worldwide.

China will promote large-scale BDS applications and encourage their market-oriented, industrialized and globalized development to offer a broader range of public services of higher quality. We will further unleash market potential, expand application scenarios, increase application scale, create new mechanisms and dynamics, improve the industrial system, strengthen international industrial cooperation, and forge a fuller, more resilient industrial chain. The goal is to share our achievements in BDS development with people all over the world for their benefit.

We will establish a comprehensive national system for positioning, navigation and timing services, develop a variety of navigation methods, and pursue cross-sector innovation in cutting-edge technologies, synergy of different methods for higher performance, and multi-source information fusion and sharing. We will extend BDS services to provide underwater, indoor and deep space coverage, and offer integrated spatiotemporal information services that are based on unified reference and seamless coverage, and are flexible, intelligent, secure, reliable, convenient and efficient. This will contribute to building a global community of shared future and make the world a better place to live.

II. A World-Class Navigation Satellite System

Aiming to build a world-class global navigation satellite system, China has adhered to an innovation-oriented approach, pursued excellence and kept improving its technologies. BDS is now a top-class system characterized by cutting-edge technologies, pioneering design, and powerful functions.

1. Independently Developed Core Technologies

China has achieved innovations in the constellation configuration, technology systems and service functions of the navigation satellite system conforming to international norms. It has made breakthroughs and reached a world-leading level in several core technologies in terms of hybrid constellation, inter-satellite links, and signal structure.

Innovative constellation configuration. China is the first country to adopt a hybrid navigation constellation in medium and high earth orbits. A satellite in a high orbit covers a larger area and has a better anti-shielding capability; those in medium orbits offer global coverage, and are core to providing global services. By complementing each other, satellites in multiple orbits have a greater capability to serve not only the region, but also the entire world.

Inter-satellite links. This is China's first inter-satellite and satellite-ground joint network, thus realizing high-precision measurement and data transmission through inter-satellite links, and providing global services based on domestic ground stations.

Optimized signal structure. With breakthroughs in core technologies such as modulation, multiplexing, and channel coding, BDS takes the lead in using triple-frequency signals, in integrating navigation and positioning with communication functions, and in providing both basic navigation information and differential augmentation information. It has reached world-class level in signal ranging accuracy, anti-interference performance, and anti-multipath capabilities. It is compatible with other navigation satellite systems and capable of providing diversified and specialized services.

2. Innovative System Configuration

BDS is composed of a space segment, a ground segment, and a user segment:

– The space segment comprises 30 satellites located in three types of orbit – MEO, GEO and IGSO;

– The ground segment mainly consists of the operation control system, the telemetry tracking and command system, the inter-satellite link operation management system, and various service platforms for international search and rescue, short message communication, satellite-based augmentation, and ground-based augmentation.

– The user segment consists of terminals and applications compatible with other navigation satellite systems.

Building the BDS integrated inter-satellite and satellite-ground network, China's first aerospace system offering global network services, has led to remarkable improvements in China's aerospace R&D capability, and leapfrog progress in China's aerospace technology.

Outstanding batch production capability. Innovations have been introduced in the research and manufacturing of satellite-ground equipment as well as satellites and launch vehicles. Carrier rocket upper stages and navigation satellite platforms have been developed to enable batch production, intensive launch of satellites and rockets, and fast constellation deployment. In less than three years, 18 rockets deployed 30 satellites into orbit, a pace unmatched by any other country.

Independent development and operation of key components. Components such as aerospace-grade memory chips, satellite-borne processors, high-power microwave switches, traveling-wave tube amplifiers, and solid-state amplifiers have been developed and produced independently by China. The 100 percent independent development and operation of BDS core components has laid a solid foundation for its widespread use.

3. Quality and Diverse Services

With its powerful functions and reliable performance, BDS is able to provide a wide range of services to meet various requirements. It mainly provides positioning, navigation, timing, international search and rescue, and short message communication services to global users, while it offers short message communication, satellite-based augmentation, precise point positioning, and ground-based augmentation services to users in the Asia-Pacific.

Positioning, navigation and timing. Through 30 satellites, BDS offers free services to users across the world. Its positioning accuracy is better than 9 meters horizontally and 10 meters vertically, its velocity measurement accuracy is higher than 0.2 meters per second, and its timing is accurate to less than 20 nanoseconds.

International search and rescue. Through six MEO satellites, BDS provides, free of charge, a global distress alert service that meets international standards. Return links have been designed so that rescue requesters can receive confirmation messages.

Global short message communication. BDS is the first navigation satellite system to provide a global short message communication service. Through 14 MEO satellites, it provides a global random-access service to specific users with a maximum single message length of 560 bits (40 Chinese characters).

Regional short message communication. BDS is the first navigation satellite system to provide a regional short message communication service for authorized users. Through three GEO satellites, it provides a data transmission service to users in China and neighboring areas with a maximum single message length of 14,000 bits (1,000 Chinese characters). It can transmit texts, graphics and audio.

Satellite-based augmentation. Through three GEO satellites, BDS provides users in China and neighboring areas with a Category I precision approach service that meets international standards. It supports both single-frequency and dual-frequency multi-constellation augmentation, providing greater security for the transport sector.

Precise point positioning. Through three GEO satellites, BDS provides users in China and neighboring areas with a cost-free high-precision positioning augmentation service. Its positioning accuracy is better than 30 centimeters horizontally and 60 centimeters vertically, and its convergence time is less than 30 minutes.

Ground-based augmentation. Network ground stations have been built across China to provide real-time meter-level, decimeter-level, centimeter-level, and post-processing millimeter-level positioning augmentation services for industrial users and the general public.

III. Improving BDS Operation Management

As a major player in the aerospace industry that takes its responsibilities seriously, China continues to improve BDS operation management and the system's performance. It ensures continuous and stable operation, open and transparent information, and sustained, healthy and rapid development of the BDS system, so as to provide reliable, secure and high-quality spatiotemporal information services.

1. Ensuring Operational Reliability

Stable operation is vital to a navigation satellite system. Applying systems thinking, China has built a BDS operation management system with Chinese characteristics, organized on the basis of multi-party support, providing a joint inter-satellite and satellite-ground network control as its system feature, and hardware-software coordination and intelligent operation and maintenance as its technical feature. The system integrates regularized operation management support, smooth transition, comprehensive monitoring and assessment, and intelligent operation and maintenance, providing basic support for continuous and stable operation.

Strengthening regularized support. China is improving the mechanisms for multi-party joint support, consultation on operation status, and equipment inspection and maintenance, and building a smooth and coordinated workflow that shares information and facilitates efficient decision-making, to constantly improve regularized support for BDS operation management.

Ensuring smooth transition. In terms of the space segment, ground segment and user segment, China has realized smooth and orderly transition from BDS-2 to BDS-3 and ensured that users do not need to replace equipment and can enjoy upgraded services at minimal cost.

Reinforcing monitoring and assessment. China is improving resource allocation for continuous global monitoring and assessment of BDS. It carries out comprehensive and regularized monitoring and assessment of the configuration status, signal accuracy, signal quality and service performance of the system, to obtain timely and accurate information on its operation and service status.

Boosting operation and maintenance. China makes full use of big data, artificial intelligence, cloud computing and other new technologies to build a BDS data pool. It integrates data from multiple sources such as system operation, monitoring and assessment, and space environment, provides on-demand information sharing, and strengthens intelligent operation management of the system.

2. Improving BDS Service Performance

Higher accuracy and reliability are constant priorities. Always seeking progress while ensuring stability, China makes constant efforts to improve the BDS system status, provide a better spatiotemporal reference, and increase application scenarios. It will continue to raise the capability of the system, expanding its service domains and upgrading its service quality.

Upgrading the system. China will upgrade and transform ground-based facilities, renew the software of in-orbit satellites as needed, and refine satellite-ground processing models and algorithms. It will continue to strengthen the capacity of the integrated inter-satellite and satellite-ground network, and elevate the accuracy and quality of space signals, to ensure a steady improvement in BDS service performance.

A better spatiotemporal reference. China will establish and maintain a high-accuracy BDS time reference and carry out the monitoring of clock bias against other navigation satellite systems. Time biases will be broadcast in navigation messages. It will increase interoperability between the BDS time and the time of other navigation satellite systems. The BDS coordinate system will remain aligned with the International Terrestrial Reference Frame, and increase interoperability with other navigation satellite systems in this regard.

Expanding service domains. China will strengthen the multi-approach navigation capability of BDS and enable the system to provide flexible positioning, navigation and timing services. It will carry out exploration and tests of cislunar space service applications, and extend the BDS service capacity into deep space. It will work for breakthroughs in key technologies in integrating navigation and communication, and improve the system's capacity to provide services in complex environments and densely populated areas.

3. Releasing the Latest Information on BDS

Releasing system information is a basic means of strengthening users' understanding of the navigation satellite system and increasing their trust. With regard to BDS, China applies the principle of openness and transparency. It is building information dissemination platforms, improving dissemination mechanisms, and publishing timely, authoritative and accurate information on the system, so as to provide services to global users in a responsible manner.

Building multi-channel information releasing platforms. Through these platforms, China publishes information on BDS construction and operation, application and promotion, international cooperation, and relevant policies and regulations. These platforms include the official BDS website (www.beidou.gov.cn), monitoring and assessment websites (www. csno-tarc.cn; www.igmas.org) and the BDS WeChat official account (beidousystem).

Releasing BDS service documents. China regularly updates and releases interface control documentation on BDS open services, defines the interface specifications between BDS satellites and user terminals, and specifies the signal structure, basic characteristics, ranging codes, navigation messages and other content, so as to provide inputs for global BDS product development efforts. It updates and releases the open service performance standards, and specifies the coverage area and performance indexes of BDS open services.

Releasing information on system status. China releases timely system status information about satellite launches and commissioning, in-orbit tests, monitoring and assessment outcomes, and decommissioning. It also issues notifications to domestic and foreign users when appropriate before carrying out plans and operations that might affect user services.

IV. Promoting Sustainable Development of the BDS Applications Industry

In the new era, China has synergized the development and application of BDS. It has made continuous efforts to refine the products supporting the BDS industry, expand application fields, improve the industry ecosystem, and promote large-scale applications. BDS applications have been better integrated into the overall development of the national economy to promote the sound development of the BDS applications industry, so as to inject strong impetus into socioeconomic development.

1. Putting in Place Industrial Development Strategies

China has placed equal importance on the development and application of BDS, and promotes development through applications. It has made a well-conceived blueprint for the development of the BDS applications industry. China strives to push forward BDS applications across industries and regions through various projects, promotes use of the BDS system, and boosts high-quality development of the BDS industry.

Working out an innovative outline for BDS applications. Faced with new circumstances and requirements in the new era, China has focused its efforts on securing the industry ecosystem, developing basic and general-purpose technologies, and promoting the BDS applications industry. It has pooled strength from all sectors to create a new development dynamic based on concerted efforts and joint management.

Strengthening the planning and design of industrial development. China has formulated and implemented the Overall Plan for Comprehensively Promoting BDS Industrial Applications and a special plan for the development of the BDS industry. Various sectors and regions have made special plans and launched campaigns accordingly to improve the systems of industrial innovation, integrated applications, industrial ecosystems, and global services.

Implementing major projects of BDS industrial development. Focusing on ensuring security, encouraging innovation and developing industry, China has given play to the leveraging role of major projects to expedite the formation of a market-oriented and enterprise-based BDS industrial development framework. These efforts have advanced with a category-based approach following the principles of overall planning, intensive utilization, and prioritization.

2. Laying a Solid Foundation for Industrial Development

In developing BDS applications, China has focused on infrastructure, basic products, and basic software. With strengthened efforts in developing basic platforms for BDS applications and intensified support for application technology R&D, a solid foundation has been laid for the steady development of the BDS applications industry.

Improving infrastructure for BDS applications. China has established a set of platforms featuring BDS services including international search and rescue, short message communication, satellite-based augmentation, and ground-based augmentation. Featured BDS services have been more deeply integrated with various communication channels. With their expanding scope and depth, BDS applications have provided users with more efficient and convenient services.

Developing basic products for BDS applications. China has developed a series of basic products such as chips, modules and antennas, and realized 100-million-scale manufacturing of BDS products. In addition, basic products that integrate satellite navigation and inertial navigation, mobile communication, visual navigation, and other means have also been developed to strengthen the resilience of BDS application solutions.

Developing basic software for BDS applications. Through intensified efforts in independent research and development, China has made progress in turning basic generic technologies in areas such as positioning solutions, model development, data analysis, design, and simulation into software and tools, and ensuring that such software programs are functioning and easy to use.

3. Fostering a Sound Ecosystem for Industrial Development

By developing standards and norms, intellectual property rights, testing and certification, and industrial assessment in a systematic manner, China has created a sound industrial ecosystem for BDS applications with all necessary factors and a strong innovation capacity. With synergy across supply chains, industrial chains, innovation chains, and policy chains, the clustered development of the BDS applications industry has been pushed forward.

Advancing standardization. Leveraging the foundational and guiding role of standardization, China has updated the BDS standards system, and expedited the formulation and revision of standards concerning BDS applications. To promote industrial upgrading, China has made continuous efforts to form a comprehensive and sound BDS application standards system that covers organizational, sectoral, national and international standards, and ensures that all these standards are integrated and compatible with each other.

Strengthening intellectual property protection. China has raised the quality and efficiency of BDS-related patent examination to strengthen the BDS patent portfolio. The stakeholders of innovative BDS applications have been motivated to create, utilize, protect and manage intellectual property rights, laying solid foundations for the future development and exploitation of China's satellite navigation patents.

Improving product testing and certification systems. China has strengthened top-level design for the testing and certification of BDS-related navigation products and has built a network of public service platforms for product testing and certification. In order to improve the quality of BDS applications and ensure security and reliability, testing and certification of BDS products has been organized in key industries and fields.

Establishing an industrial assessment system. To ensure the healthy and sustainable development of the BDS applications industry, China has worked to improve the feedback mechanism for BDS applications and established an assessment system for key industries and fields, major regions, mass applications, and international applications.

Reinforcing collaborative efforts. To better meet market demand, China has encouraged the building of a BDS industry alliance to expand channels that bring together enterprises, universities, research institutes, and end-users. Relevant industry associations and societies have been mobilized to play their role in bringing together the government and enterprises, so as to facilitate communication and cooperation while improving industry self-discipline.

Building industrial clusters. Key regions and cities have been encouraged to deploy BDS applications extensively based on their own resource endowment, with due consideration given to national strategies. The objective is to consolidate the distinctive strengths of each region and create BDS industrial clusters with R&D institutions, key enterprises, and industrial parks as the mainstay.

4. Ways and Means to Promote Industrial Development

BDS has been widely used in various industries and fields in China's socioeconomic development. It has been deeply integrated with emerging technologies such as big data, the internet of things, and artificial intelligence, fostering new business forms based on BDS. Together these have underpinned digital socioeconomic transformation with improved quality and efficiency, adding convenience and color to people's lives.

Giving full play to the leading role of key industries. Some key industries that have the potential for scale application and significant socioeconomic benefits have been selected as pilot entities for BDS applications, along with their respective regions, with due consideration to national development strategies. In this way, China has worked out comprehensive solutions to push forward large-scale application of BDS.

Entering key fields. BDS has been swiftly applied to key fields that have a vital bearing on the national economy, people's lives, public interest, national security, public security, and economic security, and has effectively improved the reliability and security of these fields.

Empowering various industries and sectors. BDS has been deeply integrated into new infrastructure such as information infrastructure, integrated infrastructure, and innovative infrastructure, and has been widely used in key sectors such as transport, energy, agriculture, communica-

---

The Fast Growing BDS Applications Industry

In 2021, the total output value of China's satellite navigation and location-based service industry reached RMB470 billion.

In terms of product manufacturing, breakthroughs have been made in a series of key BDS technologies such as chips and modules, which has effectively driven up the shipment volume. By the end of 2021, there were more than 1 billion terminals using the BDS positioning function nationwide.

In terms of its applications, BDS has been widely applied to various industries and sectors, generating significant socioeconomic benefits. As of the end of 2021, BDS had been installed in more than 7.8 million road transport vehicles nationwide. Approximately 8,000 BDS terminals were in use on the country's railway network, and more than 100,000 agricultural machines were equipped with self-driving systems based on BDS. BDS-based services in health care, epidemic prevention, remote monitoring and online services sectors were worth almost RMB200 billion.

BDS-based applications have shown their growing relevance in scenarios closely related to daily life, notably in smartphones and smart wearable devices. BDS has been widely supported by products from international mainstream chip manufacturers, including smartphone device suppliers. In 2021, 324 million Chinese smartphones supporting BDS services were shipped, accounting for 94.5 percent of the country's total.

tions, meteorology, natural resources, the eco-environment, emergency management, and disaster mitigation, helping to reduce costs and increase efficiency.

Serving everyday life. Through applications such as smartphones, vehicle terminals, and wearable devices, BDS has been widely applied in daily life, the sharing economy, and areas that are important to public wellbeing. It comprehensively serves every aspect of people's everyday life such as green travel, food delivery, elderly and child care, health care, and education.

V. Upgrading BDS Governance

China constantly upgrades its BDS governance in the new era. It has made consistent efforts to bring forward innovative ideas on systems, mechanisms and development methods, to improve policies and regulations, to optimize organization and management, to build up strengths in high-caliber professionals, to promote technological innovation through reform, and to better combine a well-functioning market with competent government.

1. Updating the Systems and Mechanisms of Management

Based on BDS development needs, China makes overall plans, improves relevant mechanisms, and maximizes its system strength in pooling resources from government, market and social sectors to achieve synergy in developing BDS.

Improving management of the BDS project through innovation. To ensure that the BDS project is operating in a smooth, concerted, efficient, orderly and rule-based manner, China gives full play to the role of the project's leading group, and has set up a management system in which various departments work in concert with clear divisions of tasks and responsibilities. It has also established a mechanism for promoting the coordinated progress of the project, its applications, and international cooperation.

Establishing a mechanism for overall planning and coordination. China makes systemic plans for BDS infrastructure construction, application and promotion, international cooperation, management of satellite radio frequencies and orbits, intellectual property rights protection, standards formulation, and human resource development, and ensures their concerted progress, creating a closely connected and well-coordinated framework.

2. Promoting Technological Innovation Through System Reform

In advancing its innovation-driven development, China relies on innovation in both technology and systems. To speed up technological innovation, it has established and is now improving a mechanism for propelling innovation in satellite navigation technology.

Establishing a mechanism for original, integrated and collaborative innovation. Following the principle of independent innovation while remaining open to exchanges, China fosters original innovation bases for satellite navigation technologies, plans strategic, fundamental and forward-looking research, and builds up advanced systems for tackling key technological problems and promoting R&D in new products. To meet the need to fully integrate BDS with new-generation information technology, China adopts an approach of phased and incremental development and multifunctional integration, and operates a collaborative innovation mechanism across disciplines, subjects and fields to concentrate resources and factors for innovation and stimulate exponential development through innovation.

Improving an incentive mechanism that encourages competition. Upholding the principles of transparency, fair play, and mutual learning, China operates a competitive mechanism in which the best products are selected from multiple enterprises based on comparison of specifications and comprehensive assessment. This can apply appropriate pressure on market players while maintaining their enthusiasm, and thus help to achieve sustainable development, high quality and efficiency, and low cost.

Upgrading the system for organizing research and production. China strengthens the leading role of digitalization and other new technologies, and builds smart systems of testing, verification and assessment.

It optimizes the research and production procedures that evolve from R&D, verification, improvement to reverification, under a new model that adapts to synchronous R&D and batch production of multiple satellites, multiple rockets, and multiple stations, and increases the capability for fast deployment between space and ground.

3. Advancing Rule of Law in Satellite Navigation

In order to create a favorable domestic and international environment for the sustainable and healthy development of BDS, China has established a comprehensive legal framework for satellite navigation and taken part in global governance balancing considerations of development and security, current and future interests, and laws governing domestic and foreign-related matters.

Accelerating satellite navigation legislation. China is constantly building up the legal system of satellite navigation. The Regulations of the People's Republic of China on Satellite Navigation has been promulgated to regulate and strengthen the management of relevant activities. Support rules concerning system construction, operation and services, applications management, international cooperation, and security guarantees have also seen substantial improvement.

Continuing to improve the business environment. Committed to a business environment that is based on market principles, governed by law, and meets international standards, China has taken measures to regulate satellite navigation market order, create an enabling environment to protect market players' rights and interests, and improve government services. These have provided a stable, fair, transparent and predictable business environment, boosting market dynamism and development drive.

Regulating satellite navigation activities. Accurate and full information about BDS satellites is reported in a timely manner in line with the provisions on the registration of objects launched into outer space. Licenses for BDS radio frequencies, space radios, and ground stations are also issued in accordance with the law. The radio frequency bands used by BDS are protected by law, and the production, sale, or operation of any type of jamming equipment that interferes with satellite navigation is strictly prohibited and will be investigated and punished in accordance with the law.

Taking part in global governance of satellite navigation. In this field, China follows the principle of achieving shared growth through consultation and collaboration in global governance. It handles affairs concerning international interests within the framework of the International Committee on Global Navigation Satellite Systems (ICG) and participates in formulating relevant international rules, contributing to a fairer and more equitable international order in satellite navigation.

4. Fostering Talent for BDS

Talent is the resource of paramount importance for development and innovation. BDS always cultivates, attracts and guides talented individuals through its development, and encourages them to succeed. It has consistently expanded its personnel pool and given full play to their strengths, sustaining the industry with quality human resources.

Training competent professionals. China has updated its talent training framework in the fields relating to BDS positioning, navigation and timing. It has improved talent training, exchange and incentive mechanisms, set up platforms for talent growth, built national key laboratories, and enlarged the team of professionals with interdisciplinary training and a global vision.

Creating academic prosperity. To meet the requirements in developing frontier technologies in positioning, navigation and timing and the satellite navigation industry, China has strengthened research on basic theories and applications, and increased academic exchanges to raise the capacity for scientific and technological innovation.

Spreading scientific knowledge. China is continuing to build popular science bases, create immersive scenarios for experiential learning, carry out relevant activities, and publish content-rich books to spread knowledge about positioning, navigation and timing, and arouse the public's interest in science, especially in the fields related to time and space.

VI. Contributing to Building a Global Community of Shared Future

Navigation satellite systems are the common wealth of humanity. Following the principles of openness, integration, coordination, cooperation, compatibility, complementarity and sharing, China has carried out active international cooperation on BDS and advanced its international applications. This will enable the system to better serve the world, benefit humanity, and contribute to building a global community of shared future.

1. Increasing Compatibility and Interoperability of Diverse Systems

In order to provide users with more high-quality, diverse, secure and reliable services, China is active in advocating and advancing the compatibility and interoperability of different navigation satellite systems, carrying out coordination and consultation on the utilization of frequency and orbital slot resources, and working with other countries to make improvements.

Stepping up cooperation for better compatibility and interoperability. China continues to promote compatibility and interoperability between BDS and other navigation satellite systems and satellite-based augmentation systems, and to strengthen the compatibility and joint applications with other navigation satellite systems, so as to achieve resource sharing, complementarity and advances in technology. China works to establish bilateral and multilateral cooperation mechanisms in the field of satellite navigation, coordinates compatibility and interoperability efforts, and carries out active cooperation and exchanges with other countries on navigation satellite systems and satellite-based augmentation systems, in a bid to achieve common development of all navigation satellite systems around the world.

Carrying out coordination and consultation on the utilization of frequency and orbital slot resources. Abiding by the International Telecommunication Union rules, China works to safeguard the international order in terms of satellite network application and coordination and to facilitate coordination and consultation on navigation satellite frequencies and orbital slots through bilateral and multilateral negotiations. China is also an active participant in technological research and standards formulation led by international organizations, and joins with other countries to safeguard, utilize and expand navigation satellite frequency and orbital slot resources.

2. Promoting International Cooperation and Exchanges

China continues to expand the circle of international BDS friends and improve its global applications through measures such as strengthening cooperation mechanisms, increasing cooperation channels, and establishing cooperation platforms and windows.

Stepping up participation in international satellite navigation affairs. China has attended activities under the framework of the United Nations, and hosted ICG meetings. It also participates actively in research projects and proposes cooperation initiatives in this area, and works with other countries to promote global satellite navigation through extensive consultation.

Carrying out bilateral and multilateral cooperation and exchanges. China conducts cooperation and exchanges with regional organizations such as ASEAN and the League of Arab States, and countries in Africa, Latin America and elsewhere. It holds BDS/GNSS cooperation forums and provides application scenarios and solutions, so as to expand international applications of BDS.

Extending cooperation in testing and assessment. China collaborates with other countries to conduct testing and assessment on the performance of BDS and other global navigation satellite systems in positioning, navigation, timing, short message communication, international search and rescue, and other areas. It issues testing and assessment reports to increase users' knowledge and confidence about the conditions and performance of navigation satellite systems, strengthening cooperation in this area.

Establishing international education and training platforms. China continues to promote academic education of international students, especially at master's and doctoral levels, in disciplines related to satellite navigation. Relying on platforms such as the Regional Center for Space Science and Technology Education in Asia and the Pacific (China) affiliated to the United Nations, the BeiDou International Exchange and Training Center, and various BDS/GNSS centers, China actively carries out satellite navigation training activities to cultivate talent and build professional capacity in the field for the international community and in particular for developing countries.

Conducting international academic exchanges. Through strengthening international exchange platforms such as the China Satellite Navigation Conference and the International Summit on BDS Applications, China has constantly expanded the global influence of BDS. China also takes an active part in international academic exchange events in the field of satellite navigation and makes contribution to advances in satellite navigation technology worldwide.

3. Promoting the Ratification of BDS by International Standards

China is making every effort to have BDS ratified by international standards organizations and standards organizations in the industrial and specialized application sectors, so that the system can better serve global users and support relevant industries.

International civil aviation standards. The technical indicators of BDS have passed the authentication of the International Civil Aviation Organization, indicating that the system conforms with international civil aviation standards and is qualified to provide positioning, navigation and timing services for global users in the civil aviation sector.

International maritime standards. BDS has become an integral part of the global radio-navigation system and gained legal status in maritime applications worldwide. China has released the official standards for BDS shipborne receiver equipment, providing criteria on the design, production and testing of relevant maritime equipment for global manufacturers. The BDS short message communication service is making steady progress in aligning with the global maritime distress and safety system of the International Maritime Organization.

International search and rescue standards. China has issued an international standard for satellite emergency locators. It is also endeavoring to enable the BDS return link service to be ratified by the Cospas-Sarsat, and working on international compatibility and joint application of the return link service.

International mobile communication standards. The 3rd Generation Partnership Project has issued technical, performance and consistency testing standards that support BDS signals, enabling 2G, 3G, 4G and 5G networks and terminals to use BDS to achieve aided positioning and high-accuracy positioning.

International data exchange standards. China is working to incorporate BDS into international general standards for data receivers in fields such as high-accuracy differential positioning services, general data exchange formats, and positioning information output protocols.

4. Enabling BDS Development to Benefit the Whole World

China is working to expand and extend the international application of BDS products, services and industries, and accelerate the large-scale application of BDS worldwide, for the purpose of boosting economic and social development and improving public wellbeing across the globe.

Increasing the contribution of BDS products to the world. China is speeding up the integration of BDS products such as chips, modules and terminals into the international industrial system, enabling them to meet international requirements and align with international standards. Efforts are also made to give full play to the unique strengths of BDS products and enable them to integrate into local industries, upgrade services, and boost economic and social development.

Promoting BDS services overseas. China has set up an international satellite navigation application and service network, and joined with other countries to build satellite navigation service platforms and provide international services and applications such as global search and rescue, short message communication, satellite-based augmentation, and ground-based augmentation to meet the diverse demands of global users.

Expanding international cooperation on satellite navigation. China engages in active cooperation with other countries and international organizations on technology R&D and the satellite navigation industry. It has set up overseas BDS application and industrialization promotion centers, and strives to build solid foundations for the satellite navigation industry. It is strengthening cooperation with regional organizations such as ASEAN, the African Union, the League of Arab States, and the Community of Latin American and Caribbean States, and releasing BDS-based solutions in the fields of smart cities, public security, precision agriculture, digital transport, and disaster prevention and mitigation, which are being piloted in Asia, Africa, and Latin America.

Conclusion

To explore the cosmos has been the dream of the Chinese nation for millennia. From observing Beidou (Chinese pinyin for the Big Dipper) to developing and using BDS, from gazing at the stars to utilizing the space, the Chinese people have shown their great potential and created a promising future. China is committed to independent innovation, building a comprehensive spatiotemporal system that is more extensive, more integrated, and more intelligent on the next generation of BDS, and continuing to advance human progress in exploring the universe.

The universe is vast enough to accommodate exploration and utilization by all countries; by the same token, it demands global cooperation. China is ready to share its achievements in developing BDS, and it will work with all countries to promote the development of navigation satellite systems, venture into deeper space, and make an even greater contribution to building a global community of shared future and a better world.

Jointly Build a Community with a Shared Future in Cyberspace

The State Council Information Office of
the People's Republic of China

November 2022

Preface

The internet is an important human achievement and a symbol of the arrival of the information age. As a new round of technological revolution and industrial transformation accelerates, the internet has turned the world into a global village, and the international community is becoming more and more interconnected, with a shared future becoming more apparent. It is the responsibility of all of humanity to develop, use, and manage the internet well and make it more beneficial to mankind.

Since China gained full access to the internet, it has always been committed to promoting internet development and governance. Since the 18th National Congress of the Communist Party of China (CPC) in 2012, the CPC Central Committee with Comrade Xi Jinping at the core has adhered to the philosophy of people-centered development and attached great importance to the internet. China engages in vigorous development, active use, and effective governance of the internet, and has made historic progress in relevant undertakings. Hundreds of millions of Chinese people have a greater sense of gain from sharing the achievements of internet development, and have contributed to building a peaceful, secure, open, cooperative and orderly cyberspace.

With the rapid development of the internet, the governance of cyberspace is facing ever more prominent problems. General Secretary Xi Jinping has proposed the important concept of building a community with a shared future in cyberspace, and elaborated a series of major principles and proposals for global internet development and governance. His proposal conforms to the development trends of the information age and of human society. It responds to the risks and challenges facing cyberspace, demonstrates the CPC's commitment to contributing to human progress and world harmony, and reinforces China's sincere desire to strengthen internet development and governance cooperation with other countries. In the new era, China's international cooperation in cyberspace, under the vision of building a community with a shared future in cyberspace, has continued to achieve new progress, new breakthroughs, and new prospects.

This white paper introduces China's vision of internet development and governance in the new era and its actions, shares its achievements in promoting the building of a community with a shared future in cyberspace, and outlines the prospects for international cooperation.

I. Building a Community with a Shared Future in Cyberspace Is Essential in the Information Age

Interconnection is the basic nature of cyberspace. Sharing and co-governance is the common vision of internet development. With the rapid development of global information technology, the internet has penetrated into all aspects of human life and work. As a consequence, humanity is increasingly confronted with development and security challenges in cyberspace, which must be addressed through joint efforts.

1. A community with a shared future in cyberspace is an important part of a global community of shared future

The world is presently undergoing a period of profound changes on a scale unseen in a century. A new revolution in science, technology and industry is gaining momentum. The Covid-19 epidemic has had a far-reaching impact, while the forces of unilateralism, protectionism, and opposition to globalization are on the rise. The world economic recovery is sluggish, frequent regional conflicts and turmoil erupt, and global problems are intensifying. The world has entered a new period of turbulence and change.

Problems with the internet such as unbalanced development, unsound regulation, and unreasonable order are becoming more prominent. Cyber-hegemonism poses a new threat to world peace and development.

Certain countries are exploiting the internet and information technology as a tool to seek hegemony, interfere in other countries' internal affairs, and engage in large-scale cyber theft and surveillance, raising the risk of conflict in cyberspace.

Some countries attempt to decouple with others, and create schism and confrontation in cyberspace. The increasingly complex cybersecurity situation calls for more just, reasonable and effective cyberspace governance. Global threats and challenges in cyberspace necessitate strong global responses.

China is the world's largest developing country and the country with the largest number of internet users. It understands the underlying trends of the information age; upholds a people-centered approach; and supports global governance based on extensive consultation, joint contribution, and shared benefits. China insists that the building of a community with a shared future in cyberspace should be based on multilateral and multiparty participation and consultation, respect for cyber sovereignty, and a spirit of partnership; and the international community should be encouraged to expand pragmatic cooperation and jointly deal with associated risks and challenges. The goal of building a community with a shared future in cyberspace conforms to the developments of the information age and meets the needs and expectations of the people throughout the world. It is a plan that China contributes to the global efforts to promote the development and governance of cyberspace on the basis of respecting cyber sovereignty.

The community with a shared future in cyberspace is an important part of a global community of shared future. Related concepts and proposals on development, security, governance and universal benefits are in conformity with the concepts of a global community of shared future and the distinctive features of cyberspace; and promoting a community with a shared future in cyberspace will provide abundant digital impetus, a solid security safeguard, and a broader consensus on cooperation to this end.

2. Build a community of development, security, responsibility and shared interests

To build a community with a shared future in cyberspace, we should hold to a vision of extensive consultation, joint contribution and shared benefits in global governance, and promote a multilateral, democratic and transparent international internet governance system. We strive to realize the goals of innovation-driven development, security, order, equality, respect, openness, and shared interests in cyberspace, so that cyberspace will be a community that benefits all of humanity.

Build a community of development. As the integration and innovation of a new generation of information and communication technologies accelerates, digital, networking and intelligent technologies have increased their penetration throughout the economy and society, profoundly changing people's approaches to life and work. However, imbalances in internet penetration, infrastructure construction, technological innovation and creation, the digital economy, digital literacy, and skills affect and restrict IT development and digital transformation around the world, especially in developing countries. To build a community of development, we should adopt more active, inclusive, coordinated, and beneficial policies to accelerate the construction of global information infrastructure and provide developing countries with accessible, affordable and useful internet services. We will give full play to the role of the digital economy as an engine in global economic development, and actively promote digital industrialization and industrial digital transformation.

Build a community of security. Security is a prerequisite for development. A secure, stable and prosperous cyberspace is of great significance to all countries. Cybersecurity is a global challenge, and no country can remain in isolation. Safeguarding cybersecurity is the shared responsibility of the international community. Building a community of security is to uphold the concept of open and cooperative cybersecurity, attach equal importance to security and development, and encourage and regulate both. We will strengthen international cooperation in protecting critical information infrastructure and data security, maintain information technology neutrality and industrial globalization, and jointly curb the abuse of information technology. We should strengthen strategic mutual trust, share timely information on cyber threats, effectively coordinate the handling of major cybersecurity incidents, cooperate to combat cyber terrorism and crimes, and jointly safeguard peace and security in cyberspace.

Build a community of responsibility. Cyberspace is a common space for human activities, and it should be jointly controlled by all countries. To build a community of responsibility is to adhere to multilateral participation and multiparty participation, and actively promote reform and development of the global internet governance system. We should leverage the role of the United Nations as the main channel in international cyberspace governance, and give play to the role of government, international organizations, internet companies, technical communities, social organizations and individual citizens to promote mutual trust and coordinated and orderly cooperation. To make the governance system more just and equitable, we should improve dialogue and consultation mechanisms, jointly study and formulate norms for cyberspace governance, and reflect the interests and concerns of all parties in a more balanced way, especially those of developing countries.

Build a community of shared interests. The achievements of internet development and governance should be shared by all countries to ensure that different countries, ethnic groups, and peoples all enjoy the dividends of internet development on an equal basis. Building a community of shared interests means putting people first, promoting science and technology for good, and making the digital economy more inclusive. We should step up policy support to help micro, small and medium-sized enterprises use new-generation information technology to promote innovation in products, services, processes, organizations and business models, so that these enterprises can share more opportunities from the development of the digital economy. We should attend to the protection of vulnerable groups on the internet, strengthen the cultivation of internet ethics and civilization, promote the healthy development of internet culture and foster a sound cyber environment. We should promote inclusive development on a global scale, reinforce the cyber development capabilities of developing countries, bridge the digital divide, share the achievements of internet development, and facilitate the effective implementation of the United Nations 2030 Agenda for Sustainable Development.

3. Basic principles for building a community with a shared future in cyberspace

To build a community with a shared future in cyberspace, we should adhere to the following basic principles:

Respect cyber sovereignty. The principle of sovereign equality, as enshrined in the UN Charter, is a fundamental norm governing contemporary international relations in cyberspace. The rights of all countries to choose their own path of network development and governance model, and to equally participate in international governance in cyberspace should be respected. All countries have the right to formulate pubic policies, laws, and regulations on cyberspace in the context of their national conditions and international experience. No country should seek cyber hegemony; use the internet to interfere in other countries' internal affairs; engage in, incite, or support cyber activities that endanger other countries' national security, or infringe on other countries' key information infrastructure.

Safeguard peace and security. A secure and stable cyberspace is important for the common wellbeing of humanity. All countries should persevere in resolving disputes and differences through dialogue and consultation, comprehensively addressing traditional and non-traditional security threats, and ensuring peace and security in cyberspace. Countries should oppose hostile cyber actions and aggression, prevent arms race and armed conflicts in cyberspace, and prevent and oppose terrorism, obscenity, drug trafficking, money laundering, gambling, and other criminal activities in cyberspace. All parties should abandon the Cold War mentality, zero-sum game and double standards; seek peace through cooperation; and strive to achieve their own security through common security.

Promote openness and cooperation. Openness is a prerequisite for international cooperation in cyberspace and an important condition for building a community with a shared future in cyberspace. All countries should uphold the concept of openness, pursue open policies, improve the level of openness, and jointly promote the sound development of the internet. We will actively build bilateral, regional and international cooperation platforms; increase the complementarity of resource strengths; maintain a global system of coordinated innovation; and promote the inclusive development of different systems, ethnic groups, and cultures in cyberspace. We oppose politicizing cybersecurity issues. We oppose trade protectionism. We oppose narrow-minded factionalism. We oppose dividing the internet and exploiting one's own strengths to undermine the security of other countries' supply chains in information and communications technology (ICT) products and services.

Maintain good order. Cyberspace, like the real world, values both freedom and order. Freedom is the purpose of order, and order is the guarantee of freedom. It respects the rights of netizens to exchange ideas and express their wishes, and seeks a sound cyber order in accordance with the law. Cyberspace is not an "extrajudicial place". Cyberspace is virtual, but the users of cyberspace are real and they should abide by the law and the rights and obligations of all parties should be clarified. We will continue to manage, run, and use the internet in accordance with the law, and ensure that the internet operates in a sound manner based on the rule of law. We will strengthen the development of cyber ethnics and civilization, employ the guiding role of moral education, and use the outstanding achievements of human civilization to nourish cyberspace and preserve the online environment.

II. Development and Management of the Internet in China

China regards the internet as a platform for opening up and cooperation, where good order and positive energy benefit the people. In the new development stage and guided by the new development philosophy, the country is building a new development dynamic. It is set to build up its strength in cyberspace and digital technologies. Progress has been made in boosting the digital economy, building a clean and sound online environment, and guarding against risks to cyberspace security. This has provided sound services, support and a guarantee for high-quality development, and laid solid foundations for building a community with a shared future in cyberspace.

1. Booming digital economy

China has advanced the construction of information infrastructure and spread the application of the internet. Driven by information technology (IT) innovation, it is growing new industries, new business forms, and new business models, and moving faster to develop the digital economy for deeper integration with the real economy, and to foster new growth drivers for new development. According to the statistics provided by research agencies, by 2021, the value of the digital economy had reached 45.5 trillion yuan, accounting for 39.8 percent of GDP and becoming a major growth engine. China's digital economy has ranked second worldwide for many years.

The scale of information infrastructure construction continues to grow. By June 2022, there were 1.05 billion internet users in China, and the internet penetration rate had reached 74.4 percent. A total of 1.85 million 5G cell towers had been built with 455 million 5G cell phone subscribers. China hosts the world's largest 5G network and becomes one of global leaders in 5G standards and technology. China also takes the lead in realizing the large-scale commercial use of standalone (SA) 5G. China has conducted international cooperation in 5G technological innovation, development, and construction, and made important contributions to global 5G penetration. It has updated the Internet Protocol Version 6 (IPv6) on its backbone networks, metropolitan area networks, and LTE networks, and increased the IPv6 support of main internet websites and applications. By July 2022, China had 697 million active IPv6 users.

The BeiDou-3 global navigation satellite system is now operational, and began to provide global services in July 2020. In 2021 China's satellite navigation and positioning services generated 469 billion yuan of industrial output. By year end there were more than one billion terminal products with BeiDou positioning functions in use, and more than 7.9 million automobiles and 100,000 automatic driving farming vehicles had installed the BeiDou system. Moreover, medical and health devices, remote monitoring, online services and other downstream service sectors reported nearly 200 billion yuan of output value. The BeiDou industrial system is in place and provides notable economic and social benefits.

Digital technological innovation and application continue to make progress. China vigorously cultivates new technologies and applications such as artificial intelligence (AI), Internet of Things (IoT) and next-generation communication networks to accelerate the transformation from digitalization and network-based service to artificial intelligence in various economic and social sectors. Innovation has become a defining feature in the country. The big data industry is growing swiftly, with a compound annual growth rate exceeding 30 percent during the 13th Five-year Plan period (2016-2020). In 2021 large internet companies and related service businesses generated 1.55 trillion yuan of revenue, up 21.2 percent year on year. The fields such as smart industry, smart transport, intelligent health, and smart energy have become areas of rapid growth in the number of industrial IoT connections.

The industrial internet has grown rapidly, and the digital transformation of manufacturing industry continues. By February 2022, 55.3 percent of the key processes of large industrial enterprises had become digitally controlled, and the application of digital R&D tools was as high as 74.7 percent. The Action Plan for Industrial Internet Development (2018-2020) was formulated, and an innovation and development initiative for the industrial internet has been carried out, stimulating nearly 70 billion yuan of investment and incubating four national industrial internet demonstration bases and 258 pilot projects. The Action Plan for Innovation and Development of the Industrial Internet (2021-2023) is now being implemented. Compatible industrial internet infrastructure has boosted the connectivity between enterprises, equipment, and products, as well as contacts between people.

The digital transformation of agriculture is making steady progress. 5G, the IoT, big data and AI have been applied in agricultural production and management, and key technological development and innovative application research for intelligent agriculture and farming machinery have been strengthened. China has launched pilot agricultural IoT projects, carried out smart irrigation projects, digital management and smart renovation of public irrigation infrastructure, promoted big data application in agriculture and rural areas, and built an information service system covering the whole agricultural production process. China has built the world's second largest databank and information system of species resources, developed the "golden seeding platform", and spread digital management services for agricultural equipment.

Digitalization and the provision of digital capacity continue to grow. E-commerce is flourishing. In 2021, China's online retail sales stood at 10.8 trillion yuan, up 12 percent year-on-year and accounting for 24.5 percent of the total retail sales of consumer goods. The turnover in China's cross-border e-commerce reached 1.92 trillion yuan, up 18.6

percent year-on-year. The scale of third-party payment transactions continues to expand. New methods have been introduced to upgrade commercial models of the service industry, and internet-based medical services, online education, and remote working have accelerated the digitalization of the service industry. The capacity in cross-border payment for digital services keeps increasing. In 2021, China's trade in digitally deliverable services reached 2.33 trillion yuan, up 14.4 percent year-on-year.

2. Digital technology benefits the people

China has developed the internet extensively, with the aim of benefiting the people. As part of its efforts to implement the UN 2030 Agenda for Sustainable Development, guided by the people-first development philosophy, China has promoted internet application in education, medical services, poverty alleviation, and other public services, improved digital technologies to make such services inclusive and benefit all, and extended the public's digital literacy and skills.

The internet has helped achieve good results in China's targeted poverty alleviation. The country implemented the Action Plan for Internet-Aided Poverty Alleviation, making extensive use of the internet in five poverty alleviation projects – internet coverage, rural e-commerce, raising education and skills, information services, and public welfare. China has extended internet access to all poverty-stricken areas. By the end of 2020, 98 percent of all poverty-stricken villages had access to optical services, and more than 12 million people in poverty had benefited from lower internet access fee. Online retail sales in rural areas amounted to 2.05 trillion yuan in 2021, up 11.3 percent year-on-year, and more than 2,400 county-level e-commerce public service and logistic delivery centers had been built across the country, with over 148,000 village e-commerce service outlets. An initial online information service system for poverty alleviation has been established. By the end of 2020, 454,000 information service outlets had been set up to provide services to villagers, remote medical services were available in the hospitals of all poor counties, and basic financial services covered 99.2 percent of all administrative villages. The online sales platform for farm and sideline products from poor regions covered all 832 poor counties across China, more than 90,000 products on the platform for sale, with a transaction value exceeding 9.97 billion yuan. The Social Assistance of China website has 65.34 million registered users, publishing 7.37 million notes of commodity demand, 5.84 million of which successfully matched.

IT application in education has improved. Focusing on information networks, platforms, digital resources, smart campus, innovative applications, and reliability and safety, the construction of new education infrastructure has been accelerated to build a high-quality education support system. The school network connectivity initiative had been completed. By the end of 2021, all primary and middle schools in China had internet access, 99.95 percent of which now have 100M bandwidth. More than 210,000 schools had wireless network services, and 99.5 percent of all schools had multi-media classrooms.

China has launched a national education digitalization initiative. Smart Education of China, an online public service platform, opened in March 2022. This platform merges the resources of national smart education platforms for primary and secondary education, vocational education, and higher education as well as the 24365 online platform that provides employment services for college graduates. To date it has connected 529,000 schools and colleges, reaching 18.44 million teachers, and 291 million students and other learners. It now provides 34,000 videos, articles and handbooks in basic education, 6,628 vocational training courses, and 27,000 higher education courses.

Better IT-based services for people with different needs. Barrier-free access to information services has been increased to help the elderly and people with disabilities enjoy a digital life. Diverse measures have been adopted to create barrier-free conditions for information exchanges among people with disabilities. Effective methods have been introduced to help the elderly with travel, medical services, shopping, cultural, and entertainment activities, and to handle other affairs in their daily life, solving their problems by using smart technology. The internet has also been utilized to protect women's rights and interests in relation to health, education, and the environment. Notable progress has been made with internet-related protection of minors.

Panel 1　Action Plan for Internet-Aided Poverty Alleviation

Giving full play to the internet in poverty relief, China carried out the Action Plan for Internet-Aided Poverty Alleviation. It includes five projects:

(1) expanding internet coverage in poor areas, accelerating R&D and application of mobile terminals, developing mobile applications for poverty alleviation, and promoting R&D of audio-visual technology using the languages of minority ethnic groups;

(2) developing rural e-commerce, holding online fairs for poverty alleviation, and expanding internet financial services into poverty-stricken areas;

(3) developing internet-based education and skills improvement programs, including internet-based remote education, training of local people and government employees, and helping college graduates work as village officials or start internet-related businesses in rural areas;

(4) launching information service projects, including building a unified poverty alleviation big data platform, featuring one platform for each county, and one outlet for each town, assigning one leading figure in each village, opening one terminal and keeping one record book for each household, fostering a contingent of workers devoted to poverty alleviation, and building a social security network in the poor regions;

(5) carrying out public welfare programs for poverty alleviation, providing paired assistance to poor regions and launching branding campaigns for this purpose.

---

3. Steadily improving legal framework for cyberspace

China governs cyberspace in accordance with the law, and applies the rule of law as a fundamental measure to develop a sound digital industry and build a standard-based and orderly online environment. It is steadfast in applying the law in governing, running and using the internet, to ensure that the internet develops within the bounds of the law.

A complete cyber law system. China has formulated and enforced a number of fundamental and comprehensive laws that affect the overall situation, including the Electronic Commerce Law of the People's Republic of China, Electronic Signature Law of the People's Republic of China, Cybersecurity Law of the People's Republic of China, Data Security Law of the People's Republic of China, and Personal Information Protection Law of the People's Republic of China. These laws serve as key pillars of the cyber legislation framework in which the Constitution plays a cardinal role, laws and administrative, divisional, and regional regulations serve as important support, traditional legislation lays the foundations, and specialized cyber laws governing online content management, information technology development, cybersecurity and other elements function as the backbone.

Rigorous cyber law enforcement. China has established a robust mechanism for coordinating cyber law enforcement to crack down on telecom and online fraud, online gambling, online pyramid selling, internet misinformation, cyberbullying, and other crimes. It has taken further steps to enforce the laws for protecting personal information, managing online information and content, and safeguarding cybersecurity and data safety. It always enforces laws in a precise and prompt manner to deter and curb illegal online activities and create an increasingly rule-based and orderly cyberspace.

Introducing new ideas and measures for cyber judiciary work. China actively employs information technology while furthering judiciary reform to make judiciary work more internet-based and transparent. Smart courts and smart procuratorates have been launched to serve the public, rules for online judicial proceedings are being improved, and a new mechanism for internet courts to adjudicate online cases online is becoming increasingly mature.

Spreading knowledge about cyber laws. China prioritizes its efforts to spread legal knowledge and takes law and order as a fundamental task for strengthening the rule of law. It consistently publicizes legal information through online channels. Information on the Constitution, the Cybersecurity Law, Data Security Law, and Personal Information Protection Law and other laws and regulations has been spread on various important occasions like the National Constitution Day, National Security Education Day, National Cybersecurity Week, and Intellectual Property Rights Week. Laws are clearly explained in the form of case studies to raise the public's legal awareness in cyberspace and web literacy and morality, especially among teenagers. A sound online and social atmosphere for respecting, learning, abiding by, and using the law is taking shape.

4. Rich and varied digital content

Positive and mainstream ideas and opinions are spreading online. New Marxist theories adapted to the context of contemporary China have struck their roots in the hearts of the people. The core socialist values guide online culture. The internet has become a new platform supporting cultural prosperity, a new spiritual home for the public, and a new place for building consensus and concentrating positive energy. Through the internet, China is presenting an accurate, multidimensional and panoramic image to the outside world.

Vigorous positive energy on the internet. Mainstream public opinion is growing in strength; positive and healthy content is increasing; popular views in support of the CPC, socialism, reform and opening up, our great country, and all ethnic groups are resonating among internet users; advanced cultural elements are filling cyberspace. The internet in China is open, harmonious and orderly. In cyberspace, more than one billion Chinese netizens learn what is happening across the world, express and exchange views, participate in state and social governance, build consensus, strength, and unity, and strive for a better future.

Diverse cyberculture. Online videos and audios, literature, music and interactive entertainment are expanding rapidly in China, producing huge volumes of cultural content, and providing the people with rich intellectual nourishment. Digital libraries, museums on "cloud", online theaters, exhibitions and concerts, VR travel – these high-quality cultural services allow people to enjoy themselves at their homes. A diverse cyberculture also gives birth to various new business modes.

Upgraded means of online communication. Big data, cloud computing, artificial intelligence, virtual reality, augmented reality and other information technologies are making great progress and expediting innovations in the means and channels of online communication. The public communication media are relying more on mobile devices, employing more engaging ways of expression, and diversifying in form. More and more integrated media products that employ advanced technologies and original designs have emerged. The Party's voice is spreading faster, farther, and wider, becoming the strongest on the internet in China, and winning wide popular support.

5. Cleaner cyberspace

Cyberspace is a common space for internet users. A clean and sound cyber environment is in the interests of the people, whereas a polluted and degenerate one is against the public interests. China is committed to creating a healthy, civilized, clean and righteous cyber ecosystem.

Launching Operation "Qinglang". China has launched the campaign to rectify the disorder in cyberspace, which has caused strong public concern. It has tightened regulation, taken rigorous action against online activities that violate the law and regulations, and striven to rein in chaotic fandom culture. The emphasis has been on cleaning up illegal and immoral content, including "porn, obnoxious, abnormal, fake, vulgar and gambling-related content", and on tackling chronic malpractice on online platforms, with a focus on live-streaming and short video platforms. Efforts have been made to bring under control "internet trolling", and suppress the operation of antisocial internet accounts. Through these efforts, online disorder has been contained and cyberspace has been cleansed.

Promoting internet civilization. China regulates the production, release, and dissemination of online content, as well as internet philanthropy. It has hosted the Internet Civilization Conference, and taken measures to build a civilized internet, so as to foster a wholesome, inspiring and righteous internet culture. We give full play to the main roles of government, platforms, social organizations, and internet users to jointly promote the civilized operation and use of the internet, share the achievements and build a healthy community online and offline.

6. More standardized operation for online platforms

In recent years, platform economy has been growing vigorously, with new business forms and models mushrooming in China. The platforms have played important roles in promoting quality social and economic development and meeting people's increasing desire for a better life. Meanwhile, problems such as monopoly and algorithm abuse have undermined fair competition and damaged consumers' rights and interests. China has been actively developing its legal system to make it compatible with the platform economy, improving its regulatory mechanism to boost business development, and fostering a sound environment for the digital economy so as to promote fair competition and orderly development on social media platforms.

Anti-monopoly review and supervision. A number of policies and regulations have been devised to provide clear guidance for the sound operation of the platforms, such as Guidelines of the Anti-monopoly Commission of the State Council for Anti-monopoly in the Field of Platform Economy, and Measures for the Supervision and Administration of Online Transactions. Investigations have been conducted on platform behaviors that hamper fair competitions and infringe upon the rights and interests of the consumers and employees, such as compelling platform users to choose one platform rather than another, engaging in big data-enabled price discrimination against existing customers, and blocking certain URL links. Administrative penalties have been imposed to protect the rights and interests of market players including small and medium-sized enterprises, employees and consumers.

Stepping up regulation related to new technologies and applications. China has steadily improved rules and regulations regarding new technologies and applications such as artificial intelligence, big data, and cloud computing. It has strengthened the regulation of services involving block chain and algorithm-based marketing and taken legal action against conduct such as algorithm abuse and illegal processing of personal information, so as to ensure that new technologies and applications better serve the people.

Advancing industry self-discipline. China's internet social organizations and industry associations have given full play to their roles in formulating self-discipline convention and guidance in urging internet companies to operate properly, actively take their social responsibilities, and accept public supervision, so as to create a healthy market order characterized by honest operation, positive interaction, and fair competition.

7. Effectively guaranteed cybersecurity

China has further consolidated its lines of defense against cyber threats. Top-level cybersecurity design has been strengthened, a basic legal framework including the Cybersecurity Law, Data Security Law, and Personal Information Protection Law is in place, and China's capacity to safeguard cybersecurity is improving steadily.

Intensifying efforts to protect critical information infrastructure. China has promulgated the Regulations on the Security and Protection of Critical Information Infrastructure. China coordinates the strengths of its government and social sectors through various measures so that all relevant sectors are working in synergy, taking on their respective responsibilities to protect critical information infrastructure in accordance with the law. It is intensifying risk assessment and safety inspection, increasing capacity in supervision and early-warning, establishing the mechanism for cybersecurity information sharing, identifying risks in a timely manner, conducting analysis and assessment, and engaging in emergency response at the earliest possible time.

Ensuring the regulated development of cyberspace. China balances internet development with law-based administration. It encourages online platforms to play a bigger role in technological innovation, increasing economic vitality, and benefiting the people with information technologies. At the same time, it is taking action against unfair competition by some platforms which abuse their strengths in data, technology, market share and capital, and it is making every effort to build a market environment for fair competition, inclusive development and open innovation.

Promoting the integrated development of cybersecurity studies, technology and industry. Cybersecurity studies have been categorized as a primary discipline. The country has selected a number of pilot colleges for cybersecurity studies, and established a special fund. More than 60 universities now have cybersecurity colleges, and over 200 have undergraduate courses in cybersecurity. The industrial ecosystem for cybersecurity is also improving. A basic industrial system has taken shape, and different cybersecurity products have been developed for different fields and so have different technologies to meet different needs. China has set up the National Cybersecurity Talent and Innovation Base and is build-

---

Panel 2   China Cybersecurity Week

Netizens' cybersecurity awareness and capability concerns not only their immediate interests, but also national cybersecurity. To raise the public's awareness and increase their skills, China has had a cybersecurity week every year since 2014. Themed "Cybersecurity: for and by the People", the event provides activities such as exhibitions, theme days, forums, public service advertising, featured programs, solicitation of good ideas, competitions, online classes, and awards for exemplary performance. During the week, local governments and industry regulatory authorities should hold relevant activities within their jurisdiction.

---

ing national cybersecurity industrial parks and pilot areas for integrating cybersecurity studies, technology, and industry, so as to create an environment for different sectors to reinforce each other.

Strengthening personal information protection. China continues to improve the legal framework protecting personal information. It promulgated the Personal Information Protection Law to address prominent problems like collecting excessive personal information and illegally obtaining or trading it, thereby providing an all-round and systematic legal guarantee for protecting personal information. To protect privacy, China has also taken firm action against mobile apps that illegally collect and use personal data, and other crimes.

Increasing the ability to ensure data safety. China has moved swiftly to handle the challenges to data safety posed by the digital transformation of the economy and society. It has promulgated the Data Security Law, setting out the legal framework for administration of data. It has established a sound basic system for categorized and tiered protection of data, supervision and early warning on risks, emergency response, data security review, and administration of cross-border data security. With increasing strength, it can effectively prevent and reduce threats to data security.

Combating cybercrimes and cyberterrorism. China has taken tough actions against cybercrimes in accordance with the law, and cut through the interest chains behind the criminality, so as to protect the netizens' legitimate rights and interests in cyberspace. It has launched the "Clean Cyberspace" campaign and other special campaigns against cybercrimes like hacking, telecom and online fraud, and online infringement and piracy, restricting the space available for internet crimes, and working to build a clean cyberspace. China is resolute in implementing relevant UN resolutions. It firmly fights against terrorist activities planned and executed online, eliminates audio and video files promoting terrorism from the internet, disseminates anti-terrorism information. The goal is to build an online counter-terrorism system in which the government serves to guide, internet enterprises assume the main responsibility, and social organizations and the public participate.

III. China's Contribution to Building a Community with a Shared Future in Cyberspace

Upholding the principle of extensive consultation, joint contribution, and shared benefits, China has continued to strengthen bilateral, regional and international dialogue and cooperation in cyberspace, and committed itself to forming extensive partnerships with parties throughout the international community. It has engaged in active cross-border collaboration in terms of the digital economy, cyberspace security, and reform and development of global cyberspace governance to promote inclusive development of the internet. All these efforts contribute to building a community with a shared future in cyberspace.

1. Expanding cooperation on the digital economy

China actively participates in international cooperation on the digital economy. It has played an active part in constructing information infrastructure, promoting the integrated growth of the digital and the real economy, and accelerating global cooperation on digital governance, thereby contributing substantially to the development of the digital economy worldwide.

(1) Construction of information infrastructure

Along with the international community, China has played an active part in constructing information infrastructure and expanding internet coverage and application, for greater connectivity of global digital infrastructure.

China has contributed to the laying of optical cables and submarine cables worldwide. Chinese enterprises have provided support for many countries in constructing information and communications infrastructure, opening up digital information expressways for other developing countries. By laying cables and building base stations, China has helped expand the coverage of optical communication in these countries, giving a powerful boost to local telecommunications. As a result, users now enjoy faster internet connection at substantially reduced prices.

China has contributed to expanding internet coverage and application. It has launched the construction of overseas nodes of the national top-level domain name system platform across five continents, providing uninterrupted and stable national domain name services to global users, and worked to spread the application of IPv6 technology. A global IPv6+ network base has been built for the in-depth integration and transformation of enterprise communication technology, information technology, and cloud computing and big data technologies, to support the construction of the digital Silk Road and find new areas of IPv6+ application. The CT-EC Express Connect service used SRv6 technology for the first time in the international cloud interconnection target network. With it, users can access various public and private clouds in China and abroad, and realize end-to-end cross-domain deployment and service provisioning within minutes. More than 10 countries and regions in Europe, Asia and Africa now benefit from this technology.

The BeiDou Navigation Satellite System has become an important component in global positioning and timing infrastructure. Its products and services now serve the entire planet, and have been exported to half the world. China has continued to carry out cooperation and exchanges in satellite navigation with the Arab League, Association of Southeast Asian Nations (ASEAN), and countries in Central Asia and Africa. A bilateral cooperation mechanism has been established to coordinate the compatibility and interoperability of satellite navigation systems.

BeiDou will apply to join the International Standardization Organization and other industry and specialized application standardization bodies, for it to improve its services to global users and support the development of relevant industries.

China has contributed to global digital connectivity. China has expanded the construction of its 5G network and engaged in active international cooperation on 5G technology innovation and development. China's enterprises helped South Africa set up Africa's first 5G commercial network and its first 5G laboratory. To realize large-scale connectivity among countries participating in the Belt and Road Initiative (BRI), China has helped to construct main arteries like national highways, railways, ports, bridges, and communication cables and networks, forming a connectivity framework consisting of six corridors, six routes and multiple countries and ports.

On this basis, it has also helped upgrade infrastructure such as ports and railways with digital application. The construction of smart ports is expected to become a new engine of high-quality development, by further integrating the internet, big data, and artificial intelligence technologies with all areas of port operation, to improve the efficiency of services and clearance and realize paperless processes through all the major filing and certification procedures.

(2) Driving global economic growth with digital technology

Fully leveraging digital technology to boost the economy, China has continued to expand global e-commerce cooperation and facilitate the digital industry and industry digitalization. It calls for joint efforts to coordinate the transformation towards digitalization and green growth.

Silk Road e-commerce cooperation has been fruitful. Since 2016, China has set up bilateral e-commerce cooperation mechanisms with 23 countries across five continents, and e-commerce cooperation dialogue mechanisms with Central and Eastern European countries and five Central Asian countries. Multilevel exchanges and cooperation are promoted through government-business dialogue, co-research, and capacity building, to create a sound climate for development and a new pattern for digital cooperation. As China's e-commerce enterprises move faster to go global, Chinese businesses in cross-border logistics and mobile payments have thus been able to reach out to the world. China has been an active participant in e-commerce-related discussions under multilateral and regional trade frameworks such as WTO, G20, APEC, BRICS and SCO, and along with its partners in free trade, it has set the norms for a high-quality digital economy. There has been a breakthrough in the formulation of international e-commerce rules, with the e-commerce chapter in the Regional Comprehensive Economic Partnership (RCEP) becoming by far the most extensive and most used set of e-commerce rules.

China has made new breakthroughs in the development and application of cloud computing and AI technologies. In 2020, China began to provide support for the cloud services in countries in Africa, the Middle East, and Southeast Asia, and those participating in the Belt and Road Initiative. Based on the World Data Center for Microorganisms, China has employed cloud service platforms to set up a global microorganisms data-sharing network involving 141 partners from 51 countries, and initiated the Global Catalogue of Microorganisms in order to enable the efficient utilization of global microorganisms data resources.

China aided Thailand in building a 5G demonstration plant, empowering new 5G technology usage in the industrial sector. In order to raise the digitalization level in agriculture, China has actively cooperated with Israel and other countries. Under the APEC framework, China has proposed to coordinate the transformation towards digitalized development and green growth. In May 2015, China and UNESCO joined to host the International Conference on ICT and Post-2015 Education in Qingdao, Shandong Province. It adopted the Qingdao Declaration, which played a significant role in boosting the digital development of education in the international community. In May 2019, the International Conference on Artificial Intelligence & Education was held in Beijing with joint support from China and UNESCO. This event led to the Beijing Consensus, which establishes a vision for education in the AI era. Subsequently, the two parties worked together to hold the International Forum on AI and

Panel 3   Silk Road Cloud Lecture

In 2020, in order to mitigate the impact of Covid-19, China launched a skills-building cooperative project – Silk Road Cloud Lecture – for e-business representatives from Belt and Road countries. The live-streamed lectures explained the local rules, regulations, approaches and strategies in Belt and Road countries for the benefit of partner governments, chambers of commerce, and enterprises. The project has held 51 live-streamed lectures for more than 6,000 trainees and 100,000 online spectators, on topics including the export of agricultural products from Latin America and products from SCO countries.

Silk Road Cloud Lecture has provided a new platform for participants to develop their digital literacy. The initiative has been widely welcomed and had a positive impact. At a special event for Silk Road e-commerce businesses, part of the Third "Reliable Brand – Quality Life" shopping festival, the average daily sales of participating retailers rose by almost 21 percent than before. The turnover of promoted products doubled, and coffee from Rwanda, fruit and vegetable juice from Argentina, and wines from Chile became online hits. In 2022, at the live-streaming event promoting goods from SCO countries, eight products from Uzbekistan became the top-selling items. At a special event for African enterprises, part of the fourth "Reliable Brand – Quality Life" shopping festival, the turnover of star products from more than 20 African countries on major online e-business platforms rose substantially from the same period in the previous year. Sales increased by as much as 50 percent for 18 countries. The Silk Road Cloud Lecture has initiated an efficient new way to share the dividends brought by the digital economy and promote closer people-to-people ties worldwide.

Education in 2020 and 2021, representing a major contribution to the digitalization of global education.

(3) Active participation in governing the digital economy

China has actively participated in the governance of the digital economy under international and regional multilateral mechanisms, raising and advancing initiatives, declarations, and proposals in the interest of most participating countries. It has also strengthened cooperation with specialized international organizations to contribute to governing the global digital economy.

China has contributed to the progress of digital economy cooperation among APEC members. In 2014, as the host country, it introduced the internet economy into the APEC cooperation framework by initiating the APEC Initiative of Cooperation to Promote the Internet Economy and overseeing its approval. In 2019, after the APEC Digital Economy Steering Group was set up, China actively pushed the full and balanced application of the APEC Internet and Digital Economy Roadmap. Since 2020, China has proposed several initiatives – "using the digital economy to improve Covid-19 response and economic recovery", "optimizing the digital business environment to activate market vitality", "strengthening digital capacity-building in the post-pandemic era to bridge the digital gap" – all of which were adopted by APEC.

China has been an active participant in digital economy cooperation under the G20 framework. In 2016, the 11th G20 Summit was held in China. Thanks to China's efforts, the summit listed "the digital economy" as a major item in the G20 Blueprint for Innovative Growth and adopted the G20 Digital Economy Development and Cooperation Initiative, the first digital economy policy paper signed by state leaders. Since then, the digital economy has become a core topic for the G20. In recent years, China has actively attended G20 ministerial meetings on the digital economy and related negotiations of the G20 Digital Economy Task Force. China has also played a part in upgrading the Digital Economy Task Force to the Digital Economy Working Group in order that the fruits of the digital economy will benefit the whole world.

China has continued to expand cooperation with BRICS countries on the digital economy. In 2017, the Ninth BRICS Summit was held in China and announced the BRICS Leaders Xiamen Declaration, which proposed to expand practical collaboration in the areas of information and telecommunications technology, e-commerce, and cyberspace. In 2019, the China branch of the BRICS Institute of Future Networks was established in

Shenzhen City in southern China's Guangdong Province. In 2022, the 14th BRICS Summit agreed on the BRICS Digital Economy Partnership Framework. China has held several important events such as the Dialogue on Digital Economy of BRICS, opening a new chapter for cooperation on the digital economy among BRICS countries.

China has strengthened cooperation on the digital economy with ASEAN. The year 2020 marked the China-ASEAN Year of Digital Economy Cooperation under the theme "combating the pandemic together for common development", and the two sides held dialogues on internet affairs. The 23rd China-ASEAN Summit issued the China-ASEAN Digital Economy Partnership Initiative, aimed to further strengthen digital economy cooperation.

China has actively sought to advance cooperation on the digital economy within the WTO. In 2017, China formally announced its entry to the WTO Friends of E-commerce for Development (FED), in order to work with the other developing members in support of negotiations about e-commerce issues. In 2019, China joined 75 other WTO members, including Brazil, Myanmar, Nigeria, Russia, Singapore, European Union and the United States, to issue a Joint Statement on Electronic Commerce, confirming their intention to begin WTO negotiations on trade-related aspects of electronic commerce. In 2022, China and other WTO members jointly released the Work Programme on Electronic Commerce, Ministerial Decision to exempt taxes on digital transmission, in a bid to facilitate the growth of the global digital economy.

China has furthered cooperation with the World Economy Forum (WEF) and the Global System for Mobile Association (GSMA). It has supported GSMA in holding the Mobile World Congress in Shanghai several times since 2015. GSMA, a frequent co-organizer of the World Internet Conference, has strengthened its cooperation with China in the realm of cyberspace and particularly in new technologies and applications for the mobile internet.

**Panel 4   The Belt and Road Digital Economy International
Cooperation Initiative**

To expand cooperation on the digital economy, China, Laos, Saudi Arabia, Serbia, Thailand, Turkey and United Arab Emirates jointly launched the Belt and Road Digital Economy International Cooperation Initiative at the Fourth World Internet Conference on December 3, 2017. According to the initiative, the digital economy has become an important driver of global economic growth. As members under the Belt and Road Initiative framework, the participating countries will strengthen policy coordination, infrastructure connectivity, unimpeded trade, financial integration, and people-to-people ties, based on the principles of connectivity, innovative development, openness and cooperation, inclusiveness, and shared benefits. They agreed to extend their cooperation in the digital economy, in order to build an interconnected Digital Silk Road and create a community of shared interests and shared future through win-win cooperation and for common prosperity.

Accordingly, the parties proposed cooperation in 15 areas:
• expanding broadband access and improving the quality;
• promoting digital transformation;
• encouraging e-commerce cooperation;
• supporting internet-based entrepreneurship and innovation;
• facilitating the development of micro, small and medium-sized enterprises;
• strengthening digital capacity building;
• promoting investment in the ICT sector;
• promoting inter-city cooperation on the digital economy;
• promoting digital inclusiveness;
• encouraging transparent digital economy policies;
• promoting cooperation in international standardization;
• fostering confidence and trust;
• advocating cooperation and respecting every country's independent choice of development path;
• jointly establishing a peaceful, safe, open, cooperative and orderly cyberspace;
• creating a multilayer communication mechanism.

2. Stronger cybersecurity cooperation

Cybersecurity is the shared responsibility of the international community. China has actively fulfilled its international responsibilities, expanded international cooperation in cybersecurity emergency response, and worked with the international community to increase the level of cooperation in data security and personal information protection, and to combat cybercrime and cyberterrorism.

(1) More partnerships in cybersecurity

China has played an active part in facilitating cybersecurity cooperation among BRICS countries. In 2017, BRICS countries agreed on the Roadmap of Practical Cooperation on Ensuring Security in the Use of ICTs. At its eighth meeting in 2022, the BRICS Working Group on Security in the Use of ICTs unanimously adopted the report on the implementation of the roadmap, which summed up the lessons learned and progress made over the past five years and reached consensus on the direction of future cooperation. China has been deeply involved in work on cybersecurity by the Shanghai Cooperation Organization. In 2021, the SCO Expert Group on International Information Security unanimously adopted the Joint Action Plan on Ensuring International Information Security for 2022-2023. In 2021, China and Indonesia signed the Memorandum of Understanding on Cooperation in Developing Cybersecurity Capacity and Technology. In 2022, China and Thailand signed the Memorandum of Understanding on Cybersecurity Cooperation.

China has carried out international cooperation in cybersecurity emergency response. CNCERT conducts exchanges with major national CERTS, government departments, international organizations and alliances, internet service providers, domain name registries, academic institutions, and other internet-related businesses and organizations. As of 2001, CNCERT has established partnerships with 274 CERTS in 81 countries and territories and signed cybersecurity cooperation memorandums with 33 of them. The China-ASEAN Cybersecurity Exchange and Training Center has been established to increase cybersecurity capabilities.

(2) Higher-level cooperation in data security and personal information protection

China adopts an attitude of openness and inclusion in global data security governance, and cooperation on personal information protection. It works to achieve a reasonable balance between data security and the orderly flow of data. Conditional on maintaining the security of personal information and important data, China has carried out exchanges and cooperation with countries throughout the world and jointly explored rules on data security and personal information protection that reflect the common concerns and meet the common interests of the international community. In September 2020, China launched the Global Data Security Initiative, which provides a blueprint for developing global data security rules. In March 2021, China and the League of Arab States (LAS) Secretariat released the China-LAS Cooperation Initiative on Data Security, highlighting the high-level consensus of the two sides on digital governance. In June 2022, the third China + Central Asia (C+C5) Foreign Ministers' Meeting adopted the Data Security Initiative of China + Central Asia, marking an important step in cooperation among developing countries to promote global digital governance. China supports discussions on the protection of privacy in the United Nations General Assembly and the Human Rights Council, advocates the establishment of principles on privacy protection in cyberspace, and encourages countries to take steps to prevent the use of the internet to infringe on privacy.

(3) Jointly combating cybercrime and cyberterrorism

China has always supported international cooperation in combating cybercrime and advocates a global convention against cybercrime under the framework of the United Nations. From 2011 to 2021, China facilitated seven meetings of the United Nations Open-Ended Intergovernmental Expert Group on Cybercrime, making a significant contribution to the adoption of relevant resolutions on the drafting of a United Nations convention on cybercrime.

Within the framework of the Shanghai Cooperation Organization

(SCO), China has signed important documents such as the Astana Declaration of the SCO Heads of States, and the Statement by the SCO Heads of Member States on Joint Counteraction to International Terrorism to combat terrorism, separatism, and extremism, including cyberterrorism. China has hosted and actively participated in the meetings of the BRICS Counter-Terrorism Working Group (CTWG), shared its approach to combating cyberterrorism, and presented proposals for strengthening cooperation and exchange on combating cyberterrorism among BRICS countries.

3. Actively participating in cyberspace governance

Cyberspace is a shared space for human activities; it needs to be developed and managed by all countries. China has actively participated in global internet governance mechanisms, and initiated international exchange platforms such as the World Internet Conference. It has strengthened exchanges and cooperation with other countries in cyberspace, driving the reform and development of the global internet governance system.

(1) Active participation in global internet governance

China firmly safeguards the international system with the United Nations at its core, the international order underpinned by international law, the basic norms governing international relations based on the purposes and principles of the UN Charter, and on these foundations, the formulation of universally agreed international rules in cyberspace.

China has always upheld the principles enshrined in the UN Charter, including sovereign equality, non-use or threats of force, and the peaceful settlement of disputes. It respects the rights of individual countries to independently choose their own path of cyber development, model of cyber regulation, and internet public policies, and their right to equal participation in international governance of cyberspace.

It has been China's consistent view that all countries, big or small, strong or weak, rich or poor, are equal members of the international community and are entitled to equal participation in developing a global order and international rules, to ensure that the future development of cyberspace is decided by people of the world. In September 2020, China released its position paper on the 75th anniversary of the United Nations, calling on the international community to step up dialogue and cooperation on the basis of mutual respect and mutual benefit, and to use cyberspace for the purposes of economic and social development, international peace and stability, and wellbeing for all. It also called on all countries to oppose cyber warfare and a cyber arms race, and to foster a peaceful, secure, open, cooperative and orderly cyberspace.

China has actively participated in the UN process of cyberspace governance. China and other SCO member states jointly submitted the International Code of Conduct for Information Security to the UN General Assembly, with an updated version submitted in 2015. It was the first systematic international document dedicated to norms of behavior in cyberspace.

China has been a constructive participant in the UN's Open-Ended Working Group (OEWG) and Group of Government Experts (GGE) on information security, and pushed for a successful OEWG-GGE final report, laying the foundations for formulating international cyberspace rules and building global cybersecurity governance mechanisms. China is fully engaged in the UN Internet Governance Forum (IGF). Chinese representatives have actively participated in the IGF's Leading Group and Multistakeholder Advisory Group (MAG), having hosted open forums, seminars, and other breakout activities during the IGF for several years, and engaged in extensive exchanges and discussions with representatives of politics, business, academia, and non-governmental organizations from all over the world.

China has continued to expand cooperation with specialized agencies of the UN on cyber affairs. The International Telecommunication Union (ITU) and World Intellectual Property Organization (WIPO) have co-hosted the World Internet Conference for several years. In July 2019, China signed a memorandum of understanding with the WIPO and officially authorized the WIPO's Arbitration and Mediation Center to conduct extensive cooperation in formulating domain name rules and dispute resolution in the field. China has taken an active part in formulating UNESCO's Recommendation on the Ethics of Artificial Intelligence. At the end of 2019, the UNESCO's International Center for Higher Education Innovation (UNESCO-ICHEI) worked with four Chinese higher education institutions, 11 Asia-Pacific and African higher education institutions, and nine partner enterprises, to set up the International Institute of Online Education (IIOE), which supports the digital transformation of higher education institutions and faculty in developing countries through open online platforms.

China has actively participated in the operation of global internet organizations. It has actively participated in the activities of platforms and organizations such as the Internet Corporation for Assigned Names and Numbers (ICANN). It has supported reform of the ICANN governance mechanism to increase the representation of developing countries, and to bring more internet information resources under concerted global management. China has also participated in the activities of the Internet Society (ISOC), Internet Engineering Task Force (IETF), and Internet Architecture Board (IAB). It has played a constructive role in facilitating community exchange, promoting technical R&D and application, and becoming closely involved in the formulation of relevant standards and rules.

(2) Extensive international exchanges and cooperation

On the basis of mutual respect and equality, China has strengthened exchanges and cooperation in cyberspace with countries worldwide. With common progress and win-win results as the goals, it has championed mutual confidence and shared governance.

In March 2017, China released a white paper – *International Strategy of Cooperation on Cyberspace* – which for the first time made proposals on promoting international exchanges and cooperation in cyberspace in a comprehensive and systematic manner. This sent a positive signal to the world on China's dedication to peaceful development and win-win cooperation in cyberspace.

China has carried forward high-level Sino-Russian cooperation on cyber affairs and information technology. Within the framework of the Sino-Russia comprehensive strategic partnership of coordination for a new era, the two sides have followed through on agreements for cooperation reached by the two heads of states, to advance bilateral cooperation on cyber affairs and information technology. In 2015, the two sides signed the Agreement Between the Government of the Russian Federation and the Government of the People's Republic of China on Cooperation in Ensuring International Information Security, which set the direction for bilateral cooperation in this area.

In 2021, on the occasion of the 20th anniversary of the signing of the Sino-Russian Treaty of Good-Neighborliness and Friendly Cooperation, China and Russia issued a joint statement in which both sides reaffirmed their commitment to strengthening international information security at bilateral and multilateral levels, and to further contributing to a global information security system based on the principles of preventing conflict in cyberspace and encouraging the peaceful use of information and communication technologies. Since 2016, they have co-hosted five China-Russia Internet Media Forum to strengthen new media exchanges and cooperation between the two sides. Through the Sino-Russian Information Security Consultation Mechanism, they have constantly enhanced their coordination and cooperation on information security.

China has applied an open and inclusive attitude to its cooperation with Europe on cyber affairs and information technology. By holding China-European Commission (EC) high-level dialogues in the digital sector, the two sides focused on digital cooperation and carried out pragmatic and constructive discussions on the standards of communication technology and artificial intelligence, among other issues. China worked with the EC in setting up the China-EU Digital Economy and Cybersecurity Expert Working Group, which has held four meetings. The China-EU Taskforce was set up in 2012. It has now held eight meetings. Under the framework of the taskforce, the two sides have continued to strengthen discussions and cooperation on cyberspace. China has carried out bilateral cyber affairs dialogues with the UK, Germany, France and other countries. China has intensified its exchanges and dialogue with European think tanks. It co-hosted the 2019 China-Germany Dialogue on the Internet Economy, and jointly issued the outcome document of the dialogue. It has also co-hosted several China-UK Internet Roundtables, and reached agreements in fields such as the digital economy, cybersecurity, online protection of children, data, and artificial intelligence.

China has strengthened cooperation on cyber affairs and information technology with neighboring countries and other developing countries. The success of a series of China-ASEAN Information Harbor Forums has continued to promote China-ASEAN cooperation in the digital sector. The China-ASEAN Cyber Dialogue Mechanism and the China-Japan-ROK Trilateral Cyber Consultation Mechanism were set up. China and the Republic of Korea have co-hosted the China-ROK Internet Roundtable. China hosted the China-Africa Internet Development and Cooperation Forum, which released the Initiative on Jointly Building a Community with a Shared Future in Cyberspace, and proposed the China-Africa Partnership Plan on Digital Innovation. A series of activities, including the China-South Africa New Media Roundtable, the Meeting for China-Tanzania Cyber Cultural Exchange, and the Symposium on China-Kenya Cooperation and Development of the Digital Economy have strengthened China-Africa exchanges and cooperation in new media, cyber culture, the digital economy and other sectors. China has hosted a series of online Silk Road expos, to facilitate pragmatic cooperation with Arab countries in information infrastructure, cross-border e-commerce, smart cities and other sectors. It has also hosted the China-Cuba Internet Development Forum and the China-Brazil Internet Governance Seminar to promote dialogue and exchanges on the development and governance of the internet in the information era.

China has discussed the rule of law in cyberspace with Asian and

African countries. In April 2015, the 54th Annual Meeting of the Asian-African Legal Consultative Organization (AALCO) was held in Beijing. At the suggestion of China, the AALCO decided to set up the Working Group on International Law Concerning Cyberspace, which would carry out in-depth discussions on relevant issues.

Panel 5   China-Africa Internet Development and Cooperation Forum

---

On August 24, 2021, the China-Africa Internet Development and Cooperation Forum, on the theme of "Pursuing Common Development and Security, Jointly Building a Community with a Shared Future in Cyberspace", took place via video link. Around 100 representatives from the African Union and 14 African countries, including Senegal, Rwanda, Democratic Republic of the Congo, Nigeria, Tanzania, Cote d'Ivoire, attended the forum online.

During the forum, the Chinese side put forward the Initiative on Jointly Building a Community with a Shared Future in Cyberspace. It welcomed support for and participation in the initiative by African countries. It also expressed its willingness to work with the African side to jointly formulate and implement the China-Africa Partnership Plan on Digital Innovation, and to design measures for pragmatic cooperation in the digital sector in the next three years, which would be incorporated in the outcome document of the next meeting of the Forum on China-Africa Cooperation (FOCAC). The African representatives responded in a positive manner, saying that they would take the forum as an opportunity to further strengthen mutually beneficial cooperation between Africa and China, promote the digital economy in Africa, jointly safeguard cybersecurity, and jointly build a community with a shared future in cyberspace.

During the forum, China's National Computer Network Emergency Response Technical Team/Coordination Center signed a memorandum of understanding on cooperation with the National Computer Emergency Response Center of Benin.

China has carried out dialogue and exchanges with the United States in the spirit of equality and mutual respect. On the basis of respecting each other's core concerns and properly managing differences, China has been committed to carrying out dialogue and exchanges with the US in the internet sector, in order to create a sound market environment for businesses from all over the world, including the US, to develop in China. These have promoted bilateral cooperation on cyber affairs and information technology. However, in the more recent past, the US has adopted misguided China policies that have resulted in serious setbacks in China-US relations. The US government has also continuously carried out cyber attacks and cyber theft activities. China will adhere to the principle of independence and self-reliance, and firmly safeguard its sovereignty, security and development interests in cyberspace.

(3) World Internet Conference

Every year since 2014, China has hosted the World Internet Conference in Wuzhen, Zhejiang Province, to build an international platform for greater connectivity between China and the world, and a Chinese platform for all to benefit from a global internet. Representatives from governments, international organizations, internet companies, think tanks, industry associations, and technology communities have come together to share their views on the further development of the global internet. The conference model provides a variety of innovative activities, such as sub-forums, Release & Presentation of Success Stories of Jointly Building a Community with a Share Future in Cyberspace, the Release Ceremony for World Leading Internet Scientific and Technological Achievements, the "Light of Internet" Expo, and the "Straight to Wuzhen" competition. These have drawn wide attention from the public.

The organizing committee of the conference has released Jointly Build a Community with a Shared Future in Cyberspace, a concept document, and the Initiative on Jointly Building a Community with a Shared Future in Cyberspace. It has also publicized the best practices on explaining the concept of building a community with a shared future in cyberspace. Every year, the organizing committee of the conference releases the blue books of the *World Internet Development Report* and the *China Internet Development Report*, to review internet development in China and around the world, in order to present facts, experiences, and guidance for global internet development. The Wuzhen Outlook is released by the High-level Advisory Council of the conference to share with the international community its views on the current trends in cyberspace and the future outlook.

Over the past eight years, the successful conferences have contributed significantly to close contacts and in-depth communication among

---

Panel 6   Initiative on Jointly Building a Community with a Shared Future in Cyberspace

On November 18, 2020, the Organizing Committee of the World Internet Conference released the Initiative on Jointly Building a Community with a Shared Future in Cyberspace, calling on all governments, international organizations, internet companies, technical communities, social organizations and individuals to take an approach to global governance based on extensive consultation, joint contribution, and shared benefits, to uphold the philosophy of "achieving shared development, ensuring common security, realizing joint governance, and enjoying benefits together", and to work together to build cyberspace into a global community where development and security are advanced for all and benefits as well as responsibility are shared.

The initiative consists of 20 proposals in four categories:

1. to adopt more proactive, inclusive and coordinated policies that benefit all, speed up global information infrastructure construction, promote innovative development of the digital economy and enhance public service capacity;

2. to advocate a cybersecurity vision that features openness and cooperation, and encourage internet development while laying equal emphasis on cybersecurity so as to jointly uphold peace and security in cyberspace;

3. to stay committed to a multilateral and multiparty approach to cyberspace governance, and step up dialogue and consultation for a more just and equitable governance system in cyberspace;

4. to advocate "Tech for Good" with a people-centered approach, narrow the digital divide, and achieve common prosperity.

---

all countries in the internet sector. They have vigorously transformed China's experience, ideas, and wisdom around building a community with a shared future in cyberspace from conceptual consensus into concrete practice, boosting the confidence and enthusiasm of people from all over the world in this regard, and contributing to a fairer and more equitable global internet governance system.

In response to calls to upgrade the World Internet Conference, the international organization of the World Internet Conference was inaugurated in Beijing in July 2022 with concerted efforts. The goal of the organization is to build a global internet platform featuring extensive consultation, joint contribution and sharing of benefits, to help the international community to adapt to the trends of digital, internet-based, and intelligent technologies, meet security challenges together, bring more benefits to the people, and jointly build a community with a shared future in cyberspace.

4. Promoting inclusive global development

China upholds "Tech for Good" with a people-centered approach. In response to the needs of the international community, China has worked with other countries to promote the implementation of the United Nations 2030 Sustainable Development Agenda in order to bridge the digital divide. It has promoted online cultural exchanges and mutual learning among civilizations and strengthened support for vulnerable groups to help people in different countries and regions share the benefits of the internet.

(1) Active international cooperation in poverty alleviation through internet access

China has always associated its own future with that of the peoples of the world. It has consistently advocated, promoted, and contributed to international poverty reduction. While using the internet to eliminate poverty, China has used technology to help developing countries improve broadband access in the poorest areas and areas with low population density. It has worked to provide universal and affordable internet access in the Least Developed Countries (LDCs), in order to eliminate poverty caused by lack of network facilities. In June 2021, China hosted the APEC Digital Poverty Reduction Seminar both online and offline, making a positive contribution to poverty eradication in the Asia-Pacific region. RuralStar, a solution put forward by a Chinese firm, allows a simple and small base station to be deployed on a wooden pole. The base station has its own power supply and consumes limited power, enabling mobile communication in remote areas of developing countries to function quickly and at a low cost. China has provided financing support for IT projects in African countries, modernized their IT services, and helped alleviate local poverty. In addition, China has provided cross-network, multi-business services for Africa and helped build network infrastructure in remote areas, making an important contribution to poverty reduction elsewhere in the world.

(2) Helping improve digital public services

China has actively developed digital public products and expanded cooperation in digital public services. The Arab-China Digital Library project, a joint initiative, provides digital resources and cultural services in Chinese and Arabic for Chinese and LAS users. Network and information technology has been used to build a platform for cooperation in international education. ChinesePlus was launched in collaboration with educational institutions and social organizations in Japan, the United Kingdom, Spain and Thailand as a platform for teaching service and information exchanges in Chinese language education. Since the global outbreak of Covid-19, pandemic forecasting platforms and robocalls developed in China have helped control and mitigation in other countries. In October 2020, the China-ASEAN Public Private Cooperation Forum on Combating Covid-19 Digitally was held. China has also donated remote video conferencing systems to other countries and provided technology, equipment, and solutions such as medical systems, AI-assisted Covid-19 diagnosis and treatment, and 5G driverless cars.

(3) Promoting online cultural exchange and mutual learning among civilizations

Online cultural exchange platforms have been created for exchange and mutual learning among civilizations. In June 2020, China Pavilion Online was launched to release information, host exhibitions, facilitate copyright trading, and promote communication. It has become a platform for the exhibition and exchange of audiovisual programs and equipment among relevant institutions from various countries. Travel Silk Road, a multilingual digital heritage and tourism information service platform, has been created to promote 1,500 heritage and tourism sites in countries along the Silk Road. Images, audios, and videos are used to highlight their scientific, aesthetic, historical, cultural and artistic value. In September 2020, the Treasure Hunt Relay: Global Museum Director's Choice was held online, in which 16 national museums from 15 countries on five continents participated. To promote the digital presentation and dissemination of Dunhuang culture, an online symposium – Sino-French Cultural Talk: the Digital Effort and Communication for Dunhuang Studies – was held in May 2021 in conjunction with a French museum. Its goal was to identify new directions, models and plans for the digital protection and dissemination of Dunhuang cultural heritage preserved in France.

IV. China's Proposals on Creating a Community with a Shared Future in Cyberspace

The internet is the shared home of all of humanity. It is the common responsibility of the international community to make this home cleaner, safer, and more prosperous. China will join other countries to build a community with a shared future in cyberspace so that the fruits of internet development can benefit everyone. As always, China will do so based on its national conditions and in the spirit of people-centered, open, and win-win cooperation.

1. Respecting network sovereignty

China advocates respect for the cyber sovereignty of all countries. It respects the right of every country to independently choose its path of cyber development, model of network management, and public policy on internet issues, as well as its right to equal participation in international cyberspace governance. China firmly opposes all forms of hegemony and power politics, interference in other countries' internal affairs, and double standards. It does not support, engage in, or conspire around cyber activities that undermine national security in other countries.

China advocates that the principle of sovereign equality established by the UN Charter be applied to cyberspace and that a just and rational international order in cyberspace be built on the basis of national sovereignty.

2. Maintaining peace, security and stability in cyberspace

Cyberspace is interconnected, resulting in the deep integration of the interests of all countries. Peace, security, and stability in cyberspace are the common wishes of people all over the world. China maintains that all governments should abide by the purposes and principles of the UN Charter, make peaceful use of the internet, and settle disputes by peaceful means. China opposes the so-called absolute security for some at the expense of the interests of others, and any form of arms race in cyberspace. China advocates that the cybersecurity concerns of all countries, large or small, strong or weak, rich or poor, should be noted and addressed, and that countries should make peaceful use of cyberspace to promote economic and social development and conduct cooperation and dialogue at all levels – global, bilateral, multilateral, and multiparty – to jointly safeguard peace and stability in cyberspace.

3. Creating an open, fair, just and non-discriminatory digital environment

The global digital economy is an open and closely connected whole. Those who build walls and barriers and call for decoupling and severing supply chains will hurt not only others but also themselves. Win-win cooperation is the only way forward. Creating an open, fair, just and non-discriminatory environment for digital development is a requirement for stronger global digital economic cooperation, which will promote the recovery and development of the global economy. China opposes the politicization of technological issues and the containment of other countries' enterprises by abusing state power and violating market principles and trading rules. China advocates that all governments should actively maintain open, secure, and stable global supply chains for IT products and services, strengthen collaborative R&D on new generations of information technology, and integrate into the global innovation network. Governments, international organizations, businesses and think tanks should discuss and develop international rules of digital governance that reflect the wishes of all parties and respect the interests of all, to promote the healthy and orderly development of the digital economy.

4. Strengthening international cooperation in protecting critical information infrastructure

Critical information infrastructure is one of the foundations for the normal operation of the economy and society of all countries in the information age. It is the common responsibility of the international community to effectively address any security risks in this regard. China firmly opposes the use of information technology to undermine the critical information infrastructure of other countries, steal their data, or engage in any other form of zero-sum game. The international community should advocate the concept of cybersecurity based on openness and cooperation, and oppose network eavesdropping and cyberattacks. Governments and relevant authorities of all countries should strengthen cooperation on early warning, risk prevention, information sharing and emergency response, and actively share experience on protecting critical information infrastructure.

5. Maintaining the security and stability of the core-resource management system for the internet

The core-resource management system for the internet is the cornerstone of internet operations. It should be guaranteed that those institutions hosting the management systems operate with full credibility and do not pose a threat to the top-level domains of any country just because of the jurisdictional demands on some other country. China advocates guaranteed availability and reliability of core internet resources – to be used by all countries and jointly managed and fairly distributed by the international community, so that the technological systems for the resources, including the domain name system, are secure, stable, and resilient. There should be a guarantee that services will not be interrupted or terminated due to any political or human factors. China advocates that governments, industry authorities, and businesses work together to accelerate the use of IPv6 technology and applications.

6. Cooperation in combating cybercrime and cyberterrorism

Cyberspace should not be a wrestling field for countries fighting against each other, nor a hotbed for crimes. Currently, cybercrime and cyberterrorism have become a global scourge, and they must be fought against through international cooperation. China proposes that governments of all countries should work together within the framework of relevant laws and international conventions to crack down on all forms of cybercrime. China calls for removing the hotbed for cybercrime and severing all criminal links, and building a better mechanism for judicial and law enforcement cooperation against cybercrime and cyberterrorism. China is an active supporter and participant in negotiations on a United Nations Convention against Cybercrime, and calls for an international cyberspace counter-terrorism treaty. China would like to coordinate with other governments in drafting laws and taking actions to jointly tackle the threat of cybercrime and cyberterrorism.

7. Promote data security, development and utilization

Data are a new type of production factor – the basis for digital, internet and smart technologies. Data have been integrated into various areas of production, distribution, circulation, consumption and social service management, profoundly changing people's approach to work, daily life, and social governance. China supports the flow, development, and utilization of data, and promotes data sharing, and would like to actively work with other countries, international organizations, enterprises, and think tanks, engaging in exchanges and cooperation to safeguard data security, development and utilization, promoting relevant international rules and standards under bilateral and multilateral frameworks, and steadily ensuring the interoperability of different data protection rules to promote the safe and free flow of data across borders.

8. Build a fairer and more rational cyberspace governance system

Cyberspace is globally interconnected, so no country can effectively govern it alone. China supports the United Nations as the main player in international cyberspace governance. China upholds genuine multilateralism and opposes any form of unilateralism, camps or coteries targeting specific countries. China champions multilateral participation, leveraging the role of various parties including governments, international organizations, internet companies, technology communities, non-governmental organizations and individuals. Following the principles of extensive consultation, joint contribution, and shared benefits, the international community should step up communication, exchange, and pragmatic cooperation, improve dialogue and consultation mechanisms on cyberspace, and formulate global internet governance rules, so that the global internet governance system becomes fairer and more rational and reflects the aspirations and interests of the majority of countries in a more balanced way.

9. Jointly building a better cyberspace

Internet civilization is an important symbol of the progress of modern society. To meet netizens' desire for a better life it is imperative to step up the construction of internet civilization. China respects the diversity of internet culture, and holds that all countries should tap their own excellent cultural resources, support the digitalization and online dissemination of their quality cultural products, encourage online cultural exchange and learning between the civilizations of various countries, regions and nations, and promote the co-existence and common development of all civilizations. China proposes that countries should cooperate with each other, industry organizations and companies should strengthen self-discipline, and individuals should improve their digital literacy, combining to counter fake online information, strengthen cyber governance, maintain sound online order, and enrich cyberspace with the excellent fruits of human civilization.

10. Sharing the benefits of the internet

The internet develops through joint efforts and its fruits should also be shared. China proposes that the international community should make joint efforts to advance the construction of information infrastructure and bridge the digital divide, step up support and help to vulnerable groups, and promote digital literacy and skills for the general public. Internet and digital technology should play a full role in combating epidemics, improving people's lives, and eliminating poverty. The international community should promote new technologies and applications for the common good, provide more innovative digital products, and promote open, inclusive, sharing, balanced and sustainable development. Efforts should be made for more countries and people to benefit from the information technology, enjoy the fruits of internet development, and actively contribute to the implementation of the United Nations 2030 Agenda for Sustainable Development.

Conclusion

The internet is the common home of mankind. Everyone shares weal and woe in cyberspace no matter how innovative digital technology develops and how the international situation changes. Building a peaceful, secure, open, cooperative and orderly cyberspace is important for the future development of human civilization, and is the common aspiration of all countries.

In an era of both challenges and hope, China would like to work with other countries to foster an open, inclusive, and vibrant cyberspace that is fairer, more secure, and more stable. Let us join hands together to build a community with a shared future in cyberspace and create a better world.

责任编辑：刘敬文

图书在版编目（CIP）数据

中国政府白皮书汇编.2022 年/中华人民共和国国务院新闻办公室 著. —北京：人民出版社，外文出版社,2023.4
ISBN 978－7－01－025730－3

Ⅰ.①中…　Ⅱ.①中…　Ⅲ.①国家行政机关-白皮书-汇编-中国-2022　Ⅳ.①D63

中国国家版本馆 CIP 数据核字(2023)第 089078 号

中国政府白皮书汇编（2022 年）
ZHONGGUO ZHENGFU BAIPISHU HUIBIAN（2022NIAN）
中华人民共和国国务院新闻办公室

人民出版社
外文出版社 出版发行
（100706　北京市东城区隆福寺街 99 号）

中煤（北京）印务有限公司印刷　新华书店经销

2023 年 4 月第 1 版　2023 年 4 月北京第 1 次印刷
开本:889 毫米×1194 毫米 1/16　印张:27.5
字数:281 千字

ISBN 978－7－01－025730－3　定价:135.00 元

邮购地址 100706　北京市东城区隆福寺街 99 号
人民东方图书销售中心　电话（010）65250042　65289539